# MINNESOTA
# HISTORY
# ALONG THE
# HIGHWAYS

**North Central / West**

Kittson
Roseau
Lake of the Woods

Lake of the Woods

Marshall

Pennington

Red Lake

Polk

Clear-water

Koochiching

Upper Red Lake

Lower Red Lake

Beltrami

Itasca

St. Louis

Lake

Cook

**Northeast**

Norman
Mahno-men

Clay

Becker

Hubbard

Cass

Mississippi

River

Aitkin

Carlton

Wadena

Crow Wing

Mille Lacs Lake

Wilkin

Otter Tail

Todd

Morrison

Mille Lacs

Kana-bec

Pine

St. Croix River

Grant
Douglas

Traverse

Stevens
Pope

Stearns

Benton

Big Stone

Swift

Kandi-yohi

Meeker

Wright

Sher-burne

Isanti

Chisago

Anoka

**Metro**

Lac qui Parle

Chippewa

Renville

McLeod

Carver

Henne-pin

Ramsey

Washington

Yellow Medicine

Minnesota River

Sibley

Scott

Dakota

Lincoln
Lyon
Redwood

Nicollet

Le Sueur

Rice

Goodhue

Mississippi River

Brown

Wabasha

Pipe-stone
Murray
Cotton-wood
Waton-wan
Blue Earth
Wa-seca
Steele
Dodge
Olmsted
Winona

Rock
Nobles
Jackson
Martin
Faribault
Freeborn
Mower
Fillmore
Houston

Red River

**Southern**

# MINNESOTA HISTORY ALONG THE HIGHWAYS

## A Guide to Historic Markers and Sites

## ★ Revised and Expanded ★

Compiled by Sarah P. Rubinstein

Minnesota Historical Society Press

www.mnhs.org/mhspress

Manufactured in Canada

10 9 8 7 6 5 4 3 2 1

International Standard Book Number 0-87351-456-4

⊖ The paper used in this publication meets the minimum
requirements of the American National Standard for Information Sciences—Permanence for Printed Library Materials,
ANSI Z39.48-1984.

**Library of Congress Cataloging-in-Publication Data**

Rubinstein, Sarah P. (Sarah Paskins), 1942–
    Minnesota history along the highways : a guide to
    historic markers and sites / compiled by Sarah P.
    Rubinstein.—Rev. and expanded ed.
        p. cm.
    Includes index.
    ISBN 0-87351-456-4 (pbk. : alk. paper)
        1. Historical markers—Minnesota—Guidebooks.
        2. Historic sites—Minnesota—Guidebooks.
        3. Minnesota—Guidebooks.
        4. Minnesota—History, Local.
        I. Title.
F607.R83 2003
917.7604'54—dc21                                    2002155776

# MINNESOTA HISTORY ALONG THE HIGHWAYS

# INTRODUCTION

Highways crisscross Minnesota's landscape, zipping drivers through forests and prairies, past hills and lakes. We hurry along them, seldom taking the time to look around us and think of the other people who have also called this place home. But the very roads beneath us were established by generations of Dakota and Ojibwe people, whose trails found the shortest and easiest routes.

And along these highways there are markers to remind us of these people and others who came before us. Fur traders and explorers, farmers and loggers, politicians and entrepreneurs, laborers and miners, authors and teachers, soldiers and clergymen—their stories are captured in the inscriptions of Minnesota's highway markers.

This book, a revised and expanded edition of the popular *History Along the Highways,* contains the texts that tell those stories on 29 state monuments, 60 markers describing Minnesota's geology, and 259 historical markers. Each entry provides a location for the marker and keys it to a regional map.

These three types of markers have different origins and appearances. State monuments, authorized by statute, were funded by the Minnesota legislature, which usually appointed a commission to oversee their erection. A typical Minnesota state monument is a stone shaft from six to fifty feet in height; they were erected between 1873 and 1984.

The Geological Society of Minnesota erected the first of its 60 markers in 1949. Highlighting places of particular geological interest for both residents and visitors, the society installed bronze marker tablets with the help of the Minnesota Department of Highways and other agencies at carefully chosen locations on state highways or in city and state parks. Most of the tablets are mounted on concrete slabs attached to limestone-block walls.

While this book includes all known state monuments and geological markers, the listing of historic markers must be more selective. By 2002 Minnesota had more that 1,700 markers of varying historical interest, erected by state agencies, county and local historical societies, patriotic organizations, and other private groups. In general, only markers approved, erected, or maintained by a state agency with public funds are listed here. The name of the sponsoring group and the year of establishment appear at the end of the marker text. If no name is listed, then the Minnesota Historical Society—the organization responsible for Minnesota's marker program—is the erecting agency; if no date is listed, the year is unknown.

The historical markers chosen for inclusion in this book were found to meet three criteria:

**(1) Significance.** A marker must possess unquestioned historical associations with events, people, or places of lasting significance to the state, region, or nation. Markers calling attention to places, events, or people of primarily local or county interest were excluded.

**(2) Adequacy of identification.** The marker inscription must be reasonably accurate and informative. Misleading, incomplete, or otherwise inadequate texts disqualified a number of markers that might otherwise have been included in this book. Readers should be aware that the inscriptions on monuments and markers were written by an earlier generation, and some phrasings may now appear insensitive. Those texts, when read in the context of their times, illuminate both the place itself and the perspectives of those writing the text.

**(3) Accessibility.** The third criterion was interpreted to include markers maintained on state highways or in state parks that met the other tests. Those on a number of county roads are also listed, but several on roads maintained by townships and not readily found by the motoring public were omitted. In the interest of safe driving, markers located in waysides and other areas with parking facilities received first consideration.

The first systematic efforts to mark state historic sites began in 1930 with a cooperative arrangement between the Minnesota Historical Society and the Minnesota Department of Highways. Between 1930 and 1940, the society designated 112 sites and prepared suitable inscriptions, and the highway department erected signs along roads maintained by the state. Many markers were steel plates, three by five feet in size, with white backgrounds and black lettering. They proved to be impermanent, subject to chipping and rusting. Other markers were bronze plaques affixed to large granite rocks or limestone walls.

In 1941 the legislature created the Minnesota Historic Sites and Markers Commission, thus formalizing and extending the cooperative arrangement between the society and the highway department. The commission, which never received any state funding, had one member each from the society, the highway department, and the division of state parks. Under the law, the commission's approval was to be obtained before markers could be erected, and it approved the markers established in state parks and along highways maintained by the state. Since the commission favored the erection of permanent markers of bronze or other metals, it was relatively inactive during the metal-short years of World War II. After 1943, when the legislature authorized county boards to acquire and maintain historic sites, county historical societies and other agencies, with the commission's approval, erected a number of markers.

In the 1950s the commission made an effort to replace the old steel signs with more permanent markers and to locate them in waysides or rest areas for convenience and highway safety. In this period, the markers were cast of various metals, chiefly aluminum. While the plan to locate markers in overlooks, wayside parks, and other off-the-road areas remained in effect, the style of marker again changed. Those erected in the 1960s had baked enamel finishes in various colors; many incorporated maps or other pictorial representations of the subjects in question.

The passage by the legislature of the Omnibus Natural Resources and Recreation Act of 1963 stimulated renewed activity in historic sites. Under the provisions of this law, historic sites were included in the list of natural resources and, for the first time, funds were appropriated for the their development. The 1960s were also a period of great activity for the Minnesota Historical Society historic sites department, which acquired its first site in 1958.

In 1965 the legislature turned its attention specifically to markers. It abolished the Minnesota Historic Sites and Markers Commission and transferred its functions to the governor, who was the state planning officer. He placed the responsibility for designating historic sites and erecting or approving markers with the Minnesota Historical Society.

In the Minnesota Historic Sites Act of 1965, the legislature defined state historical monuments, state historical markers, and state archaeological and geographical sites. It stated: "A 'state historical marker' is a plaque, sign, or marker authorized by the Minnesota Historical Society and . . . includes roadside markers maintained by the department of highways, the department of conservation, or other departments or agencies of the state and its governmental subdivisions."

The 1969 legislature made the Minnesota Historical Society solely responsible for the state historical markers program. With expanded staff, the society's historic sites department began a determined effort to mark neglected sites of statewide importance. The society marked some sites for the first time and replaced damaged markers at others. In this continuing program, several markers appeared not on highways but on hiking trails or islands and portages, reflecting the mobility and the increasingly diverse interests or Americans.

In 1987, the Minnesota Historical Society created the Markers Committee, which drew up a formal policy in 1992 on what should be marked and what information should be in the text. Recent markers are of cast aluminum, black with gold letters. One of the committee's principal efforts was to place a marker in each of the rest areas along the interstate highways, a project that was completed by 2000.

While every effort has been made to ensure accuracy of texts and locations, the reader should be aware that seemingly permanent markers are subject to the vagaries of human vandalism, natural changes, and highway construction.

We hope that this new book will introduce Minnesotans and visitors to the North Star State to the many interesting aspects of the American heritage preserved in these markers. So pull over at that wayside or rest area, read the marker, and look out at the setting of a Minnesota story. Our history is all around us.

State monuments are indicated by 🖺, geological markers by △, and Minnesota Historical Society Historic Sites by Ⓜ.

# MINNESOTA
# HISTORY
# ALONG THE
# HIGHWAYS

# METRO REGION

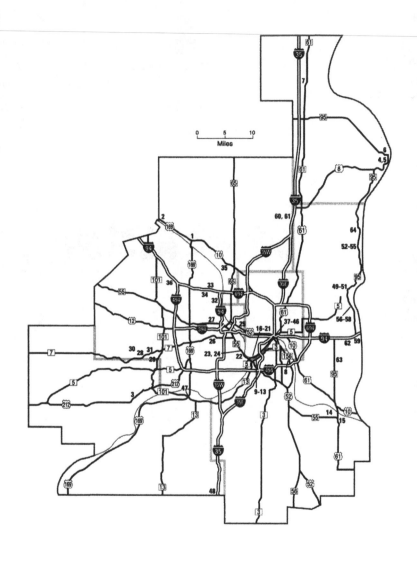

Metro Region
Markers 1–64

# ANOKA COUNTY

## 1. FATHER LOUIS HENNEPIN'S EXPLORATION IN 1680
*Located at Anoka City Hall at First Street East and East Main in Anoka*

Father Louis Hennepin, Belgian Recollect missionary accompanying Sieur de la Salle's expedition to the Mississippi River region, left Fort Crevecoeur, Illinois, on February 29, 1680, for an exploration of the upper Mississippi River. On April 11, he and his two French companions were captured by a Dakota (Sioux) war party. Leaving the river near present-day St. Paul, the Indians took their captives on a grueling five-day march to their encampment on the shores of Mille Lacs Lake.

In early July Father Hennepin accompanied a Dakota hunting party down the St. Francis (Rum) River. On the fourth day the group camped on the west bank of the Mississippi just opposite the mouth of the Rum River in present-day Champlin. A day or so later Father Hennepin viewed the falls to which he gave the name St. Anthony of Padua.

On July 25, some miles below Lake Pepin, Father Hennepin and his two companions were rescued by five Frenchmen led by Daniel Greysolon, Sieur Du Luth, who had come from Lake Superior by way of the Brule and St. Croix rivers. The Indians and Frenchmen now returned to Mille Lacs Lake.

Late in September Father Hennepin and Sieur Du Luth set out on their homeward voyage. They wintered at Mackinac and reached Quebec in the spring of 1681. Father Hennepin returned to France, where, in 1683, he published his widely-read *Description of Louisiana*.

Erected in the Tricentennial Year 1980 by the Anoka Senior Citizens Club.

## 2.   ITASCA VILLAGE TOWNSITE

*Located on U.S. highways 169 and 10 in Dayton Port Road-side Park near the western border of Anoka County*

Itasca grew up around an Indian trading post which was established 800 feet east of here in 1849 by Thomas A. Holmes and James Beatty. At the suggestion of Territorial Governor Alexander Ramsey, the settlement was named in honor of Lake Itasca, the source of the Mississippi River. In 1852 a substantial hotel was built, the village was platted, and Itasca boasted the first post office in present Anoka County. There was even an unsuccessful attempt to locate the territorial capital here.

Itasca was a stopping place on the heavily traveled Red River Oxcart Trail between Pembina, North Dakota, and the steamboat landing in St. Paul. In 1857 cargoes of fur, buffalo robes, and meat valued at $120,000 arrived at St. Paul, and in 1858 more than 600 carts plied the trade. Traces of the old trail can be seen a few feet west of this marker.

Drivers pose with Red River oxcarts

The village's prosperity began to wane in 1856, when the removal of the roving Winnebago Indians from the Long Prairie Reservation took away the mainstay of local trade. By the early 1860s the town was virtually deserted.

Itasca remained a post office until 1879, and it was the first mailing address of the Order of the Patrons of Husbandry, better known as the National Grange. This farm organization was founded by Oliver H. Kelley, who opened a Grange office in his home near here in 1868. For two years he mailed through the Itasca post office vast amounts of literature encouraging farmers to join the Grange.

Erected by the Anoka County Historical Society. 1966

# CARVER COUNTY

### 3. LITTLE RAPIDS FUR POST
*Located on U.S. highway 212, 1 mile west of Chaska*

By 1804 Jean B. Faribault was trading in furs for the Northwest Company near the "Little Rapids" of the Minnesota River, 5 miles south of this point, and in this vicinity.

His fur post of 1842 on the site of Chaska became the nucleus for the first Catholic mission in Carver County under Father Ravoux.

# CHISAGO COUNTY

### 4. GLACIAL POTHOLES  △
*Located on U.S. highway 8 in Interstate State Park near the park interpretive center*

The potholes at the St. Croix Dalles have their origins in a tale of fire and ice. They are carved in a dark volcanic rock called basalt, which erupted as lava 1.1 billion years ago. This basalt is related to lava flows that line the North Shore of Lake Superior. About 500 million years ago, when shallow tropical seas covered this area, the basalt was buried beneath a thick blanket of sand, which later became sandstone.

During the last two million years, glaciers have advanced from the Ontario region through the Lake Superior basin, repeatedly covering the Taylors Falls area. About 12,000 years ago, near the end of the most recent glaciation, meltwater collected at the southwestern edge of a glacial lobe as the lobe receded into the Superior basin. This water formed a growing Glacial Lake Duluth. When Glacial Lake Duluth drained, great floods flowed southward through the St. Croix River valley, forming Glacial River St. Croix. The largest of these floods was perhaps a hundred times the volume of modern ones. At this time, Glacial Lake Duluth drained only via Glacial River St. Croix, because ice still blocked the Superior basin's eastern outlet to the lower Great Lakes.

Rapid erosion of drainage spillways around the edge of Glacial Lake Duluth released tremendous amounts of water in a short time. These torrents of meltwater readily cut through the glacial sediments and the sandstone, deepening the St. Croix valley. Fierce rapids developed where the rushing current encountered the hard, resistant basalt. The rapids increased the speed and turbulence of the water, and a heavy sediment load provided powerful abrasive action—all necessary to carve potholes into the basalt.

Potholes commonly occur behind the base of a large boulder or other flow obstruction. They are made when turbulent water forms an eddy, or whirlpool, strong enough to swirl pebbles and cobbles around in one spot. There the swirling stones grind a cylindrical hole down into the bedrock. The exceptional depth and abundance of potholes here attest to the enormous power of Glacial River St. Croix.

Erected by the Geological Society of Minnesota in partnership with the Minnesota Department of Trans-

portation, the Minnesota Geological Survey, and the
Minnesota Department of Natural Resources. 2003

## 5.  GEOLOGY OF THE TAYLORS FALLS REGION  ⌂
*Located on U.S. highway 8 and state highway 95 in a
scenic overlook .2 mile south of Taylors Falls*

About 1.1 billion years ago, a great rift valley formed
across the North American continent from the Lake
Superior region southwest to Kansas. As this rift valley
opened, basaltic lavas erupted into it, accumulating to
a thickness of up to 20 kilometers in the Lake Superior
region. The dark-grey basalt rocks that form the St.
Croix River gorge are made from these rift lava flows.
Continental rifting with volcanism is common in the
geological record and often leads to the breakup of con-
tinents and the formation of intervening ocean basins.
For reasons not completely understood, the Midcontinent Rift here in North America failed to evolve to the
stage of complete continental separation.

About 520 million years ago in the Late Cambrian
period, the North American continent was positioned
with Minnesota near the equator. Shallow seas covered
the region, into which great thicknesses of mainly
quartz sand were deposited. These deposits are now the
sandstone bluffs along this river valley and the rock
faces exposed on the highway road cuts south of this
marker. Although most of the region then lay flat, the
basalts in the Taylors Falls area stood high as rocky,
cliff-ringed islands in a tropical sea.

The most recent geological event recorded here
occurred about 12,000 years ago during the end of the
Ice Age of the last two million years. As the last of the
glaciers melted and receded to the north, tremendous
quantities of sediment-laden glacial meltwaters were
channeled into the St. Croix River valley. Here at Taylors Falls, a colossal torrent of abrasive currents carved
down through the Cambrian sandstones and deep into
the rift basalts now seen on the valley floor. The spec-

tacular potholes in the lava rock, found in Interstate
Park about 0.4 kilometer north of this site, attest to the
high velocity of the raging glacial waters that carved
the St. Croix River gorge.

Erected by the Geological Society of Minnesota in
partnership with the Minnesota Department of Transportation, the Minnesota Geological Survey, and the
Minnesota Department of Natural Resources. 1998

## 6.  FOLSOM HOUSE  🏠

*Minnesota Historical Society Historic Site*
*Located at 272 W. Government Street, Taylors Falls,*
*north of U.S. highway 8*

William Henry Carman Folsom, St. Croix River Valley
lumberman and land speculator, chose this imposing
site for his home in 1854. He, his wife Mary Jane, and
their two small sons lived in an open barn on this

property to prove up
the claim while the
five-bedroom home,
reflecting both Federal
and Greek Revival
styles, was con-
structed. In 1855, after
the family moved in,
Mary Jane wrote to rel-
atives in Maine, "We
shall have plenty of
room for as many as
will come."

W. H. C. Folsom
arrived in Taylors Falls
in 1850 and actively

William Henry Carman Folsom, about 1855

involved himself in both the business and community
development of his new home. Although he ran a store
for 24 years, Folsom also helped operate a gristmill, a
copper mining company, a bridge company, and a

cemetery association. A member of the 1857 state constitutional convention, Folsom served five terms as state senator and one as representative. In his spare time, he wrote "Fifty Years in the Northwest," which is still a respected source of information on the early years of settlement in the area.

Once a wagon shed and stable, barn, icehouse, chicken coop, outhouse and wellhouse surrounded the main building. Of these, only the wellhouse remains, although the present garage was made with timbers from the barn. 1970

### 7. MINNESOTA'S ARROWHEAD REGION: A TOURIST MECCA

*Located on I-35 (north bound) at Goose Creek rest area*

"The North Country is a siren/Who can resist her song of intricate and rich counterpoint?" (Grace Lee Nute, *The Voyageur's Highway,* 1941)

Lured by America's premier wilderness canoe region, Lake Superior's rugged shoreline and cascading streams, and Duluth's reputation as America's great inland seaport, tourists have been coming to northeastern Minnesota since the 1890s. In recognition of this great natural treasure, President Theodore Roosevelt established the Superior National Forest in 1909.

Tourists first came by steamship and rail. But it was the advent of the automobile and the building of roads, particularly the Lake Superior International Highway (the North Shore Drive), dedicated in 1925, and the Gunflint Trail, built during the 1920s, that opened what came to be called the Arrowhead Region. The region's civic leaders, quick to take advantage of this new opportunity, organized the Arrowhead Association in 1924 to promote the area's recreational opportunities. Thanks in part to the organization's efforts, the North Shore Drive soon came to be known as one of the nation's most scenic highways. Americans, infatuated with the freedom and adventure of automobile travel, came in large numbers. In 1938, an estimated 1,000,000 tourists visited Split Rock Lighthouse, and in 1940 the U.S. Coast Guard declared it to be "probably the most visited lighthouse in the United States."

Numerous resorts were developed during the 1920s to accommodate the ever-increasing number of tourists. The State of Minnesota acquired several scenic areas along the North Shore for parks: Gooseberry Falls in 1933, Cascade River in 1934, and Temperance River in 1936. In 1926 the federal government moved to preserve the pristine lakes and forests of the boundary region as a wilderness canoe county.

This region remains a favorite destination for travelers from all over the world who heed the captivating call of the Arrowhead Region. 1996

# DAKOTA COUNTY

### 8.  KAPOSIA VILLAGE
*Located on state highway 156 at county 4 (Concord Street and Butler Avenue) in South St. Paul*

Here on the Mendota trail, from 1839 to 1852 stood the Sioux village of the Little Crow family. An attempted Chippewa attack in 1842 precipitated the Battle of Kaposia across the river. After the treaty of Mendota in 1851 the band moved up the Minnesota River to the Lower Sioux Agency region near Redwood [Falls].

### 9.  SIBLEY HOUSE  Ⓜ
*Minnesota Historical Society Historic Site*
*Located on state highway 13 at 1357 Sibley Memorial Highway in Mendota*

From 1910 to 1996, the Minnesota Society of the Daughters of the American Revolution (DAR) volunteered time, money, and leadership to restore and care for this historic site.

The Minnesota Chapter of the DAR was established in 1891 for the purpose of fostering patriotism, historic preservation, and education. Its members formed the Sibley House Association (SHA) in 1910 to preserve the then abandoned home of Henry Hastings Sibley, Minnesota's first governor and a descendant of Revolutionary War veterans. Envisioned as "Minnesota's Mount Vernon," the Sibley House Museum opened to the public with great fanfare on June 14, 1910. Admission was ten cents.

For the next 85 years, the DAR worked to make the house and its history available to Minnesotans. It raised funds, coordinated restoration work, collected photographs and artifacts, and a operated successful tour program. During that time it also added two other Mendota properties to the site. The house built in 1854 by Sibley's secretary, Hypolite DuPuis, was purchased in 1922, and operated as the popular Sibley Tea House until 1973, providing funds to run the museum. The 1839 house of Jean Baptiste Faribault, a long-standing Mendota fur trader was acquired in 1936 and restored with the help of the Works Progress Administration.

After 86 years of restoration and care of the Sibley Historic Site, the Sibley House Association of the Daughters of the American Revolution generously donated its properties and collections to the State of Minnesota in 1996.

### 10.  HENRY HASTINGS SIBLEY
*Located on state highway 13 in Mendota at west end of Sibley Historic Site*

To the glory of God and in memory of General Henry Hastings Sibley. Born February 20, 1811. Died February 18, 1891. A great patriot-soldier-statesman. This historic marker is built of the only remaining stone from the pioneer church erected by General Sibley in 1847 as a

place of worship "for Christians of all denominations."
The church stood upon a high hill opposite this site.
Dedication services in holiness unto the Lord, Sunday
June 5, 1955 and Monday June 6, 1955.

Given by Nathan Hale Chapter Number 178. National Society Daughters of the American Revolution,
St. Paul, Minnesota.

## 11.  ST. PETER'S CHURCH
*Located on the east end of the Mendota Bridge on state
highway 13 in Mendota Heights*

Here at Mendota (where the rivers meet) missionaries
ministered to both Indians and settlers, enduring the
hardships of a sprawling wilderness that was the Minnesota country. In 1842, Father Lucien Galtier built a
small, log chapel with only two windows, where the
Catholics of St. Peter's Parish worshipped for nearly
eleven years.

In 1844 Father Augustin Ravoux, who had already
spent three years in the area, arrived at Mendota to assist
Father Galtier. When Father Galtier left to serve another
parish in the fall of that year, Father Ravoux assumed
full responsibility for ministering to the thriving Mendota
community, which was the American Fur Company's
chief trading center with the Dakota (Sioux) Indians in
Minnesota territory.

Father Ravoux had this church constructed in
1853. Built of limestone quarried nearby and roofed
with hand-split pine shingles, the entire structure
measures only 35 by 75 feet, and the rear portion was
originally used as living quarters for the pastor.

The steeple has been twice replaced. The original
cross that topped the spire now hangs over the inside
door. While alterations have changed the interior, the
exterior remains much as it was in 1853.

The church still serves St. Peter's Parish and is the
oldest church in continuous use in Minnesota. From its
vantage point, it commands a spectacular view of the

Minnesota and Mississippi Rivers and of Historic Fort
Snelling. 1973

## 12. MENDOTA

*Located on state highway 13, 2 blocks north of junction
with state highway 55*

Mendota—in the language of the Sioux means the mouth
of a river—was the earliest permanent white settlement
in southern Minnesota. A pioneer center of the fur
trade—near here were signed treaties with the Indians
in 1805—1837—1851 ceding to the whites most of the
lands in Minnesota. Fort Snelling was established on
this side of the river in 1819. This region was long
known as Saint Peters.

## 13. MENDOTA

*Located on state highway 13 in Mendota*

This wide valley intersection between the two rivers
known today as the Minnesota and the Mississippi has
been a meeting place for people for thousands of years.

The Dakota people lived on these prairielands by
the 1700s. They knew this place as *Mdo'-te* or "the junction of one river with another." French explorers and
traders who were here in the late 1600s named the
Minnesota river *Sans Pierres* because the river was silty
but had few rocks. British explorers and traders who arrived a few years later misunderstood the French name,
calling the river Saint Peter's. In 1852, the territorial
legislature changed the name of the river to Minnesota,
a version of its Dakota name.

The American military arrived here in 1805 when
Lieutenant Zebulon Pike signed a treaty with the Dakota,
purchasing a parcel of land that included the river valleys and the high bluff across the river on which Fort
Snelling was built.

What had been a meeting spot for the Dakota became a trading hub for the entire region when the Amer-

ican Fur Company opened a post at Mendota. Alexis
Bailly took charge in 1826, followed by Henry Hastings
Sibley in 1834. Sibley replaced the log buildings at the
post with several permanent structures, and others were
added later. Four major structures remain today: a limestone company storehouse (1834); Sibley's limestone
dwelling and store (1836); the limestone and sandstone
house (1839) of trader Jean Baptiste Faribault; and, up
the hill, a brick house (1854) of trader Hypolite DuPuis.

Trade ended here in 1851, when the Treaties of Traverse des Sioux and Mendota resulted in the removal of
the Dakota to a reservation in the upper Minnesota
Valley. Henry Sibley resided here until 1862 and led an
active political career, serving as Minnesota Territory's
first delegate to Congress (1849–53) and the state's first
governor (1859–1860). 1997

## 14.  IGNATIUS DONNELLY'S NININGER CITY HOME
*Located on county roads 42 and 87, 3.5 miles northwest of
Hastings*

Just northwest of here, at the bottom of the hill, stood
the home of Ignatius Donnelly, author, orator, politician, reformer, and prophet who was easily the best
known Minnesotan of his time, both in the state and
throughout the world.

The Donnelly home in Nininger, about 1940

Donnelly, a lawyer from Philadelphia, moved west to Minnesota and launched a national campaign to attract settlers to Nininger City, a promising village of more than 500 residents when it was laid out around this site in 1856. After the town melted away during the panic and depression of 1857, Donnelly turned his astonishing energy to politics, serving one term as lieutenant governor and three terms in Congress. For nearly 40 years his restless search for fair and effective social and economic institutions led him to play a role in virtually every agrarian reform movement of the late nineteenth century.

In addition to his fiery campaigns on behalf of farmers and workers, Donnelly wrote several unconventional and widely read books of popular science, including *Atlantis, The Great Cryptogram, Ragnarok* and *Caesar's Column* in which he predicted the collapse of American society in the year 1988.

Donnelly lived at his Nininger City home until his death on January 1, 1901. Despite efforts to save it, the house was dismantled in 1949.

Erected by the Minnesota Historical Society on November 3, 1981 the 150th Anniversary of Ignatius Donnelly's Birth.

### 15.  DAKOTA COUNTY REGION  △

*Located in a wayside park near the junction of U.S. highway 61 and state highway 55 in Hastings*

Hastings lies just south and east of the limits of the last glaciation. About 20,000 years ago a lobe of ice, called the Superior lobe, advanced from the Lake Superior basin and crossed the ancient bedrock valley of the Mississippi River between St. Paul and Hastings. There it filled the valley with ice and sediment (silt, sand, gravel, and boulders). Glacial ice trapped in the valley was then covered by more sediment as the ice lobe slowly receded. The melting lobe deposited a large amount of sediment along its edge, creating a swath of hills of which a portion curves around the Twin Cities on the south and west. This deposit of glacial sediment is called the St. Croix moraine. Meltwater streams flowed out from the Superior lobe, breached the moraine, and built a broad outwash plain of sand and gravel. This outwash deposit buried the Mississippi River valley south of the moraine as far as Hastings.

About 16,000 years ago another lobe of ice, the Des Moines lobe, advanced from the northwest through central Minnesota and eventually extended as far south as Des Moines, Iowa. Locally, meltwater from its eastern margin drained eastward and carved a river valley to the Mississippi River at the present site of Hastings. The modern Vermillion River is but a shrunken remnant of that stream.

Ice blocks buried within the St. Croix moraine and filling the ancient bedrock valley of the Mississippi were insulated by sediment and melted very slowly. Eventually, their melting collapsed the moraine and re-established the Mississippi River valley for drainage. As the glacial lobes continued to recede, large volumes of meltwater flowed through the Mississippi again, forming numerous terraces and re-exposing the bedrock valley. When the influx of glacial meltwater ended, the volume of water in the Mississippi decreased greatly to what we see today.

Erected by the Geological Society of Minnesota in partnership with the Minnesota Department of Transportation and the Minnesota Geological Survey. 1998

# HENNEPIN COUNTY

### 16. FORT SNELLING NATIONAL LANDMARK
*Located off state highways 5 and 55 at Historic Fort Snelling*

Fort Snelling has been designated a National Historic Landmark. This site possesses national significance in

commemorating the history of the United States of
America.

National Park Service, United States Department of
the Interior. 1960

### 17.  FORT SNELLING 1861–1946  Ⓜ
*Minnesota Historical Society Historic Site*
*Located off state highway 55 at Historic Fort Snelling*

This historic ground was a pivotal place in the development of the Northwest. With the outbreak of the Civil
War in 1861, Fort Snelling expanded beyond its limestone walls into this area, formerly a part of the U. S.
Indian Agency and the location of the fort's gardens.
As the frontier moved west following the war, the fort,
as Headquarters of the Department of Dakota, administered and supplied dozens of western posts.

The military played an increasing world role after
1898, and the fort continued to grow. Handsome brick
buildings lined Taylor Avenue—a hospital, offices,
barracks, and officers' quarters. Opposite the extensive
parade grounds were the support facilities—stables,
workshops, and warehouses.

During World War I the fort was enlarged to a total
of some 400 structures. Here Minnesota's recruits for
both world wars first entered the service. Many others
served between the wars in the Third Infantry and
other units long associated with what was then known
as the "Country Club of the Army." Fort Snelling closed
in 1946, but it remains a fond memory for many who
played a part in its long history. 1989

### 18.  CAPTAIN MELVILLE WILKINSON
*Located at 6411 Taylor Avenue at Historic Fort Snelling in*
*Minneapolis*

The members of the Grand Army of the Republic resid-
ing in St. Paul and Minneapolis have erected this tablet
to the memory of their comrade, Captain Melville Cary

Wilkinson. Born in Scottsburg N.Y. Nov. 14, 1835. 1st. Lieut. 123 N.Y. Inf., May 16, 1861; Capt. 107 N.Y. Inf., Aug.9, 1862; 2nd. Lieut. 42 U.S. Inf., July 28, 1866; Assigned to 3rd U.S. Inf., Aug. 3, 1870; Captain 3rd U.S. Inf., April 24, 1886. Killed in action with hostile Indians at Sugar Point, Minnesota Oct. 5th, 1898.

Soldier rest! Thy warfare o'er,/Sleep the sleep that knows not breaking/Dream of battled fields no more,/Days of danger, nights of waking. 1899

### 19. JOSEPH HALE

*Located at 6411 Taylor Avenue at Historic Fort Snelling in Minneapolis*

The Society of the Sons of the Revolution in the State of Minnesota honors the memory of Captain Joseph Hale. Born February 1, 1839—Died October 12, 1898. Private 5th Mass. Vols. Apl. 19,–Jul. 31, 1861. Private, corporal, 1st sergeant 11th U.S. Inf. Aug. 10, 1861–May 25, 1864. Commissioned and served in 3rd U.S. Inf. 2nd Lieut. May 18, 1864, 1st Lieut. Mar. 21, 1865, Captain Mar. 2, 1885–Oct. 12, 1898.

A hero of the Civil, Indian, and Spanish Wars.

### 20. THREE ISLANDS IN THE MISSISSIPPI

*Located on Pike Island in Fort Snelling State Park*

The Mississippi River's many islands are well known to navigators, and the roles of several as accessible and safe havens for villages, camps, and forts have made them significant in Minnesota's past. Lt. Zebulon Pike chose this island, later named for him, as a camp site on his 1805 expedition to explore the upper Mississippi following the Louisiana Purchase. Pike met with Dakota Indian leaders here and purchased land which would later become part of the Twin Cities.

Grey Cloud Island, further downstream, was known to the Dakota people for its supernatural woods and its great variety of wild fruit. U.S. troops under the command of Colonel Henry Leavenworth found it a good campsite on their way up the river to establish Fort Snelling, and in 1838 Joseph R. Brown, a former fort drummer boy, established a trading post there.

The home of the Prairie Island Dakota Indian Community, who share it with a nuclear power plant, Prairie Island at the mouth of the Vermillion River may have been one of the first Minnesota locations visited by French explorers in the late 17th century. They called it Isle Pelee (Bald Island), probably because of its extensive prairie cover dotted with several lakes and sloughs. 1989

### 21. DAKOTA INTERNMENT CAMP
*Located off state highway 5 in Fort Snelling State Park*

In the winter of 1862–63 some sixteen hundred Dakota people, mostly women and children, were confined here under guard in the aftermath of the 1862 U.S.-Dakota Conflict. Frightened, uprooted, and uncertain of the fate of their missing relatives and friends, the interned Dakota suffered severe hardship. At least 130 died during the long months of captivity.

The Dakota camp below Fort Snelling in 1862

The U.S.-Dakota Conflict was the culmination of nearly a century of enforced change for the Dakota people. Pushed off their lands as whites moved into the region, they were by the 1850s confined to small reservations and under heavy pressure to give up their own culture and religion. Reacting to broken treaties, greed, and injustice just as any other people would react, many Dakota felt by August, 1862, that they must fight for their traditional way of life. In the six weeks of conflict some five hundred white settlers and soldiers and an unknown number of Dakota people died. When the fighting ended, some Dakota fled west or into Canada. Others were brought here to Fort Snelling, later to be exiled from their ancient homeland of Mini sota makoce.

In May, 1863, the surviving thirteen hundred people from the internment camp were crowded aboard two small river steamers and taken down the Mississippi and up the Missouri rivers to Crow Creek in southeastern South Dakota, a "dismal drought-stricken place" that was soon dotted with Dakota graves. Those who survived were uprooted again three years later, when most were moved to the Santee Reservation in Nebraska.

Erected in 1987, the Year of Reconciliation, by the Dakota People of Minnesota, the Minnesota Department of Natural Resources, and the Minnesota Historical Society.

## 22.  CAMP COLDWATER
*Located off state highway 55 in Minneapolis, .2 mile east on 54th Street East, .5 mile south on access road past government buildings*

On May 5th of 1820 Lieutenant Colonel Henry Leavenworth moved the 5th U.S. Infantry troops under his command to this area to escape the unhealthy conditions they had endured at their earlier stockade on the Minnesota River. The clear, cold spring water helped restore the men and their families, who lived in tents and elm bark huts here during three summers while they built the permanent stone fort nearby. The military continued to rely on the spring's fresh water through the nineteenth century, using horse-drawn water wagons and later a stone water tower and underground pipes to transport the water to Fort Snelling.

Families who left the Red River colony of Lord Selkirk were allowed by Colonel Josiah Snelling to settle near this location in 1821. Here they raised cattle and sold provisions to the army. When they were forced to vacate the military reservation in 1840, they moved downriver and helped establish St. Paul.

Blacksmith shops, stables, trading posts such as B. F. Baker's substantial stone warehouse, the St. Louis Hotel, and a steamboat landing all occupied this area, but by the time of the Civil War nearly all were gone. Today this spring is all that remains of Camp Coldwater. 1990

### 23.  MINNEHAHA DEPOT 🏛
*Minnesota Historical Society Historic Site*
*Located in Minnehaha State Park off Minnehaha Avenue in Minneapolis*

Milwaukee Road station agents affectionately referred to the quaint little Minnehaha Depot as "the Princess." Its delicate gingerbread architecture is reminiscent of the Victorian era when ladies in bustles and gentlemen in high collars traveled largely by train.

The first track connecting Minneapolis with Mendota was laid in 1865 by the Minnesota Central Railway, the predecessor of the Chicago, Milwaukee and St. Paul Railway. The Princess was built in the mid-1870s to replace a smaller station here. Throngs of picnickers and sightseers took the sixteen-minute ride from Minneapolis to Minnehaha Park and the old Longfellow Gardens Zoo, while others traveled to and from Fort Snelling and Mendota. In 1910 three trains made thirteen round trips daily to the depot. It was the scene of feverish activity during World Wars I and II because of the military traffic in and out of Fort Snelling.

The Milwaukee Road closed the station in August, 1963, and presented it to the Minnesota Historical Society in 1964. The Minnesota Transportation Museum, Inc., an affiliate of the society, has undertaken the restoration and maintenance of the depot. 1969

### 24. MINNEHAHA FALLS ⚲

*Located in Minnehaha Park, accessible from Minnehaha Avenue or West River Road in Minneapolis or from Ford Parkway in St. Paul*

Near Fort Snelling, 10,000 years ago, melt water from the Wisconsin glacier was discharged through the Mississippi River and plunged over a ledge of Platteville limestone into a gorge cut chiefly in the white St. Peter sandstone. The undercutting action in the soft sandstone caused the limestone ledge to break off with a vertical face, thus maintaining the falls, while causing them to retreat upstream. When the falls in the main channel passed the upper end of the island—where the Soldiers Home now stands—the entire flow in the river was diverted to the main gorge and the falls in the west channel were abandoned. This unique and unusual geological feature, an abandoned waterfall, is located at the north end of the former west channel which lies 200 feet east of this tablet.

The cataract in the Mississippi has migrated to St. Anthony Falls and Minnehaha has retreated from the abandoned channel to its present location, where the undercutting action responsible for the migration is apparent.

Erected by the Geological Society of Minnesota in cooperation with the Board of Park Commissioners City of Minneapolis. 1953

## 25.  THE ARMORY BUILDING, 1896–1996
*Located at 15 Church Street SE, University of Minnesota, Minneapolis*

[Front] The University of Minnesota opened in 1869, assisted by federal subsidies and with military instruction mandated by the Land Grant Act of 1862. Since 1884, the buildings used for military instruction have met additional University needs. Lt. George Morgan headed the movement to build the Armory in 1894, when the Coliseum auditorium/drill hall burned. Architecture professor Charles Aldrich designed the castle-like replacement for military and athletic instruction, and University events. In 1895, the legislature appropriated $75,000, and civil engineering students staked the layout of the 220 x 135- foot building which became the largest structure on campus. The Armory was completed in 1896 for $67,000.

The Armory featured a ramp and sally port entrance leading to a two-story assembly and drill hall. The hall had suspended galleries and moveable partitions at the ends which enclosed men's and women's gymnasiums. When fully opened as an auditorium it seated 3,700. When used as a ballroom, there was dancing space for over 300 couples. After 1929, when Northrop Auditorium was completed, the hall continued as a site for activities that ranged from military ceremonies to final exams.

The Armory's main and top floors included classrooms and offices for military instruction, and later the Aeronautical Engineering Department. A running track, gun room, and quarters for University athletic teams were at the ground level. A rifle range extended the length of the building underground. The Armory hosted University athletic events and housed physical education instruction until replaced by Cooke Hall in 1935. In the 1940s, the west balconies were enclosed to accommodate instruction for Navy midshipmen. After

World War II, the ground floor was devoted to training Air Force cadets. At the close of the twentieth century Army, Navy, and Air Force instruction continued in the Armory, along with University College and the programs of Continuing Education and Extension.

### Military Training at the University
[Back] Military training began in 1869 under ex Civil War colonel and first University president William Watts Folwell. Since then over 100,000 men and women have participated in military training programs. In 1888, the University of Minnesota Cadet Corps was formally established, and women participated in drill. In 1889, drill became compulsory for all students. Female participation ended in 1892 when physical culture classes became available, but returned in the early 1970s when women were admitted for officer training in all the military services. Drill remained compulsory for male freshmen and sophomores until 1934.

Between 1910 and 1916, the Cadet Corps trained in summer camps at Fort Snelling. The Corps was dissolved in 1916, when the National Defense Act established the Reserve Officer Training Corps (R.O.T.C.). In 1918, the World War I draft rapidly enlarged the Army,

Cadets fire a cannon salute to Gov. J. A. Johnson, 1909

and over 6,000 men came to campus for the Student Army Training Corps program of collegiate men and technical instruction.

In 1939, with World War II, the armed forces were enlarged again and Navy R.O.T.C. began at the University. When the nation entered the war, naval officer candidates received medical, dental, and engineering instruction, and naval aviators were quartered in Nicholson Hall while they took preflight training. The 88th Army Air Forces Training Detachment quartered hundreds of air crewmen inside Memorial Stadium when the men took classes on campus and flight training at Victory Field near Anoka. Army officer candidates were trained as weather forecasters in the University's meteorology program.

At the beginning of the Cold War in 1946, a program for aviator officers began under the Army Air Force. Air Force R.O.T.C. was established and became a distinct unit at the University in 1949. The three services have commissioned over 6,000 officers since 1935, and cooperate with similar programs at other universities around Minnesota, and with military reserve units in this area.

Erected by the Minnesota Historical Society and the University of Minnesota. 1996

### 26. LAKE HARRIET REGION  ⩗
*Located in Minneapolis on the northwest shore of Lake Harriet, at West Lake Harriet Boulevard and William Berry Road*

The continental glaciers spreading over Minnesota during the great ice ages brought vast quantities of rock material from the north to be dumped indiscriminately during the recession of the ice. Old river valleys were filled and belts of hills were formed as conditions changed. The Lake Harriet landscape has such an origin.

Leaving the present channel of the Mississippi
River at the Plymouth Avenue bridge, a preglacial valley runs almost directly south beneath Lake of the Isles,
Lake Calhoun and Lake Harriet to the Minnesota River
at Bloomington. This valley was mostly filled but not
completely obliterated by glacial deposits. The unfilled
portions of the valley are now basins, which are filled
by lakes perched high on the glacial debris. Lake Harriet lies directly over this ancient valley, its surface 250
feet above the valley's rocky floor, and is in a setting of
hills piled up while the ice front paused here in its final
retreat about 10,000 years ago.

Erected by the Geological Society of Minnesota and
the Board of Park Commissioners, City of Minneapolis
aided by a grant from the Louis W. and Maud Hill Family Foundation. 1955

### 27.   GOV. FLOYD B. OLSON STATE MONUMENT 🏛

*Located on Olson Memorial Highway (state highway 55)*
*(east bound) between Oliver and Penn Avenues North in*
*Minneapolis*

Floyd B. Olson, 1891–1936, Twenty-second Governor of
the State of Minnesota

### 28.   PETER M. GIDEON AND THE WEALTHY APPLE

*Located on county road 19 at Glen Road, about 1 mile north*
*of the junction of 19 and state highway 7 near Excelsior*

In 1853, Peter Miller Gideon and his wife Wealthy, arrived in Minnesota from Ohio and settled on the shores
of Lake Minnetonka. Long interested in fruitgrowing,
Peter Gideon determined to satisfy the craving of pioneer families for apples and other fruits although all
previous efforts to grow them had failed.

In 1854 he recorded that he planted one bushel of
apple seed and a peck of peach seed. For fourteen years
he planted, seeded, and grafted more than 10,000 apple,
cherry, peach, pear, plum, and quince trees; but hard

winters, blight, grasshopper plagues, and other reverses prevailed. Each year he had to start anew.

From one seed he obtained from Maine, a seedling grew that withstood the hard Minnesota winters and produced in 1868 the celebrated Wealthy apple, which was named for his wife and hailed as the "best apple produced since Adam and Eve left the Garden of Eden." From this flourished the Northwest's fruitgrowing industries.

His steadfastness and perseverance applied also to his outspoken, often inflexible, views on social issues. He condemned slavery and abuse of Indians, supported women's rights, and fought for the "advancement of moral refinement."

Within view of this monument, which is on the southeast corner of the original homestead, is the Gideon home, now more than 100 years old, and the site of the original orchards. 1965

### 29.  CHRISTMAS LAKE
*Located on state highway 7 in wayside 2.5 miles east of Excelsior*

Named for Charles W. Christmas, first county surveyor of Hennepin County elected in 1852, who platted the original town site of Minneapolis for John H. Stevens and Franklin Steele. This lake and Lake Minnetonka now occupy what in pre-glacial times was part of the channel of the Mississippi River near its junction with the pre-glacial Minnesota River. 1968

### 30.  MINNETONKA—QUEEN OF THE INLAND LAKES
*Located on county road 110 south of junction with county road 15 in Mound*

In May, 1822, a Fort Snelling drummer boy named Joseph R. Brown and his friend, William Snelling, son of the fort's commander, canoed up what is now called Minnehaha Creek to "discover" a lake long sacred to the Indian people who built burial mounds along its shores. Thirty years later, the 23-square-mile natural lake with 110 miles of indented shoreline was named "Minnetonka"—Dakota for "Great Piece of Water"—by Governor Alexander Ramsey.

By the early 1880s Lake Minnetonka had become a favorite summer resort for the rich and famous of the United States and Europe, including Presidents Ulysses S. Grant and Chester A. Arthur. The 300-foot "Belle of Minnetonka" and other excursion boats nearly as large carried thousands of visitors enjoying holidays at comfortable summer homes or elegant hotels like the Chapman House here on Cook's Bay and the prestigious Hotel Lafayette on Crystal Bay.

With the arrival of the automobile, the great hotel era faded and the summer cottages evolved into permanent homes. Lake Minnetonka is still known for its beauty and its many recreational opportunities. Erected by the Minnesota Historical Society and the Mound Historical Society. 1984

### 31.  GEOLOGY OF LAKE MINNETONKA △
*Located on Lake Street at Water Street by the municipal docks in Excelsior*

Like most lakes in Minnesota, Lake Minnetonka was formed during the Ice Age of the last two million years. During several separate glacial periods, ice advanced along different routes across the state. The glaciers, along with large volumes of sediment (clay, silt, sand, gravel, and boulders) trapped in the ice, altered the preexisting terrain and created the landscape we see today.

Before glacial action, the surface of this region consisted of sandstones and limestones which formed from sediments deposited in seas that covered the area 300 to 500 million years ago. After the seas retreated, rivers carved a valley system into the sedimentary bedrock. This ancient valley system had provided southward drainage through the region. The bedrock floor of a

The Belle of Minnetonka, about 1891

principal valley of that ancient system now lies as much as 122 meters below the surface of Lake Minnetonka.

About 25,000 years ago, at the peak of the last glacial period, or Wisconsin glaciation, an advancing glacier, which was passing over the ancient river valley that now lies beneath Lake Minnetonka, filled the valley with ice. Sediment that melted out of the overriding glacier then buried the ice trapped in the valley. The glacial ice and sediment were later covered by additional sediment from more recent glacial advances. As a result, when glaciers last receded from Minnesota 10,000 years ago, large blocks of ice were buried deep in the ancient valley under thick piles of sediment. When the ice blocks melted, the overlying sediment collapsed and created numerous depressions that filled with water, which are called kettle lakes. At Lake Minnetonka, the ice blocks were so big and close together that the depressions coalesced to form the large, composite kettle lake that we see today.

Erected by the Geological Society of Minnesota in partnership with the Minnesota Department of Transportation and the Minnesota Geological Survey. 1998

## 32. THE MISSISSIPPI FINDS A WAY ⛰

*Located off I-94 at the 53rd Avenue exit in North Mississippi Regional Park*

About 20,000 years ago, a glacier from the Ontario region passed through the Lake Superior basin and reached the Twin Cities area. As the glacial ice melted, it deposited the St. Croix moraine at its margin. A moraine is a deposit of sediment (clay, silt, sand, gravel, and boulders) left by a melting glacier. The St. Croix moraine forms a belt of hills that crosses the Twin Cities and extends northwest to St. Cloud. As the moraine was deposited, it buried some blocks of stagnant glacial ice that were left stranded in an ancient valley.

This park lies within the southernmost part of the Anoka sand plain, a vast area of sand stretching from St. Cloud to the St. Croix River valley. Much of the sand was deposited about 12,000 years ago in Glacial Lake Anoka. Fed by meltwater from glacial ice in northwestern Minnesota, the lake formed on the northern side of the St. Croix moraine. The hidden ice blocks buried earlier in the moraine eventually melted to create a gap through which Glacial Lake Anoka drained, abandoning its former outlet to the east through the St. Croix River valley. The gap, called the Camden breach, formed just downstream from here, in the area south of the Soo Line railroad bridge. The Camden breach established the general course of the Mississippi River between here and the site of Hastings.

After Glacial Lake Anoka drained, the Mississippi River upstream of the Camden breach meandered across the flat surface of the former lake bottom, from the Osseo area in the west to the Fridley area in the east. The shifting river formed two distinct terrace levels before becoming entrenched in its present narrow floodplain. Shingle Creek, to the west, generally follows the boundary of the two former river levels, at the base of the upper terrace. Across the Mississippi from this park, the river has exposed clay-rich sediment from a glacial lake that existed before Glacial Lake Anoka. The clay was mined in pits along the river for the manufacture of brick from about 1875 to 1910.

Erected by the Geological Society of Minnesota in partnership with the Minnesota Department of Transportation, the Minnesota Geological Survey, and the Three Rivers Park District. 2003

### 33.  GEOLOGY OF PALMER LAKE  △
*Located off I-94 in Palmer Lake Park in Brooklyn Center*

About 20,000 years ago, a glacier from the Ontario region passed through the Lake Superior basin and reached the Twin Cities area. As the glacial ice melted, it deposited the St. Croix moraine at its margin. A moraine is a deposit of sediment (clay, silt, sand, gravel, and boulders) left by a melting glacier. The St. Croix moraine forms a belt of hills that crosses the Twin Cities and extends northwest to St. Cloud. As the moraine was deposited, it buried some blocks of stagnant glacial ice that were left stranded in an ancient valley.

Palmer Lake lies within the southern part of the Anoka sand plain, a vast area of sand stretching from St. Cloud to the St. Croix River valley. Much of the sand was deposited about 12,000 years ago in Glacial Lake Anoka. Fed by meltwater from glacial ice in northwestern Minnesota, the lake formed on the northern side of the St. Croix moraine. The hidden ice blocks buried earlier in the moraine eventually melted to create a gap through which Glacial Lake Anoka drained, abandoning its former outlet to the east through the St. Croix River valley. With this gap, the general course of the Mississippi River was established between the sites of north Minneapolis and Hastings.

Ice blocks were also left stranded in other valleys, where they became buried below the Anoka sand plain. Like most other lakes in the Twin Cities area, Palmer Lake formed in a depression created by the melting of buried ice. Palmer Lake is shallow because the hole left by the melting ice was probably filled in as it formed, first by sediment deposited in Glacial Lake Anoka, and then after the lake drained, by sediment from the Mississippi River.

The Mississippi meandered widely, as far west as the Osseo area, across the flat surface of the former bottom of Glacial Lake Anoka. The shifting river formed two distinct terrace levels before becoming entrenched in its present narrow floodplain. Palmer Lake lies within the lower terrace. The upper terrace forms the slightly higher ground on the west side of the lake.

Erected by the Geological Society of Minnesota in partnership with the Minnesota Department of Transportation, the Minnesota Geological Survey, and the City of Brooklyn Center. 2003

### 34. EARLE BROWN AND THE BROOKLYN FARM
*Located at the Earle Brown Heritage Center, 6155 Earle Brown Drive, in Brooklyn Center*

Although this site is known today as the Earle Brown farm, it originally belonged to Captain John Martin, who was involved in steamboating, lumbering, banking, flour milling and railroading. In the mid-1880s, he purchased 420 acres of rich Hennepin County farmland. Martin sold the farm to his grandson, Earle Brown in 1901. Brown gradually increased the size of the farm to about 750 acres.

Aspiring to be a gentleman farmer, Brown initially used the land to breed award-winning Belgian Horses. But the farm was destined to become famous for activities unrelated to agriculture. In 1911, the village of Brooklyn Center was formed at a meeting held at the Brown Farm. As the nation became interested in aviation during World War I, Brown offered his farm and its buildings as a training field for U.S. military aviators. Though this offer was declined, the Brown farm did become the first commercial flying field in Minnesota in the summer of 1918, when hangars were

erected and pilots began using the site as a training facility and airport. Although planes had previously
landed on Minneapolis lakes and at the Parade (grounds)
near Dunwoody Institute, no formal air fields had been
constructed. In 1920 Brown was elected Hennepin
County sheriff, a position he held twice, from 1920–1929
and then from 1943–1947. In 1929 he organized the
Minnesota Highway Patrol, which used the farm as a
training facility. In 1932 he unsuccessfully ran for state
governor, and lost to Floyd B. Olson. Brown lived on
the Brooklyn Farm until his death in 1963, raising horses
and collecting carriages.

In 1949, Brown willed the farm to the University of
Minnesota, hoping that it would become the University's Agricultural Extension Center upon his death.
After Brown died, however, the University sold the land
and used the income to build the Earle Brown Continuing Education Center of the St. Paul Campus.

In 1985 the City of Brooklyn Center acquired the
buildings and property of the original homestead. Preserved for the people of Minnesota, it is a tangible link
to the agricultural heritage of what is now an urban
area. It is also a memorial to an important figure in
Minnesota history. 1998

Earle Brown at his farm in 1932

## 35.  GEOLOGY OF THE COON RAPIDS DAM AREA △

*Located off West River Road on the bank of the Mississippi River near the Coon Rapids Dam*

About 20,000 years ago, a glacier from the Ontario region passed through the Lake Superior basin and reached the Twin Cities area. As the glacial ice melted, it deposited the St. Croix moraine at its margin. A moraine is a deposit of sediment (clay, silt, sand, gravel, and boulders) left by a melting glacier. The St. Croix moraine forms a belt of hills that crosses the Twin Cities and extends northwest to St. Cloud. As the moraine was deposited, it buried some blocks of stagnant glacial ice that were left stranded in an ancient valley.

This park lies within the southern part of the Anoka sand plain, a vast area of sand stretching from St. Cloud to the St. Croix River valley. Much of the sand was deposited about 12,000 years ago in Glacial Lake Anoka. Fed by meltwater from glacial ice in northwestern Minnesota, the lake formed on the northern side of the St. Croix moraine. The hidden ice blocks buried earlier in the moraine eventually melted to create a gap through which Glacial Lake Anoka drained, abandoning its former outlet to the east through the St. Croix River valley. With this gap, the general course of the Mississippi River was established between the sites of north Minneapolis and Hastings.

After Glacial Lake Anoka drained, the Mississippi River meandered across the flat surface of the former lake bottom. The shifting river formed two distinct terrace levels before becoming entrenched in its present narrow floodplain. The terraces can be seen about two kilometers west of here on 109th Avenue, where a northwest-trending slope separates Champlin Park High School on the upper terrace from Jackson Middle School on the lower terrace. As the Mississippi cut below the lower terrace, it encountered many boulders in the glacial sediment just upstream from this dam. The boulders formed a barrier to erosion on the river bottom, creating the Coon Creek rapids, now submerged behind the dam.

Downstream from the dam, the river has cut its channel into reddish, clay-rich sediment from a glacial lake that existed before Glacial Lake Anoka. The red clay was mined along Coon Creek just north of this park by various companies from just before 1880 to about 1910.

Erected by the Geological Society of Minnesota in partnership with the Minnesota Department of Transportation, the Minnesota Geological Survey, and the Three Rivers Park District. 2003

### 36. PRESERVING THE PAST
*Located on I-94 (east bound) in the Elm Creek Rest Area*

Beneath the surface of our cities, farms, and highways lie clues to Minnesota's past. Those clues may be bison bones from a 12,000-year-old hunting camp, a broken pipe from a trash pit left by fur traders in the 1700s, or the foundation of a log home abandoned by an immigrant farmer years ago. From such evidence, archeologists piece together the stories from our cultural heritage.

To protect our cultural resources from destruction, the U.S. government and the Minnesota Legislature passed a series of laws in the 1960s and 1970s. One of those laws, the federal Department of Transportation Act of 1966, requires careful planning of highway construction projects to minimize damage to historic sites, defined as "all districts, sites, buildings, and objects significant in American history, architecture, archeology, and culture."

To comply with the new law the Minnesota Department of Transportation—in cooperation with the Minnesota Historical Society and the Federal Highway Administration—created an archeological survey program in 1968 for state highway construction projects. A similar program for county and municipal highways followed in 1975. The programs share a common mission—to find, study, and preserve cultural remains that lie in the path of highway construction.

Before construction can begin, archeologists, using a combination of research, site inspection, and excavation, determine what cultural resources are present, assess their importance to Minnesota's history, and make recommendations for their preservation.

If possible, construction plans are changed to avoid destroying important sites. When a site cannot be saved, archeologists collect material and record data about the site for future study.

Only by such means can we ensure that irreplaceable chapters in the story of Minnesota's past are not lost. 1997

# RAMSEY COUNTY

### 37.  ST. PETER SANDSTONE  △
*Located off U.S. highway 61 in Battle Creek Regional Park near the eastern edge of St. Paul*

The white sandstone that forms the walls of this ravine was made from sand that originated in what is now the Lake Superior region. About 460 million years ago, this sand was carried southward by rivers and strong winds to the edge of a warm, shallow sea that covered much of North America. When the sand reached the sea, storm waves and nearshore currents dispersed it along the coastline. As the sea level changed over time, the shoreline migrated across the region of southeastern Minnesota. At that time, southeastern Minnesota may have looked like the sandy coast of the Gulf of Mexico today.

The St. Peter Sandstone was named after the St. Peter River (now called the Minnesota River). It is composed almost entirely of similarly sized and well-rounded quartz sand grains, which are pitted or frosted. The pitting and frosting probably occurred in large dune areas along the shoreline where the sand was blown by the wind before being submerged. The sandstone crumbles easily because its grains are poorly cemented together with minerals that were precipitated from water flowing between the grains. The St. Peter Sandstone is nearly 99 percent pure quartz (crystalline silica) and has been used as a raw material for glass manufacture and metal casting molds.

The St. Peter formation reaches a thickness of up to 58 meters in the Twin Cities area and has been excavated to hold an extensive system of tunnels for water, sewer, and communication cables. Extending across the Midwest and from Michigan south to Arkansas, the St. Peter Sandstone is one of the most widely distributed, high-purity quartz sandstone formations in North America.

Erected by the Geological Society of Minnesota in partnership with the Minnesota Department of Transportation, the Minnesota Geological Survey, and Ramsey County Parks and Recreation. 2003

### 38.  INDIAN MOUNDS PARK  ⚠

*Located in Indian Mounds Park on Mounds Boulevard at Earl Street in St. Paul*

This point commands a view of one of the great water courses of North America. The stream which once filled this valley, named the River Warren, was larger than any river on the continent today.

During the past million years, Minnesota has been partly covered by glaciers at least 4 times. The short summers and long winters of the great ice ages caused an accumulation of snow and ice to a thickness of several thousand feet.

As the climate moderated and glaciation came to an end, enormous quantities of water were released to flow in rivers away from the ice field. The valley of the Mississippi visible from this point, was eroded by such a stream about 12,000 years ago. Scoured to a depth of

100 feet below the present river surface, the valley was
later filled by sand and gravel as the force of the torrent
subsided.

Erected by the Geological Society of Minnesota and
the Department of Parks, City of St. Paul aided by a
grant from the Louis W. and Maud Hill Family Foundation. 1954


**39.  CARVER'S CAVE**

*Located on Mounds Boulevard between Plum and
Cherry Streets in St. Paul*

Repeated attempts were made by French and British explorers to discover a Northwest Passage. One of the most
significant of these expeditions was conceived by Major
Robert Rogers, a commandant of Fort Michilimackinac
on Upper Lake Michigan, and led by Jonathan Carver in
1766. Carver pushed westward from the fort into the
Minnesota country, reaching the Mississippi River in
late autumn.

On November 10, 1766, the explorer arrived at the
foot of the bluff, where he found a "remarkable cave of
an amazing depth." He tells us that it contained a lake
and "many Indian hieroglyphicks which appear very
ancient." The cave, he says, was called by the Sioux
"Wakon-teebe," meaning Dwelling of the Great Spirit.

In April, 1767, Carver returned to this spot with
300 Sioux, and here he took part in a great Indian
council. When he was asked to speak, the explorer
warned the Indians in their own language against al-
liances with the French and attempted to impress them
with the power of Great Britain.

When Minnesota was settled, Carver's Cave became a popular tourist attraction and was regarded a
century ago as "the foremost relic of antiquity" in the
region. Today only a debris-filled remnant of the once
large cavern remains. It was destroyed by railroad construction about 1869. 1965

### 40.  ALEXANDER RAMSEY HOUSE  🏠

*Minnesota Historical Society Historic Site*
*Located at 265 South Exchange Street in St. Paul*

Appointed by President Zachary Taylor in 1849, Alexander Ramsey came to Minnesota as the territory's first governor. Ramsey stayed in Minnesota for his remaining fifty-four years and, during a successful political career as a Whig and then a Republican, served as mayor of St. Paul, state governor, United States Senator, and Secretary of War in the cabinet of Rutherford B. Hayes. When the Civil War broke out in 1861, Ramsey was the first Union governor to offer troops to President Abraham Lincoln.

This fifteen-room house of native limestone, typical of the elegant late Victorian period, was designed in a French Renaissance style by St. Paul architect Monroe Sheire. It had been under construction for four years by 1872, when Alexander and Anna Ramsey moved in. A focus for the political, cultural, and social life of Minnesota for nearly a century, the house was occupied by three generations of Ramseys, all of whom affectionately preserved the structure and its furnishings.

Behind the main house stands an ornate two-story wooden carriage house, reconstructed by the Minnesota

Boy Scouts explored Carver's Cave, about 1935

Historical Society in 1970 from the original architectural plans preserved among Ramsey's papers. Once
used to provide quarters for the groom, stalls for the
horses and a cow, and storage for carriages and harness
equipment, the carriage house now serves as a Visitors'
Center. 1972

### 41.  THE ST. PAUL HIGH BRIDGE
*Located on state highway 149 (Smith Avenue) and*
*Mississippi River in St. Paul*

The Smith Avenue High Bridge was named for Robert A.
Smith, the mayor of St. Paul from 1887 to 1892. The
bridge was a rare example of nineteenth century bridge
technology, and provided a vital transportation link in
the City of St. Paul for 96 years. Andrew Carnegie's Key-
stone Bridge Company designed the 2,770-foot wrought
iron structure which towered from 80 feet above the
river on the north to 191 feet on the south. Construction on the bridge began in 1887 and was completed in
May of 1889. Nearly one million pieces of wrought iron
weighing more than 3,000 tons were used to build it.
     Although many repairs were made to the bridge
throughout its life, including the replacement of the five
southernmost spans after a 1904 windstorm, the appearance of the truss was never altered. The High Bridge was
recognized by the National Register of Historic Places for
the role it played in the development of St. Paul and for
its place in wrought iron bridge technology.
     Age, weather, structural deterioration, and the
stresses of modern, daily traffic took considerable toll
on a bridge originally designed for horse and wagon.
The bridge was permanently closed on July 25, 1984,
and demolished on February 24, 1985. Its wrought iron
sidewalk railings and pier stone from the river piers
were salvaged and reused in this overlook.
     Significant features of the old High Bridge were
also incorporated into the design of the new bridge.
Steel was used to reflect the use of metal in the old

bridge, and the design of the decorative sidewalk rail-
ing was chosen from the work of Cass Gilbert, architect
of the State Capitol. The bridge type was selected by
the residents of the two adjacent neighborhoods. The
bridge was designed by Strgar-Roscoe-Fausch Inc./T.Y.
Lin International under contract with the Minnesota
Department of Transportation.
    Original High Bridge, 1889–1985

**42.  GILLETTE STATE HOSPITAL FOR CRIPPLED CHILDREN**
*Located at 987 Ivy Avenue East near Phalen Park in
St. Paul*

In 1897 the Minnesota Legislature established the State
Hospital for Crippled and Deformed Children, the first
hospital in the nation to provide free care to disabled
children of low-income parents. Renamed for its first
chief of staff, Dr. Arthur Gillette, the hospital moved to
this site near Lake Phalen in 1911. Over the next 35
years, nine buildings were built to meet the growing
demand for services, necessitated by the polio epidemic
of the 1930s and 1940s.
    To serve long-term patients, the hospital added this
educational facility in 1924; it housed a school, library,
and auditorium. Named the Michael J. Dowling Memorial Hall, the building honored a benefactor who was
himself disabled. The Spanish Colonial-style structure
was designed by Clarence H. Johnston, one of Minnesota's most prominent architects. Among the hall's
distinctive features are a red-tiled roof, arched doorway,
marble columns, and decorative plaster relief sculptures.
    Due partly to the development of polio vaccines in
the 1950s, Gillette Hospital's patient load began to decline. In 1977 Gillette closed its Lake Phalen facilities
and moved to new quarters in the St. Paul-Ramsey
Medical Center. Three years later all of the buildings
except Dowling Memorial Hall were demolished.
    Several times the building was threatened with
demolition. Each time its East Side neighbors fought

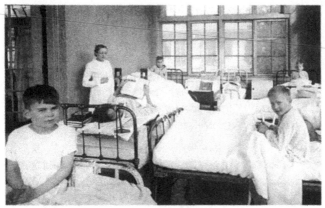

Convalescent children in the solarium at Gillette in 1937

to save it. Finally in 1995, after sitting vacant for 18 years, Dowling Memorial Hall was renovated by the Minnesota Humanities Commission for use as an office and education center.

During renovation of the hall, many visitors—some of whom had been patients at the hospital as children—stopped by to see the work—testimony to the building's deep emotional ties to the community. 1997

### 43. THE FIRST CAPITOL BUILDING [M]
*Minnesota Historical Society Historic Site*
*Located inside the Minnesota State Capitol at 75 Constitution Avenue in St. Paul*

The first capitol building constructed in Minnesota was on the site bounded by Exchange-Cedar-Tenth-and Wabasha Streets. It was begun July 21st 1851, completed in 1855 and destroyed by fire March 1st 1881.

The second capitol building on the same site was begun in 1881 and completed in 1883.

Ground was broken for this building May 6th 1896, the cornerstone was laid by Alexander Ramsey, first governor of the territory July 27th 1898, and the building was occupied January 1st 1905.

## 44. MONUMENT TO THE LIVING 🏛

*Located on the Minnesota State Capitol grounds in St. Paul*

Monument to the Living, by Rodger M. Brodin, "Why do you forget us?"

Presented by and for The Veterans of Minnesota, Dedicated May 22, 1982.

## 45. JAMES J. HILL 🏠

*Minnesota Historical Society Historic Site*
*Located at 240 Summit Avenue in St. Paul*

[Front] "Most men who have really lived here have had, in some shape, their great adventure. This railway is mine," wrote James J. Hill to the Great Northern Railway employees upon his retirement in 1912. Throughout his long working life Hill remained a titanic force in the economic transformation of the Northwest as his railroads encouraged immigrant settlement, agricultural development and commercial expansion.

Hill was born in southern Canada in 1838 and began his career in transportation as a 17-year-old "mud clerk" on the bustling St. Paul levee. He spent 20 years in the shipping business on the Mississippi and Red rivers, and in 1878 along with several other investors he purchased the nearly bankrupt St. Paul and Pacific Railroad. Hill toiled ceaselessly during the next two decades to push the line north to Canada and west across the Great Plains and Rocky Mountains to the Pacific Ocean. "When we are all dead and gone," Hill declared of the renamed Great Northern Railway, "the sun will shine, the rain will fall, and this railroad will run as usual."

"Empire Builder" Hill pursued a vast network of related businesses: coal and iron mining, electric and water-power development, Great Lakes and Pacific Ocean shipping, agriculture and milling, banking and finance. Hill supported many educational institutions and built the St. Paul Public Library along with the reference library that bears his name. He spoke at countless county fairs and civic organizations on scientific agriculture and sound business practices. Presidents sought his financial support and economic advice on national and international concerns. After amassing a personal fortune of $63 million, James J. Hill died in his Summit Avenue home on May 29, 1916, one of the wealthiest and most powerful figures of America's gilded age.

**The James J. Hill House**
[Back] The population of St. Paul expanded dramatically during the 1880s, and many business and civic leaders began building fashionable homes along the bluffs overlooking the city. Forty-six new houses were constructed on Summit Avenue between 1882–1886. James J. Hill tore down the first house ever built on Summit Avenue to construct a house that symbolized his success and suited him, his wife Mary, and their large family.

The red sandstone mansion was designed in the massive Richardsonian Romanesque style by Boston architects Peabody, Stearns, and Furber. Completed in 1891, the 36,000 square foot residence immediately became the largest and most expensive house in Minnesota. The interior featured carved oak and mahogany woodwork, stained glass, gilding, and crystal chandeliers. A two-story skylit art gallery at the east end of the first floor showcased Hill's extensive collection of French paintings. Innovative technical systems provided central heating, gas and electric lighting, plumbing, ventilation, security and communication.

Mary Hill maintained a watchful eye over the household, raising the children, hiring and managing servants, and hosting numerous social events, including a reception for President William McKinley in 1899. After her death in 1921, the children gave the house to the Archdiocese of St. Paul and until 1978 it was used as a school, residence, and office building by the church. Designated a National Historic Landmark in 1961, the James J. Hill House is now a historic site operated by the Minnesota Historical Society. 1997

## 46. ST. JOSEPH'S ACADEMY

*Located on Marshall Avenue (north side) between Virginia and Western Avenues in St. Paul*

St. Joseph's Academy, the oldest catholic educational institution in Minnesota, was founded in 1831 by four Sisters of St. Joseph of Carondelet two hundred years after the order's founding in Le Puy, France. Leaving the mother house in St. Louis at the invitation of Bishop Joseph Cretin, the nuns believed they were to start an Indian mission. Instead they established a school dedicated to their patron saint. The first classes were held in the vestry of Father Lucien Galtier's log chapel of St. Paul from which the city took its name. A year later the school was moved into a two-story brick building. In 1839, requiring larger quarters, it was relocated on the present site of St. Joseph's Hospital.

By 1863 the academy was moved to this location. The original structure (the southwest section of this complex) is thought to be the oldest remaining Catholic schoolhouse in the state. Built of yellow limestone from local quarries, its style may be classified as "Italianate." There have been four additions to the original academy which was chiefly a boarding school until about 1870 when the growth of the city improved transportation facilities. Today the institution is a day high school for girls.

# SCOTT COUNTY

## 47. POND MISSION

*Located off county road 101 on a frontage road at the east edge of Shakopee*

These foundations mark the site of a two-story frame building erected by the Reverend Samuel W. Pond in 1847. It served as a Presbyterian mission to the Shakopee Sioux, and as Pond's home until his death in 1891.

An eight-foot stockade enclosed the house and a half-acre garden.

The building was wrecked about 1907.

## 48.  THE BIG WOODS
*Located on I-35 (south bound) in New Market rest area*

When the first explorers came to what became Minnesota, they found a land with three very different personalities. To the north were the great forests of white pine and other conifers that later attracted armies of lumberjacks and made Minnesota a leading producer of lumber. To the south and west was the beginning of the Great Plains, the flat, fertile prairie that was broken into successful farms. And in what is now south-central Minnesota was the dense broadleaf forest that settlers called the "Big Woods."

The Big Woods was at the western edge of the great deciduous forest that swept over the middle United States from the Atlantic coast to the Great Plains. In Minnesota the deciduous belt ran from the northwest to the southeast, thickening in the middle to form the Big Woods. There, elm, basswood, sugar maple, and red oak covered more than 3,000 square miles, rising high in the air to form a vast canopy that nearly obliterated the sun during the leafy summer months.

Fire played a large part in determining the boundaries of the Big Woods. Prairie fires, started by lightning or by Indians for hunting purposes, kept the broadleaf trees from invading the grasslands. At the same time, natural firebreaks—lakes, rivers, and rough terrain—prevented these fires from spreading into the forest itself.

Fertile soil lay beneath the Big Woods, and, inevitably, much of the land was cleared for farming during the last half of the nineteenth century. Only a few remnants of the great forest remain today. The largest of these is in Nerstrand Big Woods State Park. 1996

# WASHINGTON COUNTY

### 49.  STILLWATER REGION  △

*Located on state highway 95, in a wayside park 1 mile
north of state highway 96*

The site of this tablet marks the northern limit of Lake
St. Croix, impounded by the natural dam of sand and
gravel, made by the Mississippi where it is joined by
the St. Croix River, twenty miles below Stillwater. The
valley, with its steep banks, is typical of youthful topography—of a young stream—and its size, compared with
the river, indicates that a much larger volume of water
flowed here when the St. Croix was an outlet of Glacial
Lake Duluth, the ancestor of Lake Superior. The highway and picnic grounds occupy a river terrace on which
the river flowed at an earlier stage. The rock walls of
the valley are chiefly sandstone formed in the sea when
it covered Minnesota during the Cambrian period 500
million years ago. Because of the thickness of the beds
and the excellence of the exposures along the river,
these formations, wherever they appear in North America, are known as the St. Croixian series.

Erected by the Geological Society of Minnesota in
cooperation with the Department of Highways, State of
Minnesota. 1950

### 50.  ST. CROIX BOOM SITE

*Located on state highway 95 in a wayside park, 1.5 miles
north of state highway 96*

Center of log and lumbering activities in this region for
over half a century prior to 1914.

Here millions of logs from the upper St. Croix and
tributaries were halted, sorted, and rafted, later to be
sawed into lumber and timber products. More logs
were handled here than at any similar place in this
section. 1940

## 51. ST. CROIX BOOM SITE

*Located on state highway 95 in a wayside park, 1.5 miles
north of state highway 96*

The St. Croix Boom Site has been designated a Registered National Historic Landmark under the provisions of the Historic Sites Act of August 21, 1935. This site possesses exceptional value in commemorating or illustrating the history of the United States.

U.S. Department of the Interior, National Park Service. 1966

## 52. MARINE MILL SITE 🏠

*Minnesota Historical Society Historic Site*
*Located on east side of Judd Street near Maple Street
(county road 4) in Marine on St. Croix*

One of Minnesota's first major industries was born here on August 24, 1839, when the slow, cumbersome up-and-down saw of the Marine Lumber Company cut the first commercial lumber in the state from trees felled in the rich white pine forests of the St. Croix Valley. The mill was built by a group of settlers from Marine, Illinois, at a site selected a year earlier by David Hone and Lewis S. Judd.

During the winter of 1839–40, the saw at Marine produced about 5,000 board feet of lumber a day. From this modest beginning, the much rebuilt and enlarged mill of the Walker, Judd, and Veazie Lumber Company was by 1877 turning out two million board feet of lumber, 500,000 shingles, and 200,000 laths a year with an average daily work crew of fourteen men.

Financial depression, a huge log jam that prevented logs from reaching the mill, extensive tornado damage, and a low-water summer combined to cause failure of the business in 1885. By 1895, after a few years of intermittent operation in the hands of other companies, the mill closed forever, and the extensive frame buildings were torn down. Only the ruins of the mill's enginehouse, which can be seen by following the path to the overlook, serve as a reminder of Minnesota's magnificent pine forests and the profitable lumber industry that built the towns and cities of an expanding nineteenth-century mid-America. 1985

A log jam at the boom near Stillwater in 1873

### 53. MARINE SAWMILL
*Located on Parker Street in a wayside off Maple Street (county road 4) in Marine on St. Croix*

The first commercial sawmill in Minnesota was erected 300 feet east of here in 1838. The lumbering industry, which monopolized the minds and talents of men in the St. Croix Valley for three-quarters of a century, was born with the erection of this mill. Lewis Judd and David Hone selected the site, and the Marine Lumber Company erected the mill which sawed the first lumber from the magnificent pine stands of the St. Croix Valley.

The village which grew up around the mill was the earliest Minnesota settlement in the valley, and was named Marine after the home of its founders in Illinois. This bell, cherished by generations of Marine residents,

was brought here from St. Louis in 1857 to serve as a
church bell. Prior thereto it had served for many years
as a steamboat bell.

### 54.  MARINE

*Located on Parker Street in a wayside off Maple Street
(county road 4) in Marine on St. Croix*

In 1857 these millstones were installed at Marine in
one of the early flour and grist mills of Minnesota Territory. Water from a stream south of this site was conveyed by a race or flume to furnish power for the
overshot mill wheel. Later, rollers were installed for the
finer grinding of wheat flour. Under various owners,
the mill continued to operate until 1930. [1950]

### 55.  THE MARINE TOWNSHIP HALL

*Located between Oak and Pine Streets in upper section of
Marine on St. Croix*

The Marine Township Hall was constructed in 1872 as a
meeting hall and jail. The building was erected on
property donated by Orange Walker. Its construction
was financed by Morgan May who took the town's
bonds for the necessary $2,000. Members of the build-
ing committee were Hans F. Boock, Porter E. Walker,
and Mathias Welshons. Gustaf Carlson, a local mason,
utilized stone quarried and cut near the village.

After the official abolishment of Marine Township
in 1895, the "Stone House" led a varied career as a
school, storage quarters, and community center.

The structure received architectural recognition in
1934 when the National Historic American Buildings
Survey chose it as an outstanding example of the
Swedish stone work of early Minnesota settlers and
recorded its architectural measurements in the Library
of Congress.

In 1963 the Town Hall became a museum operated
by the Women's Civic Club of Marine. 1968

## 56.  TAMARACK HOUSE

*Located on state highway 95 in a wayside at the north edge
of Stillwater*

Here in 1839, in Crawford County, Wisconsin Territory,
Joseph R. Brown, first settler of this valley, laid out the
town of Dahcotah. The following year as a member of
the Wisconsin Territorial Legislature, Brown secured passage of a bill setting up St. Croix County. In the election
to select a county seat Dahcotah won and here Brown
built Tamarack House to serve as a courthouse, the first
capitol building in Minnesota. [1960]

## 57.  WASHINGTON COUNTY COURTHOUSE

*Located at the corner of Fourth and Chestnut Streets
in Stillwater*

Minnesota's first courthouse, a three-room frame structure erected at the corner of 4th and Chestnut Streets
in Stillwater in 1849, had become inadequate by 1866.
On November 6 of that year, Washington County voters
approved funds for the construction of a new building.

For the magnificent sum of $5, Socrates Nelson, a
prominent Stillwater lumberman, and Mrs. Elizabeth M.
Churchill offered the city a block of property high on
"Zion's Hill." By the time ground-breaking ceremonies
were held in April, 1867, Augustus F. Knight, St. Paul's
first resident architect, had been commissioned to design
the building. His unique design reflects the Italianate
style then so popular. Constructed of native sandstone
faced with red brick, the courthouse features a projecting
portico with two tiers of ten rounded arches.

Two local contractors, George M. Seymour and
William M. May, supervised the construction which
was completed during the winter and spring of
1869–70, despite the seemingly insurmountable diffi-
culty of laying the imported English floor tiles in the
correct pattern. The courthouse stands today as "an or-
nament to the city" and "a credit to the county." 1968

## 58.   THE WARDEN'S HOUSE

*Located at 602 N. Main Street in Stillwater*

In 1849, the Governor of the new Territory of Minnesota, Alexander Ramsey, urged the Territorial Legislature to provide for a "proper and safe place of confinement" for prisoners of the territory. Because of Ramsey's request, the Legislature appropriated $20,000 for the erection of a penitentiary.

The site chosen for the penitentiary was in a ravine at the north end of Stillwater. This ravine is known as "Battle Hollow" because of the battle fought there in July of 1839 between the Dakota and the Ojibwe. It was a good location for a prison because natural cliffs bound the ravine on three sides.

In May 1851, the territory chose the firm of Jesse Taylor & Company to construct the prison building out of stone. By early 1853, the three-story prison building was completed. It contained six cells and two dungeons for solitary confinement, a workshop, and an office. The Warden's House, which sits just outside this ravine, was completed at this time also.

Francis R. Delano, the first warden, assumed office, and moved into the house on April 4, 1853. A total of thirteen wardens administered over the prison until 1914, when the last of the prisoners were moved into new facilities.

In November 1876, three notorious convicts entered the Minnesota Prison. The Younger Brothers, Cole, Jim, and Bob, were sentenced to life imprisonment for their roles in the famous Northfield, Minnesota bank robbery in which several people were killed and others wounded.

After the prison was moved south of Stillwater, the old warden's home housed deputy wardens. In 1941, Minnesota Governor Harold Stassen signed the house over to the Washington County Historical Society. Since that time the Society has operated the house as a museum.

In December 1974, the Warden's House was listed in the National Register of Historic Places and today stands as a testimony to the history of Washington County and the State of Minnesota.

Erected by the Washington County Historical Society. 1998

### 59. THE ST. CROIX RIVER VALLEY
*Located on I-94 (west bound) in Bayport rest area*

Forming a long stretch of the border between Minnesota and Wisconsin, the St. Croix is one of America's most scenic Wild Rivers. Its valley is sometimes referred to as the "New England of the West."

Along with the Brule River in northern Wisconsin, the St. Croix forms a water passageway between Lake Superior and the upper Mississippi River that was well known to the Dakota and Ojibway people and became a highway of the early fur traders. In the first half of the 19th century lumbermen found the river useful for transporting logs and lumber in huge drives from the white pine forests of the north to the booming markets of the growing Midwest.

Swedish novelist Fredrika Bremer saw the St. Croix valley as "just the country for new Scandinavia," and the first of many Swedish settlers in Minnesota built their homes near here in 1850. The Minnesota territory had been organized and named just two years earlier in a convention at the river town of Stillwater, the "Birthplace of Minnesota" some six miles north of this marker.

In the 20th century the St. Croix valley had become an important recreation area for residents of the Twin Cities. Interstate Park, located north of here, was established in 1895 as a joint enterprise of Wisconsin and Minnesota. It was the first such cooperative state park in the United States. Several other parks and forest reserves now occupy much of the land on both sides of "America's Rhine," and thousands enjoy its beauty year round. 1988

## 60. BLUE STAR MEMORIAL HIGHWAY

*Located on I-35 (south bound) in Forest Lake rest area*

National Council of State Garden Clubs, Blue Star Memorial Highway

A tribute to the Armed Forces that have defended the United States of America

Sponsored by the Federated Garden Clubs of Minnesota, Inc. in cooperation with the Minnesota Department of Highways

The *William Crooks*, Minnesota's pioneer locomotive, about 1935

## 61. RIBBONS OF STEEL

*Located on I-35 (south bound) in Forest Lake rest area*

Railroads were chartered in Minnesota as early as 1853, but it was not until 1862 that Minnesota's first railroad began to operate on ten miles of track connecting St. Paul with St. Anthony (now part of Minneapolis). In 1870, the Northern Pacific Railroad began at Carlton, Minnesota and reached Portland, Oregon by 1884. By 1871, railroad lines had reached Minnesota's southern and western borders, and by 1893 the Great Northern Railway extended from St. Paul to Seattle. Over 150 railroad companies received their charters and built rail lines into nearly every part of the state by World War I consolidating into about a half dozen major railroads. This immense transportation system was made possible by grants of public land to the railroads estimated in 1873 at over thirteen million acres worth over fifty million dollars.

Railroads were critical to the development of Minnesota; they connected its citizens, agricultural products, natural resources, and manufactured goods with the rest of the country. They promoted towns and cities along their routes, and opened new markets as goods and products were swiftly transported across the country.

The peak year of railroad trackage in Minnesota was 1929 with 9,500 miles. By the mid 1990s there were less than 5,000 miles of track remaining. Passenger service, except for the modest Amtrak effort, was discontinued by the mid 1970s. Decline and further consolidation has been the fate of Minnesota's railroads during the last several decades, and many small towns and rural areas are without rail service of any kind. Numerous miles of right-of-way, once bearing ribbons of steel, now serve recreational uses; many former railroad depots have been adapted for new uses and are tangible reminders of the past. 1997

### 62. BOLLES FLOUR MILL

*Located on state highway 95 at the north edge of Afton*

About 1843, six years before Minnesota became a territory, Lemuel Bolles erected on this creek the first commercial flour mill in the Minnesota country. Bolles salvaged wood from the shore of Lake St. Croix and carried it on his back to the mill site a mile and a half upstream. Lacking nails, he used wooden pegs in the construction of a small mill. First built for grinding corn and wheat, the mill was later remodeled and was in operation as late as 1875 when Bolles died. The stream on which the mill was built became known as Bolles Creek.

Erected by the Washington County Historical
Society in cooperation with the Minnesota Highway
Department. 1959

### 63. JACOB FAHLSTROM
*Located off Indian Trail South in Fahlstrom Preserve
cemetery in Afton*

Jacob Fahlstrom, 1795–1859; Margaret Bungo
Fahlstrom, 1787–1880
    Jacob, first Swede in Minnesota, about 1813—Fur
Trader, Mail Carrier, Farmer, First Methodist Convert in
Minnesota 1837, Methodist local preacher 20 years,
Guide, Interpreter, Missionary to the Chippewa Indians,
Lumber Camps, Settlers
    This memorial placed 1964 by the Minnesota
Methodist Historical Society.

### 64. SWEDES IN MINNESOTA
*Located on Olinda Street (county road 3) in front of the
Swedish Immigrant Heritage Museum in Scandia*

The first Swedes arrived in the territory of Minnesota in
1850, settling in Scandia. By 1920 nearly a quarter of
Minnesota's foreign-born residents were from Sweden,
making it the home of more Swedes than any other
state. About half lived in Minneapolis and St. Paul.
    Beginning in the 1850s, Swedish immigrants dis-
embarking at New York or Montreal headed for Chicago,
where they could go by train to Rock Island, then by
steamboat up the Mississippi. They were seeking to
reestablish their farming way of life in American soil.
The first Swedes reached the Chisago Lakes area in 1851,
and it subsequently became the most Swedish area of
the nation. Other early settlements developed in Goodhue and Carver counties.
    In the 1860s Minnesota lured Swedish immigrants
here to purchase railroad land grant tracts. Swedish settlements sprang up along the rail lines, westward toward

Kandiyohi County and northward towards Moorhead. The farmers supplemented their incomes by cutting timber or helping build the railroads. As the cities of Minneapolis and St. Paul burgeoned in the 1870s and 1880s, thousands of Swedish men found work there, particularly in the lumber mills and the construction industry. Women worked as domestic servants, cooks, laundresses, janitors, or seamstresses in the garment factories.

Among the most literate of immigrants, Swedes soon published newspapers in their native tongue. People tended to settle with others from the same region of Sweden, larger concentrations came from Småland, Skåne, and Dalarna. Churches were the center of most Swedish settlements, whether Lutheran, Baptist, Methodist, or Mission Covenant.

Swedish Americans have made significant contributions to education, business, industry, government, civic affairs, and cultural life in Minnesota.

Looking around from this vantage point in one of the several large concentrations of Swedish settlement in the state, one could say that Swedish author and traveler Fredrika Bremer's often quoted prediction has come true: "Hvilket herrligt Nytt Skandinavian kunse ej Minnesota bli!" "What a glorious new Scandinavia might Minnesota become!" 1996

# SOUTHERN REGION

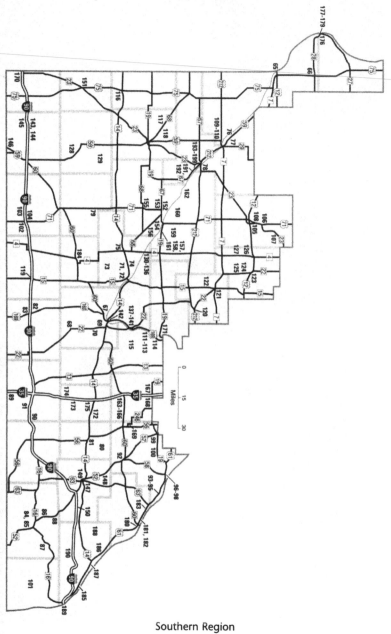

Southern Region
Markers 65–199

# BIG STONE COUNTY

### 65.  ORTONVILLE REGION  ⩙
*Located 1,000 feet west of the junction of U.S. highways 12 and 75, about .5 mile east of Ortonville*

Of all the geological agents which have played a part in shaping the face of Minnesota, the most overwhelming and powerful one is glacial ice. At least four times during the last million years, continental glaciers have spread over the state during long periods of cold climate, each advance being followed by widespread retreat.

The last glacier that invaded Minnesota from Canada came by the low valley of the Red River of the North, pushed its way southward across Minnesota and advanced as far as Des Moines. During its slow retreat, 11,000 years ago, the largest glacial river of them all, the Glacial River Warren, formed the valley in which the Minnesota River now flows. This valley, as seen from here, is an impressive reminder of the volume of water it once carried.

Big Stone Lake, now the headwaters of the Minnesota River, visible to the northwest, was formed behind a delta-like barrier of sand and silt deposited across this ancient drainage channel by the Whetstone River of South Dakota.

Erected by the Geological Society of Minnesota in cooperation with the Department of Highways, State of Minnesota. 1960

### 66.  GRACEVILLE
*Located on state highway 28 off U.S. highway 75 at west edge of Graceville*

About 1866 a trading post on the Fort Wadsworth Trail was established on Tokua [Toqua] Lakes a mile west of town. Early in 1878 Archbishop [John] Ireland, after erecting a church on the present townsite, located several hundred families in the vicinity through the

Catholic Colonization Bureau, and named the settlement for Bishop Thomas L. Grace.

# BLUE EARTH COUNTY

### 67.  SEPPMAN MILL
*Located off state highway 68 in the northwest part of*
*Minneopa State Park*

The Seppman wind powered grist mill produced flour
until it fell victim to natural disasters and new milling
technology.

Although the wind driven grist mill may still be
seen in various forms in Northern Europe, this structure is the last still standing in Minnesota. It is characteristic of the German style mills, reflecting the
builders' heritage.

Realizing the need for a local source of flour, Mr.
Louis Seppman, a stone mason by trade, undertook the
building of this mill in 1862. Utilizing local material,
he and a neighbor, Mr. Herman Hegley, began construction. Each stone was rolled up an inclined plane and
laid in place while local trees were sawed into lumber
and timbers. Two years later, the mill was operational.

The finished structure had walls that were constructed of sandstone two feet thick at the base and
eighteen inches thick at the top. The mill was thirty feet
in diameter at the base, thirty-two feet tall and twenty
feet across the top. The cap, a modified cone twelve feet
tall, could be rotated into the prevailing wind. Four sails,
each covered with thirty-five square feet of canvass, captured the wind's energy to turn the grinding stones.

Once construction of the mill was complete, Mr.
Seppman began the arduous task of learning how to
operate it. With some practice, he discovered that with
a favorable wind, he could transform about one hun-
dred-fifty bushels of wheat a day into fairly good flour.

Things went well until 1873 when lightning struck,

knocking off two of the arms and sails. These were replaced and operation continued until 1880 when a tornado again tore off two arms. These were not replaced but operation continued until 1890 when another storm finally damaged the structure beyond repair. By this time water and steam mills all over the country, together with the invention of the "roller process," had made windmills unprofitable to operate.

Over time, the mill and adjacent granary began to deteriorate. When these structures became a part of Minnesota State Parks, a renovation project was undertaken. All stone rebuilding was done to original dimensions with authentic materials so you might catch a glimpse into Minnesota's past. 1974

### 68. CRADLE OF CURLING IN MINNESOTA
*Located on state highway 22 in Mapleton*

When this area was opened to settlers in 1856 those who took claims were of several nationalities. Among them were Scots in the Mapleton Colony, who began curling before 1860 on the ice of Lura and Bass Lakes and the Maple River. The game attracted their fellow settlers and is now the chief winter sport in this community.

A curler demonstrates his form, about 1946

Plaque erected by Maple River Club, Heather Curling Club, Mapleton Civic and Commerce Association
with the cooperation of the Village of Mapleton and
the Minnesota Highway Department. 1962

## 69. VICTORY HIGHWAY
*Located on state highway 22, 4.5 miles south of Mankato*

In honor of the men and women who served in World
Wars I and II.

Sponsored by the Mankato Garden Club and the
American Legion of Mapleton with the cooperation of
the Department of Highways Centennial Year. 1958

## 70. THE WINNEBAGO AGENCY 1846–1855
*Located on county road 173 about 1 mile south of St. Clair.*

America's westward expansion came at the expense of
the American Indians. Tribes were relocated as the tide
of European settlement reached their traditional homelands, and the treaties negotiated and reservations set
aside for these relocations were seldom long lasting or
satisfying to either side. Among the many Indian nations affected were the Winnebago, whose homeland
was the area known today as southwestern Wisconsin.

In 1832 a new reservation was established for the
Winnebago along the Mississippi River near the present
Iowa-Minnesota border. They were placed at this location to serve as a buffer between the Dakota and Sauk
tribes. Only 14 years later the Winnebago people were
relocated to the Crow Wing River in central Minnesota,
centered around the present-day town of Long Prairie
in the area of the Todd County Fairgrounds. Here the
reservation population numbered over 2,500 individuals, and the more than 150 structures included a headquarters, school, church, convent, stores, and offices.

In only nine years the Winnebago were uprooted
again and moved to a new location near present-day St.
Clair in Blue Earth County. Here they remained for

seven years until, following the U.S.- Dakota Conflict of 1862 in which they took no part, they were forcibly moved along with the Dakota to Crow Creek reservation in South Dakota.

The road that had been constructed from Little Falls to the Winnebago reservation in the Crow Wing region later served settlers moving into the area. The reservation headquarters was renamed Long Prairie and eventually became the county seat of Todd County. 1990

# BROWN COUNTY

### 71. DEFENDERS' STATE MONUMENT 🏛

*Located at Center and State Streets near the Brown County Courthouse in New Ulm*

This monument is erected by the State of Minnesota to commemorate the battles and incidents of the Sioux Indian War of 1862, which particularly relate to the town of New Ulm. 1890. Honored be the memory of the citizens of Blue Earth, Nicollet, Le Sueur, and adjacent counties, who so gallantly came to the rescue of their neighbors of Brown County and by their prompt action and bravery aided the inhabitants in defeating the enemy in the two battles of New Ulm, whereby the depredations of the savages were confined to the border, which would otherwise have extended into the heart of the State.

The Sioux Indians located at the Red Wood and Yellow Medicine Agencies on the upper waters of the Minnesota River, broke into open rebellion on the 18th day of August, 1862. They massacred nearly all the whites in and about the agencies. Under the leadership of Chief Little Crow, they proceeded down the river towards New Ulm, and on the 19th of August entered the settlement of Milford, about seven miles west of New Ulm, and killed many of the inhabitants. On the afternoon of the 19th of August a force of about one hundred warriors attacked the town of New Ulm, killing several of the citizens and burning a number of buildings, but did not carry the barricades, which had been hastily thrown up.

While the battle was in progress the advance of Captain Charles E. Flandrau's company from Nicollet County, about fifteen strong under the command of L. M. Boardman, entered the town and the savages withdrew. The defense up to this time was in charge of Captain Jacob Nix. At 9 P.M. of the 19th of August, a large force, consisting of Captain Flandrau's company from Nicollet County together with a company from Le Sueur County arrived and took possession of the town; reinforcements to the number of several hundred subsequently arrived. On the 20th Captain Flandrau was chosen Commander in Chief and the defenses were strengthened.

On the 23rd the Indians, six hundred and fifty strong, again attacked New Ulm at half past nine in the morning, and besieged it until noon of the 24th. The assault was vigorously executed and desperately resisted. One hundred and eighty buildings were destroyed in the contest, leaving of the town such part only as lay within the barricades. Of the defenders thirty-four were killed and about sixty wounded. Reinforcements arrived at noon of the 24th under Captain Cox of St. Peter. On the 25th the town was evacuated and the inhabitants all safely conveyed to Mankato.

**Roster of those killed in the battles of New Ulm.**

Capt. John Belm's Co. New Ulm, 11th Reg't. State Militia,

C. W. Otto Barth, William England, Matthias Meyer, Leopold Senzke, Jacob Castor, Julius Kirschstein, August Roepke.

Le Sueur Tigers No. 1, Capt. William Dellaughter, 1st Lieut. A. M. Edwards, William Lusky.

Le Sueur Tigers No. 2, Capt. E. C. Saunders, 5th Sergt. William Maloney, Mathew Aherin, Washington Kulp.

Capt. William Bierbauer's Mankato Co.
Newel E. Houghton, William Nicholson.
Capt. Charles E. Flandrau's Co. St. Peter Frontier Guards,
1st Lieut. Wm. B. Dodd, Max Haack, Jerry Quane, John Summers, Rufus Huggins, Luke Smith. Capt. Louis Buggert's Co., Capt. Louis Buggert. New Ulm Co., Ferdinand Krause, August Riemann. Milford Co. Jacob Haeberle.

Citizens killed August 19th 1862, returning from a reconnoissance: Almond D. Loomis, Uri Loomis, William Tuttle, William Carroll, George Lamb, DeWitt Lemon, Ole Olson, Nels Olson, Tory Olson, Jan. Tomson.

Monument Commission: Hy. H. Sibley of St. Paul, Chm.[,] John F. Meagher of Mankato, A. W. Daniels of St. Peter, Wm. Pfaender of New Ulm, Secretary. [Approved by 1889 legislature; dedicated August 22, 1891]

**72.  CHARLES EUGENE FLANDRAU**
*Located on state highway 15 in Flandrau State Park in New Ulm*

The colorful frontiersman credited with giving Minnesota the nickname of the Gopher State was born in 1828 in New York City of French Huguenot and Irish ancestry. As a young lawyer he moved to Minnesota in 1853. After exploring the Minnesota River Valley for two years, he settled at Traverse des Sioux until 1864 and became known as the Defender of New Ulm in the Dakota War of 1862.

A lifelong Democrat, Flandrau rose rapidly in the frontier hierarchy. He became territorial legislator, Indian Agent, delegate to Minnesota's constitutional convention, and member of the territorial and state supreme courts (1857–1864). Like many of the state's male pioneers, he was an active member of the Minnesota Historical Society's executive council. He took his duties there seriously, drawing on personal experience to establish a considerable reputation as a historian of the young state. Flandrau authored numerous published speeches as well as such hefty tomes as *Encyclopedia of Biography of Minnesota* and *The History of Minnesota and Tales of the Frontier,* both published in 1900. Flandrau's published works earned him a piece of Minnesota immortality.

He was also known far and wide as a raconteur. When he died in St. Paul in 1903, one eulogy declared, "Minnesota owned Flandrau. They called upon him for addresses upon all sorts of occasions, whether to act as toastmaster or make a speech at a banquet, to celebrate an important historical event, to grace a reception, to make a memorial address, to preside at a convention, or to open a fair." 1996

### 73. LAKE HANSKA
*Located 4 miles west of Hanska on county road 20, then 1.5 miles south on county road 11*

The Sioux Indians called this lake "minne hanska," meaning "long water." The basin of the lake was formed 11,000 to 15,000 years ago by the Wisconsin glacier; the original hard clay bottom is now about 50 feet below the present surface of the water.

Charles Flandrau with his sons, Blair, John, and Charles M., about 1895

This area south of the Little Cottonwood River was a favorite with the Indians and is rich in legend and history. It has evidence of prehistoric habitation in the form of scattered burial mounds, and an old Indian trail once ran north of the lake.

In the spring of 1863 Fort Hanska was built on a knob near this site, as one of the fortified posts erected in southern Minnesota following the Sioux Uprising of 1862. This fort guarded the frontier between Madelia and the Big Cottonwood River. Constructed by Company B, Ninth Minnesota Volunteers, Fort Hanska was protected by an earthen wall eight feet high and topped with palisades.

The soldiers in 1863 thought the post ideally located, 25 rods from the lake, with excellent swimming and fishing, and a view over the countryside a dozen miles in any direction.

Erected by the Minnesota Historical Society and the Brown County Historical Society. 1968

### 74.  MILFORD STATE MONUMENT 🏛
*Located on county road 29 near Milford, 2.5 miles north of Essig*

Erected by the State of Minnesota in memory of the men, women and children of Milford who were massacred by the Indians Aug. 18, 1862

John M. Fink, Monika Fink, Max Fink, Carl Merkle, John B. Zettel, Barbara Zettel, Elizabeth Zettel, Stephan Zettel, Anton Zettel, Johanna Zettel, Max Zeller, Lucretia Zeller, John Zeller, Monica Zeller, Cecilia Zeller, Conrad Zeller, Martin Zeller, Anton Messmer, Mary A. Messmer, Joseph Messmer, Martin Henle, Anton Henle, Mary Henle, Frank Massapust, Mary A. Massapust, Mary Massapust, Julia Massapust, Frank Massapust, John Rhoner, Barbara Rhoner and child, Sebastian May, Barbara May, Henry May, Bertha May, Henry Heyers, Dorothea Heyers, Carl Heyers, John Heyers, Joachin Heyers, Mrs. Jos.

Stocher, Benedict Drexler, Frank Drexler, Christ. Haag, Adolph Shilling, John Kech, Brigitta Pelzl, Fred Gluth, Joseph Emmerich, George Roesser, Barbara Roesser, Florian Hartmann, Theresia Eggensdoerfer. [Approved by 1929 legislature; dedicated July 4, 1929.]

### 75. CHIEF SLEEPY EYES STATE MONUMENT 🏛
*Located off U.S. highway 14 at Oak and Fifth Streets near the railroad station in Sleepy Eye*

Ish-tak-ha-ba "Sleepy Eye"[s] always a friend of the whites died 1860. 1902

# CHIPPEWA COUNTY

### 76. JOSEPH RENVILLE
*Located at the junction of county roads 32 and 13, 2.75 miles west of U.S. highway 59, at Lac qui Parle historic site*

Joseph Renville was one of Minnesota's most prominent and influential pre-statehood citizens. The son of a Dakota woman and a French fur trader, he was born in 1779 near St. Paul. After attaining an officer's commission serving with the British in the War of 1812, he worked for the Hudson's Bay Company before helping to establish the Columbia Fur Company which dominated Upper Midwest fur trade from 1822 until it merged with John Jacob Astor's American Fur Company in 1827.

In the late 1820s, Renville built a stockaded log fort just below this road. At this wilderness settlement he extended hospitality to travellers and explorers, ruling, as one visitor commented, "in barbaric splendor quite like an African king." It was Renville's invitation that brought missionaries to his remote post, where they established the Lac qui Parle Mission in 1835. He helped them translate the Bible into the Dakota language, and his translations of Christian hymns are still in use today.

Crop failures in the late 1830s and the collapse of the American Fur Company in the early 1840s left Renville nearly penniless. Fort Renville began to decay, and Joseph Renville died in the spring of 1846, . . . "neglected by many who had profited by his generosity." 1983

### 77.  LAC QUI PARLE MISSION 1835–1854 🄼
*Minnesota Historical Society Historic Site*
*Located at the junction of county roads 32 and 13, 2.75 miles west of U.S. highway 59, at Lac qui Parle historic site*

The Protestant Mission to the Dakota Indians established here in 1835 at the request of the trader Joseph Renville became the nucleus of one of the earliest and most colorful centers of white settlement in the Minnesota River Valley. At this remote station the valley's first school and church were founded, the state's first church bell pealed, cloth was woven for the first time in Minnesota, and the Bible was first translated into the Dakota language for which the missionaries devised a written alphabet.

Among those who served here were Dr. Thomas S. and Margaret Poage Williamson, Alexander G. and Lydia Pettijohn Huggins, Sarah Poage, Gideon and Samuel Pond, Stephen R. and Mary Riggs, Jonas and Fanny Huggins Pettijohn, and Moses and Nancy Adams.

A replica of the mission church was completed by the Chippewa County Historical Society and the Works Progress Administration in 1942. Sites of original structures are marked. 1983

### 78.  A WITNESS TO TIME
*Located on U.S. highway 212 at a wayside 1.25 miles east of Granite Falls*

The Minnesota River Valley is a witness to time. Rocks formed 3.8 billion years ago—some of the oldest in the world—lie exposed on the valley floor. These grey, pink, and red granite rocks are memorials to a firey young earth when molten rocks in the planet's interior pushed against the earth's crust, deforming it, creating mountains four miles high. For eons, water and ice relentlessly eroded the mountains, eventually leaving a subdued plain.

At the close of the last ice age, 12,000 years ago, mile-high glaciers melted, forming Glacial Lake Agassiz to the north of here. The outlet for the lake was Glacial River Warren whose torrent carved the large valley you see. The abrasive current streamlined the rock outcroppings which lay in its way. The roar of rushing water and tumbling boulders would have been heard for miles. Today, the gentle Minnesota River creates barely a whisper as it flows almost unnoticed in the shadow of its prehistoric glory.

Across the river, spearheads, knives, hide-scrapers, and other stone tools have been discovered in association with extinct forms of bison. These bison-butcherings have dated human occupation of the valley to 6,400 years ago. 1992.

## COTTONWOOD COUNTY

### 79.  JEFFERS PETROGLYPHS  🖼
*Minnesota Historical Society Historic Site*
*Located 3 miles east of U.S. highway 71 on county road 10*
*and 1 mile south on county road 2*

On a glacier-scarred bedrock ridge on southwestern Minnesota's prairie, the Jeffers Petroglyphs historic site contains thousands of ancient rock carvings, or "petroglyphs." Search the rock outcroppings with guides for carvings and follow the self-guided trails through recreated prairies.

# DODGE COUNTY

### 80. WASIOJA SEMINARY
*Located off county road 16 in Wasioja*

The role of buildings in the development of a community and their significance in history is amply pointed out by the history of this structure. Anxious to promote the growth of the newly formed town, the citizens agreed to provide the Free Will Baptists with a building for a seminary. A structure of native limestone was completed in 1860, and the Minnesota Seminary opened in November of that year with an enrollment of more than 300 students. By 1861 the school had been renamed Northwestern College and offered classes on all levels from primary to collegiate. In 1862 Wasioja had a dozen stores, a hotel, a flour mill, and was surrounded by farms and quarries that promised a great future.

Then the course of history was changed. The Civil War had begun and men from Minnesota were on the battlefields. Captain James George, who had served in the Mexican War, asked the students to volunteer. Led by Professor Clinton A. Cilly, the young men marched down to Captain George's law office and enlisted. That office is preserved today by the Dodge County Historical Society. Organized as Company C of the 2nd Minnesota, they marched off to war. Just over a year later at Snodgrass Hill near Chickamauga, they stopped the Confederates' advance at a high cost. Of the eighty young men that left Wasioja, only 25 returned with life and limb intact. The town never recovered from the great loss.

The school continued to operate, although its enrollment had been cut in half, and in 1868 the Free Will Baptists ceased their sponsorship. It was reopened as the Groveland Seminary, closing in 1872 and was reopened again in 1873 by the Wesleyan Methodist Conference. The school finally closed in 1894, and in 1905 a fire destroyed the building, leaving the ruins that stand today.

Reverend A.B. Gould, a graduate and instructor of the Seminary, acquired and preserved the ruins. On his death his heirs deeded the site to Dodge County as a public park. Stabilization of the ruins and erection of this plaque were carried out in 1994. 1995

## 81. PLOWVILLE

*Located on county road 34, 1.5 miles east of Dodge Center*

The First National Soil Conservation District Field Day and Plow Matches were held here on September 6, 1952. Over 125,000 spectators saw demonstrations of new methods and new techniques for soil conservation during the event. The presidential candidates for the 1952 election spoke here on the importance of agriculture. Both Adlai Stevenson and Dwight D. Eisenhower acknowledged that the future of the country depended on the preservation of soil and water resources.

This event was held because of actions begun in the 1930s. The U.S. Congress had enacted the Soil Conservation Act in 1935, in response to the dust storms and floods that ravaged the country because of drought and poor land management practices. The legislation led to the creation of a partnership between government agencies, states, and individuals to address a broad range of resource concerns. They ranged from erosion control, contour plowing, flood prevention, water quality, wetlands, and wildlife, to recreation and community development. Today there are over three thousand conservation districts covering 98% of the privately owned land in the 50 states, and, Puerto Rico, the Virgin Islands, the District of Columbia, the Northern Mariana Islands and Guam. Within Minnesota there are 91 Soil and Water Conservation Districts that generally follow the borders of the county in which they are located. 1995

Taking a break from haying, about 1910

# FARIBAULT COUNTY

### 82. MINNESOTA AGRICULTURE
*Located on I-90 (west bound) in Blue Earth rest area*

Since its territorial days in the mid-19th century, Minnesota's identity has been rooted in agriculture. With acres of prairies and woodlands to turn into farms, the state proved attractive to waves of settlers from eastern states and other nations.

At first, family farms grew crops and raised animals for their own use. As transportation and farming methods improved, farmers began growing crops to sell. In the 1870s and 1880s, wheat was the main crop. Gradually farmers diversified, switching to other, more profitable crops. Today Minnesota is a leader in the production of sugarbeets, turkeys, soybeans, oats, flax, sunflowers, peas, and corn.

So central is agriculture to the state's economy that it has given rise to many related industries. In the late 19th and early 20th centuries, Minnesota was the flour milling capital of the world, due largely to local advancements in milling technology. Since then the state has remained in the forefront of the food processing and food science industries. Home to such corporate giants as General Mills, Pillsbury, Cargill and Hormel, Minnesota is not just an agricultural state but an agribusiness center.

Agriculture has played a role in shaping the state's cultural and political life as well. No Minnesota summer would be complete without a visit to a county fair or the Minnesota State Fair, one of the largest in the country. Two leading farm organizations, the National Grange of the Patrons of Husbandry (the Grange) and the cooperative movement (the Co-op), were formed here. Agriculture has even spawned Minnesota's unique brand of the Democratic Party—the Democratic-Farmer-Labor Party.

In recent decades Minnesota's agricultural landscape has changed. Now dotting the countryside are large, consolidated farms where crops and animals can be raised more cost-effectively. What once was the backbone of the state's farm economy—the small family farm—is gradually becoming less common. 1997

## 83.  EXPLORING SOUTHWESTERN MINNESOTA
*Located on I-90 (east bound) in Blue Earth rest area*

With the Louisiana Purchase in 1803, the United States acquired a vast area west of the Mississippi River. Eager for information about its new territory, the government dispatched a series of explorers to learn more about the land and the native peoples who lived there.

Expedition leaders recorded their observations, in words, on maps and in pictures. Each built on the work of earlier explorers until, together, their findings put Minnesota on the map.

The first to conduct a U.S. expedition from Ft. Snelling to the west was Major Stephen H. Long in 1823. Traveling with him through the Minnesota and Red River valleys were scientists, a landscape painter and an interpreter.

In 1835 the government sent English geologist G.W. Featherstonhaugh to further explore the remote region. He kept detailed journals of the expedition and later published his account. It is an important eyewitness record of a frontier in transition, as traders, missionaries, and the military gradually forced the Dakota out of their tribal lands and traditional way of life.

Another witness to those changes was the artist/author George Catlin, who traveled throughout North America making a complete pictorial record of American Indians before their culture was forever altered. In 1836 he recorded the Pipestone Quarry in what became southwestern Minnesota. His panoramic picture of the site recorded the religious rites of the Indians as they quarried the stone at this sacred site for carving and trading throughout native North America.

No other explorer did more to increase our knowledge of this region than French map-maker Joseph Nicollet. Commissioned by the U.S. Army in 1836, Nicollet and his assistant John Fremont led two surveying expeditions into the triangle of land between the Missouri and the Mississippi rivers. Nicollet's map of the area, extraordinarily accurate for its day, remains a monument to the achievements of western explorers. 1997

# FILLMORE COUNTY

### 84. MYSTERY CAVE △

*Located off county road 5 in Forestville State Park west of Preston*

Take a walk through layers of rock that were once deposits of sediment on the floor of a shallow sea that covered this area 450 million years ago. Ancient marine fossils on the cave walls and ceiling reveal part of the story of life at that time. Mystery Cave is a significant feature in the local karst terrain. This terrain consists of limestone and dolostone carbonate bedrock that lies

very close to the surface. The carbonate bedrock is riddled with features eroded by slightly acidic water: sinkholes, passageways, extensive underground water
systems, and caves.

Rainwater becomes slightly acidic by absorbing carbon dioxide in the atmosphere and, if it seeps through
the soil, by absorbing the carbon dioxide given off by
plant roots, bacteria, and other organisms. Over time,
this water following bedrock joints, or fractures, dissolves the carbonate rock and gradually enlarges the
cracks. Eventually, a system of underground drainage
will develop that bypasses the surface drainage pattern.

Mystery Cave is part of an active underground
drainage system that captures water from the South
Branch of the Root River and redirects it through a
complex, three-dimensional maze of interconnecting
passageways. Regionally aligned joints in the bedrock
direct the water flow and give a strong east-west orientation to many cave passages. The cave ranges from 10
to 50 meters below ground and has a total of more
than 20 kilometers of passageways. The underground
flow finally emerges at springs 2.4 kilometers northeast
of here.

Exploration reveals a variety of typical calcite
speleothems (mineral deposits formed by water), including stalactites (V), stalagmites (Λ), flowstone, and
many others. Also, some extremely rare features such as
organic filaments, pool fingers, and several types of
iron-cored speleothems are known only in a few other
caves in the world.

It is unknown when Mystery Cave started to form.
Research shows that some of its cave passages existed
and were filled with silt more than 200,000 years ago,
but those near the main entrance are likely to be much
younger. Continually changing, Mystery Cave holds a
unique record of time, sedimentation, glaciation, and
karst processes that makes it an important part of Minnesota's geology.

Erected by the Geological Society of Minnesota in partnership with the Minnesota Department of Transportation, the Minnesota Geological Survey, and the Minnesota Department of Natural Resources. 2003

### 85. MEIGHEN STORE  Ⓜ

*Minnesota Historical Society Historic Site*
*Located on county road 12 in Forestville State Park*
*southeast of Wykoff*

Horse medicine, school slates, eyeglasses, flour—all might have been for sale or trade in the log cabin store opened in 1853 by Felix Meighen and Robert Foster, boyhood friends from Pennsylvania. As the only store in Fillmore County, it did a thriving business and also served as a social center for the new town of Forestville. The stagecoach station stood just beyond the store, and up the hill was the schoolhouse, located now by its foundation ruins.

Interior of the Meighen store in 1978

In 1856, Meighen and Foster built the present store, constructed from the first brick made in the county. Although Foster withdrew from the partnership in 1868, the Meighen family kept the store open until 1910.

Some of the original trees still forest the Meighen homestead area; the family set aside land about a mile past the store as a park, and placed picnic tables for public use along the river bank. The Meighen store, complete with its 1910 inventory of merchandise, is now part of Forestville State Park, which includes more than 2,000 acres. 1970

## 86.  GEOLOGY OF SINKHOLES  ⋔
*Located off U.S. highway 52 in Fountain City Park*

The surrounding area and much of southeastern Minnesota are karst landscapes. Minnesota's karst landscapes consist of limestone and dolostone bedrock that lies very close to the surface. This carbonate bedrock is often riddled with features eroded by slightly acidic water: sinkholes, passageways, extensive underground water systems, and caves.

Rainwater becomes slightly acidic by absorbing carbon dioxide in the atmosphere, and if it seeps through the soil, by absorbing the carbon dioxide given off by plant roots, bacteria, and other organisms. Over time, this water following bedrock joints, or fractures, dissolves the carbonate rock and gradually enlarges the cracks. Eventually, a system of underground drainage will develop that bypasses the surface drainage pattern. Sinkholes are inlets to that system.

A sinkhole may begin to develop where joints in the bedrock intersect and the downward flow of water is more rapid. Over time, a funnel-shaped cavity often forms in the rock. Infiltrating surface water erodes the soil and moves it down the hole, thus forming a pronounced depression in the ground. When erosion into the subsurface is slow, sinkhole formation is also a slow, gradual process. When erosion is rapid, a sudden collapse of overlying sediment can occur. Sinkholes sometimes collapse suddenly after heavy rains. A sinkhole may become temporarily closed as newly collapsed sediment clogs the passageway.

In a karst landscape, water flowing into sinkholes bypasses the natural filtering action of a lengthy percolation through thick soil and sediment layers. Once in the bedrock, water can move rapidly through a complex system of passageways at rates as high as several kilometers per day. Using dye to color the water, scientists have shown that water entering this sinkhole emerges in about a day at the headwater springs of Trout Creek, about two kilometers northwest of here.

In karst terrains, bedrock aquifers, a common source for drinking water, are susceptible to rapid contamination from activities on the surface of the land. Likewise, water quality in spring-fed streams, which mark the end point of underground drainage in a karst landscape, may also be affected.

Erected by the Geological Society of Minnesota in partnership with the Minnesota Department of Transportation and the Minnesota Geological Survey. 2003

### 87.  MINNESOTA'S NORWEGIAN AMERICANS
*Located on state highway 16, 2 miles east of Lanesboro at Inspiration Point wayside*

Like immigrants from many European nations in the mid-19th century, Norwegians left their homeland to escape overpopulation, food shortages and farm foreclosures. They began arriving in Minnesota in the 1850s, drawn by rich farmland and job opportunities. Eventually they grew to become the state's third largest ethnic group, and Minnesota became a national cultural center for Norwegian Americans.

Among the first to arrive were immigrants who had first settled in Wisconsin and then migrated into southeastern Minnesota. There they formed rural communities anchored by Lutheran churches, which were social and religious centers and visible links to the traditions of Norway.

As these farming settlements grew, newcomers moved on to the prairies of central and western Minnesota. When the railroad reached Moorhead in 1872, Norwegian immigrants poured into the Red River Valley. The earliest and most numerous group of European settlers in the valley, they quickly became leaders of business and local affairs.

Norwegian immigrants in the 1880s and 1890s found other employment as good farmland became scarce. Some pioneered commercial fishing on the North Shore of Lake Superior. Others gravitated to the cities and the iron ranges, where they worked in mills and mines and as domestic servants.

To serve their growing numbers around the state, Norwegians formed their own institutions—schools, fraternal societies like the Sons of Norway, political organizations, businesses—that fostered the development of a Norwegian-American culture. Novelists like O.E. Rolvaag and Martha Ostenso wrote about Norwegian-American experiences. With an active Norwegian-American press as their forum, Norwegian-Americans rose to prominence in Minnesota politics, religion and higher education.

Immigration quotas, the Great Depression and World War II slowed the flow of new immigrants to the state. Yet Norwegian-American culture thrives in Minnesota today, supported by such organizations as the Norwegian-American Historical Association in Northfield, thanks to an enduring interest in their heritage by Minnesota's Norwegian-Americans. 1997

## 88. CHATFIELD

*Located in on U.S. highway 52 on the east edge of Chatfield*

Settled in 1853 and platted in 1854, this town from June, 1856 to November, 1861, was the Government Land Office for the southern area. The St. Paul-Dubuque stage route, opened in 1854, following the Territorial Road from Hastings, roughly the present highway, here met the line from Winona. Chatfield Academy was established in 1858. 1940

# FREEBORN COUNTY

### 89.  MINNESOTA'S ROADS

*Located on I-35 (north bound) at the tourist information center south of Albert Lea*

"A perfect highway is a thing of beauty and joy forever," enthused a speaker at Minnesota's first "Good Roads" convention in 1893. "It blesses every home by which it passes."

Early in the 1890s, even before the automobile age, bicycling Minnesotans and those interested in improved mail delivery and farm marketing were clamoring for better roads. But Minnesota's constitution, adopted with statehood in 1858, expressly prohibited the state from engaging in "works in internal improvements." The few roads of that era were of secondary importance to the river highways that had carried most early settlers into the region, and after 1865 attention was focused on the fast-growing railroad and streetcar systems. Counties and townships built the few roads and bridges that their residents petitioned for, financed by property taxes and a

A car and buggy stuck in the mud, about 1908

requirement that all able-bodied men of 21 to 50 years
of age work three days each year on the roads.

It was the automobile that finally brought good
roads to Minnesota. In 1902 Minneapolis recorded its
first automobile speeding arrest, and a new law the following year required autos to be licensed by the state
boiler inspectors. By 1909, 7,000 cars and 4,000 motor-
cycles were registered, but road construction lagged
until 1920, when there were over 330,000 licensed ve-
hicles and a constitutional amendment was finally
passed to "get Minnesota out of the mud." It allowed
the state to construct a trunk highway system of 70
numbered routes financed by vehicle taxes. Today's I-35
follows portions of the route of Minnesota Constitutional Road Number 1 from Albert Lea to Duluth. 1985

### 90.  EVERYONE'S COUNTRY ESTATE
*Located on I-90 (west bound) in Oakland Woods rest area*

Today more than one hundred parks, waysides, monuments, historic sites, and trails are operated by the
State of Minnesota. They fulfill the plea of Newton H.
Winchell, state geologist and archaeologist, who in 1889
stressed the value of a system of public parks and of
". . .the healthful resort that it would afford for those
living in the cities."

Minnesota's parks preserve portions of the state's
varied topography that ranges from forests to prairies
and wetlands to lakes. They also include vivid representations of the state's geological story by preserving evidence of volcanism, sedimentation from continental
seas, the work of numerous glaciers, and subsequent
erosion. Also, much of the history of this area is preserved within state parks; these resources include Native American earthworks, military forts, a lighthouse,
and numerous other historic places and structures.
Many of them are beautiful stone and wooden buildings constructed in the 1930s by the Works Progress
Administration and the Civilian Conservation Corps.

Minnesota's State Parks are truly "Everyone's Country Estate," a description that came from the title of Roy W. Meyer's book on the history of the state park system. Efforts began in 1885 to preserve some of the state's natural resources and to provide places for its citizens and visitors to enjoy. In that year the Minnesota State Legislature authorized the establishment of Minnehaha State Park: it never gained this status, but today it serves as one of the most important parks in the Minneapolis park system. It was in 1891 that Itasca, famed as the source of the Mississippi River, became the initial park in the statewide system, and it retains that premier position. At Itasca and the other state parks all people are given the opportunity to encounter nature and its many wonders, as well as numerous significant episodes in human history. 1997

### 91. MEXICANS IN MINNESOTA
*Located on I-90 (east bound) in Hayward rest area*

Like immigrants from many other countries, Mexicans were drawn to the United States by the promise of work. They began arriving in Minnesota in large numbers during the 1900s. Recruited from Mexico and the southwestern U.S., they found jobs at farms in southern Minnesota, the Minnesota River Valley, and the Red River Valley.

At first most of the Mexicans and Mexican Americans in Minnesota were migrant or seasonal workers, staying only for the few months they were needed in the fields of vegetables and especially sugar beets. Gradually, more and more of them "settled out," remaining over the winter to become permanent residents of the state. The story of Minnesota's Mexican community is the story of these two groups—year-round residents and migrant workers.

Many of those who stayed migrated to St. Paul, where thriving Mexican neighborhoods began to emerge. As this community grew, residents turned for support to their churches and other organizations like the West Side's Neighborhood House, which offered citizenship classes, athletics and job training. By the 1940s many resident Mexican Americans had shifted away from field work to industrial jobs in the cities, many at meat packing plants and canning factories.

Migrant workers in rural areas had fewer opportunities. Though missionaries started summer schools and some companies built housing, the workers faced many hardships—poor health care, crowded living conditions and long work days. Despite the difficulties, migrants continued to come to Minnesota for seasonal agricultural work, mostly from Texas. Conditions have slowly improved for them as Minnesotans have come to understand their needs in job placement, education and health services.

As with all immigrant groups, Mexicans in Minnesota experienced pressure to adopt new ways of living. But in the 1970s a trend emerged that continues today—preservation by the Mexican-American community of their culture and Spanish language. 1997

# GOODHUE COUNTY

### 92.  ZUMBROTA
*Located at the intersection of U.S. highway 52 and state highway 58 at a roadside park on the southwest edge of Zumbrota*

Settled by a colony that moved from Lowell, Mass. in 1856, this community takes its name from the Zumbro River which flows through it. This stream, called Riviere des Embarras by the French because of a raft of driftwood at its mouth, became mistakenly transformed into Zumbro when its French name was pronounced quickly and incompletely. To it was added the Sioux suffix, ta: meaning at, in or on. Several landmarks dramatize Zumbrota's links with the past.

The old Dubuque Trail, on which this marker is situated, linked Dubuque and St. Paul in the 1850's and was one of the major overland stage routes during the territorial period. The fare per person from St. Paul to Zumbrota was $4.50. Postal rate was 5¢ a letter up to 300 miles.

The First Congregational church, built in 1862, is a handsome structure located on East Avenue between 4th and 5th streets. It is an inspiring monument to the sturdy Yankees who founded the town.

The Old Covered Bridge is Zumbrota's proudest possession—the only such bridge surviving in Minnesota—located on the fairgrounds. This imposing 120 foot structure vividly recalls the 63 year period, 1869 to 1932, when it was located on Main Street, the gateway to the town over which hundreds of wagon loads of wheat were transported annually on their way to market and a favorite haunt for young couples until the village council ordered a kerosene lamp hung in the center.

This plaque was made possible by the sale of gold tacks by a committee of the Zumbrota Civic and Commerce Association with the cooperation of the Department of Highways and the Historical Society. Dated this 19th day of May, 1961.

### 93.  MAIDEN ROCK
*Located on U.S. highway 61 in a wayside at the junction with the south end of county road 2*

On the east shore of Lake Pepin, opposite this point juts out a high rock. From this pinnacle according to accounts of early travellers a Sioux maiden of Wabasha's band prevented from marrying the warrior of her choice, leaped to her death, that she might avoid union with another and older man. 1939

## 94.  GEOLOGY OF FRONTENAC STATE PARK  △

*Located on U.S. highway 61 in Frontenac State Park*

This site offers a magnificent view of the Mississippi
River valley. The valley is carved into rock that was deposited as sediment in a warm, shallow sea that covered the area of southeastern Minnesota and much of
North America about 500 million years ago. The upper
parts of the bluffs are composed mostly of dolostone, a
chemically altered limestone that is resistant to erosion.
The lower parts are mostly weakly cemented sandstone.
This layering of resistant rock over erosive rock helps
keep the bluffs steep.

During the Ice Age of the last two million years,
tremendous torrents of glacial meltwater repeatedly discharged from huge glacial lakes in the region of northern Minnesota and Canada. The forceful currents
eroded this river valley to its present width and flushed
it clean of sediment, right down to the bedrock. This
colossal river was much higher than the Mississippi is
today, and locally it flowed through both the main
channel before you and a secondary channel, which
passes just south of this bluff along Highway 61/63.
The spot where you are now standing was, for thousands of years, on an island between these channels.

Today, the Mississippi River is but a trickle compared to its volume when it drained meltwater from
the glaciers. Its much slower current is unable to wash
away all the sediment that tributary streams carry into
the valley, so the valley is slowly filling. Here, the valley contains Lake Pepin, a river lake formed behind the
delta of Wisconsin's Chippewa River. The Chippewa enters the Mississippi near Wabasha, about 27 kilometers
downstream. Its delta is large enough to dam the Mississippi back into this valley. Two other rivers have
built deltas into the lake near here: the Rush River to
the north on the Wisconsin side, and Wells Creek to
the south on the Minnesota side. Visible just down-

stream on the right-hand shore are Willow Point and Sand Point (more distant), both parts of the Wells Creek delta.

Erected by the Geological Society of Minnesota in partnership with the Minnesota Department of Transportation, the Minnesota Geological Survey, and the Minnesota Department of Natural Resources. 2003

### 95.  FRENCH TRADING POSTS ON LAKE PEPIN
*Located on U.S. highway 61 in Frontenac State Park,
2 miles south of Frontenac Station*

In September, 1727, a party of French soldiers and traders, under the leadership of René Boucher, Sieur de la Perrière, built a fortified post on Lake Pepin from which they traded for two years with the Dakota (Sioux) Indians. They were there to secure an alliance with the Dakota in order to gain access to the fur and possible mineral wealth of the area and to eventually press westward in search of the "Great Western Sea."

Accompanying the group were two Jesuit missionaries, Michel Guignas and Nicholas de Gonner. A letter from Father Guignas to the Governor General of New France, Marquis de Beauharnois, reported that "the day after landing axes were applied to the trees, and four days later the fort was entirely finished." Variously referred to as the "Post Among the Sioux" or "Fort Beauharnois," it included several trading houses, a guardhouse, quarters for the members of the party, and a chapel named in honor of St. Michael the Archangel.

Several trading posts were built on Lake Pepin by the French from 1686 until they abandoned the area in the 1750s during the French and Indian War. Most are believed to have been located on the east side of the lake, but the remains of only one, near Stockholm, Wisconsin, have been found. The locations of all the others, including Fort Beauharnois, are unknown. 1985

## 96.  RED WING REGION △

*Located off U.S. highways 61 and 63 in Memorial Park in Red Wing*

During the great ice ages the landscape of Minnesota was profoundly altered by continental glaciers in four major epochs of glaciation. In this area, as elsewhere, the closing stage of each epoch was characterized by the release of floods of meltwater which eroded the broad valley of the Mississippi River 200 feet deeper than the present channel. Because the tributary streams carried less water than the main river they were unable to cut down so rapidly, and consequently their valley floors had steeper slopes.

As the volume of meltwater diminished with the depletion of the ice, the velocity of the main stream was reduced and it was no longer able to remove all of the sediment contributed by its high-gradient tributaries. Thus the valley was filled to its present level and exhibits a remarkable series of meanders, oxbow lakes, side channels, sloughs, swamps, and tillable land.

Erected by the Geological Society of Minnesota and the City of Red Wing aided by a grant from the Louis W. and Maud Hill Family Foundation. 1955

Barn Bluff near Red Wing in 1898

## 97. BARN BLUFF

*Located on East Fifth Street at the U.S. highway 61
overpass in Red Wing*

"The most beautiful prospect that imagination can
form," wrote 18th century explorer Jonathan Carver
about the view from Barn Bluff. "Verdant plains, fruitful
meadows, and numerous islands abound with the most
varied trees. . . . But above all, reaching as far as the eye
can extend, is the majestic, softly flowing river."

Composed of various Paleozoic rocks, including
sandstone, siltstone, and dolomite, and capped by some
35 feet of sand, gravel, and loess deposited by glaciation,
Barn Bluff has also been known as "LaGrange," or "Twin
Mountain." Rising some 343 feet above the modern city
of Red Wing, it is one of the best known natural features
along the Mississippi and was climbed by many of Minnesota's early tourists, including Henry David Thoreau.
Topographical engineer Stephen H. Long, who climbed
it during his 1819 mapping expedition, found "the sub-
lime and beautiful here blended in a most enchanting
manner," and artist Henry Lewis called the view "incred-
ibly beautiful" while remarking unfavorably on a "mass
of rattlesnakes" to be found there.

Lewis also reported on an "Indian Legend" about
the bluff. Many hundreds of years ago, according to the
story, a mountain twice as big stood in this place. The
inhabitants of two Dakota villages quarreled over possession of the mountain, and to settle the dispute without bloodshed, the Great Spirit divided it into two
parts. He left one part here, and moved the other half
downstream to the second village. The portion that was
moved, according to Lewis's interpretation, rises above
today's city of Winona and is called Sugar Loaf. 1989

## 98. WILLIAM COLVILL
*Located off U.S. highway 61 in William Colvill Park*
*in Red Wing*

William Colvill was born in New York state on April 5, 1830. As a young lawyer he moved to Red Wing in 1854, becoming the town's first city attorney.

On April 19, 1861—one week after the Confederates fired on Fort Sumter—a citizens' meeting was held at the courthouse in Red Wing in response to a call for Union soldiers. Colvill and 49 others eagerly enlisted as members of the "Goodhue Volunteers." Colvill is said to have leaped over the backs of others attending the meeting to be the first to sign the rolls. When the men were mustered into the army as Company F, First Minnesota Volunteers, they numbered 114, and they had elected Colvill captain.

He was a full colonel when, on the afternoon of July 2, 1863, he led the First Minnesota in a bloody charge against a far larger Confederate force at Gettysburg. There the First bought for the Union Army a few minutes of precious time and thus turned the tide of battle. But 215 of the regiment's 262 officers and men, including Colonel Colvill, lay dead or wounded on the battlefield. General Winfield Scott Hancock, who ordered the charge, observed that "No soldiers, on any field, in this, or any other country, ever displayed grander heroism."

As a disabled veteran, Colonel Colvill returned to Red Wing and lived near this park at 807 East Seventh Street for a number of years. He served as a member of the state legislature in 1865 and 1878, and was attorney general of Minnesota from 1866 to 1868. He died in Minneapolis on June 12, 1905.

This memorial to William Colvill and the valiant men of the First Minnesota who were his comrades-in-arms in the Army of the Potomac was placed by the people of Goodhue County on the hundredth anniversary of the famous Gettysburg charge, July, 1963.

### 99.  WILLIAM COLVILL STATE MONUMENT 🏛
*Located on state highway 19 in Cannon Falls Cemetery,
east of Cannon Falls*

[Front] William Colvill, Col. 1st Regt. Minn. Vols. Born
April 5, 1830. Died June 12, 1905.

[Side] In Memory of Colonel William Colvill and
the 1st Reg. Minn. Vols. which he commanded at the
Battle of Gettysburg on July 2nd, 1863.

This was the first regiment tendered to President
Lincoln at the outbreak of the Civil War; and it served
three years in the Army of the Potomac, during which
time it engaged in the following battles and operations:

Bull Run, Ball's Bluff, Siege of Yorktown, Construc-
tion of "Grapevine" Bridge across the Chickahominy
River (over which McClellan moved reinforcements to
support his left wing at Fair
Oakes), Fair Oakes, Peach Or-
chard, Savage's Station,
White Oak Swamp, Glendale,
Malvern Hill, Flint Hill, Vi-
enna, South Mountain,
Antietam, Fredericksburg,
Chancellorsville, Haymarket,
Gettysburg, Bristow Station
and Mine Run.

Colonel William Colvill, about 1863

[Other side] At Gettys-
burg the loss of the Regiment
on July 2nd, 1863, in its
charge against the Confederate Brigades of General
Barksdale and General Wilcox, was 82 per cent of the
men engaged.

General Hancock says,—"I ordered these men to
charge because I saw that I must gain five minutes
time. Reinforcements were coming on the run, but I
knew that before they could reach the threatened point
the Confederates, unless checked, would seize the position. The charge was necessary. I was glad to find such
a gallant body of men at hand willing to make the terrible sacrifice."

Again on July 3rd, 1863, the regiment sustained a further loss of 15 per cent of the men engaged in resisting General Pickett's charge of 15,000 men against the left center of the Union line.

The regiment was successively commanded by Colonel Willis A. Gorman, Colonel Napoleon J. T. Dana, Colonel Alfred Sully, Colonel George N. Morgan, and Colonel Colvill, of whom the first three, through the valor of the regiment, were made brigadier generals during the service, and the last two were breveted brigadier generals at the close of the war. [Approved by 1907 legislature; dedicated July 29, 1928]

"To the Last Man"

1861 1st. Minn. Vol. 1865

1898 13th. Minn. Vol. 1899

1916 1st. Minn. Inf. 1917

1917—135th Inf. World War—1918

135th Inf. M. N. G.

Dedicated July 29, 1928

[Back] Colonel William Colvill was born in Forestville, New York, April 5, 1830. He emigrated to Red Wing, Minnesota in 1854 where he opened a law office. In 1855, he established the first local newspaper, the "Sentinel," which he edited until the outbreak of the Civil War.

In 1861, he raised the Goodhue County Volunteers and was mustered in as a captain in the First Minnesota Volunteer Infantry. He was promoted to colonel of the regiment in May, 1863. During the Civil War, Colonel Colvill was twice afflicted with wounds that would affect him the rest of his life. He was discharged with the regiment in 1864. He was mustered out of the service in May, 1865, with the brevet rank of brigadier general for gallant and meritorious service.

He resumed his law practice in Red Wing. Appointed editor of the "Republican," he held the position until his election to state attorney general, serving at that capacity from 1866–1868. In 1876, he entered the House of Representatives and served one term. In 1877, he was appointed registrar of the federal land office at Duluth. A student of astronomy, mineralogy and geology, Colonel Colvill was the author of a history of glaciers in the northwest.

In 1867, Colonel Colvill married Jane Morgan. Jane Morgan was born in Trenton Falls, New York on October 9, 1834. She was a direct descendant of Parson Brewster, the minister who served the little band of colonists who came to this country on the Mayflower. Highly regarded for her charity and her leadership in church work, Mrs. Colvill died in Duluth on November 13, 1894. She was laid to rest in the Cannon Falls Cemetery.

Colonel Colvill died on June 12, 1905. He was buried beside his wife in the Cannon Falls Community Cemetery near the graves of his aunt, two sisters and their families.

The statue of Colonel Colvill, designed by Mrs. George Backus, of St. Paul, is of bronze and mounted on a pedestal of Bedford stone. A duplicate is found at the state capitol in St. Paul, Minnesota. This monument was unveiled at a ceremony in 1909. After completing ground work including the balustrade and steps to the memorial, a plaque commemorating the Colonel and the First Minnesota was unveiled at a dedication ceremony on July 29, 1928. President and Mrs. Calvin Coolidge along with Minnesota Governor Christianson were in attendance. The memorial stairway and balustrade were designed by St. Paul architect J. C. Neimeyer.

This statue is the only state monument dedicated to a Civil War Veteran. July 31, 1994

### 100.   VASA: MATTSON'S SETTLEMENT
*Located at 15359 Norelius Road (county road 7) in Vasa at the east side of Vasa Lutheran Church*

Founded in 1853 and called "Mattson's Settlement" after its first resident, Hans Mattson, the community was renamed Vasa in 1856 in honor of Swedish King Gustav Vasa. Once called "the most Swedish colony in

America," the town prospered as an agricultural community until its two general stores, creamery, and post
office were closed in the 1950s. It has continued to
serve as a religious center, and its ethnic heritage has
been carefully preserved.

Two men played major roles in Vasa's development.
Mattson was one of the earliest promoters of Swedish
immigration to the United States. He organized and led
a company of Swedish volunteers in the Civil War and
later became Minnesota's first commissioner of immigration in 1867 and its secretary of state in 1869. He
later served as U.S. Consul General to India and in
1888 was named national chairman of the celebration
marking the 250th anniversary of Swedish settlement
in America.

Reverend Eric Norelius, who settled in Vasa in 1855,
established about a dozed Lutheran congregations in
southeastern Minnesota. A major force in establishing
the Minnesota Conference of the Lutheran Church—
the Augusta Synod—he also started the state's first
Swedish newspaper and one of its first colleges, Gustavus
Adolphus, now located in St. Peter. Minnesota's first
private children's home and first private high school
were both established in Vasa by Pastor Norelius, who
was later knighted for his efforts by Swedish King Oscar.

Vasa was listed on the National Register of Historic
Places in 1974. It stands today as a tribute to Amerca's
Swedish immigrants. 1988

# HOUSTON COUNTY

### 101.  BIG SPRING  ⛰

*Located in Beaver Creek Valley State Park 5 miles west
of Caledonia.*

Water bubbling out of the ground is a natural wonder.
Where does it come from? How long has it been in the

ground? To ponder these questions can be almost routine in southeastern Minnesota. Much of this area consists of karst terrain, characterized by sinkholes, underground passageways, caves, and springs. These features are formed by surface water that enters fractures in the underlying carbonate bedrock—limestone and dolostone.

Surface water is slightly acidic from absorbing carbon dioxide in the atmosphere and soil. As this water seeps into and follows fractures in the bedrock, it slowly dissolves the carbonate rock and gradually enlarges the cracks. Continued erosion along these passageways develops a system of underground drainage that bypasses the surface drainage pattern. As a result, groundwater can move quickly to replenish an underground reservoir, and then, as is the case at Big Spring, escape through porous rock layers to finally emerge as a bubbling spring.

The water of Big Spring maintains a nearly constant temperature of about 10 degrees Celsius (50 degrees Fahrenheit). This constant temperature keeps the spring from freezing and helps sustain a healthy trout population. The mineral-rich water is also ideal for watercress—the green plants with small oval leaflets floating in the creek. These plants display tiny white flowers in summer. Watercress typically grows around springs, where the water is rich in calcium and magnesium dissolved from the underlying bedrock. Its presence is a good indicator that a stream is fed by groundwater. These bright green plants flourish year-round, adding vibrant color to even the winter scene.

The water coming from Big Spring has not been in the ground for a very long time—most likely less than a year. But this reliable source of refreshing spring water has made the valley an ideal setting for people from prehistoric Native Americans, to early European settlers, to the park visitors of today.

Erected by the Geological Society of Minnesota in partnership with the Minnesota Department of Transportation, the Minnesota Geological Survey, and the Minnesota Department of Natural Resources. 2003

# JACKSON COUNTY

### 102.  JACKSON STATE MONUMENT 🏛
*Located off U.S. highway 71 in Ashley Park in Jackson*

Erected by the State of Minnesota in the year 1909, to the memory of the pioneer settlers of Jackson County, whose names are inscribed below, massacred by the Sioux Indians on March 26th, 1857, and August 24th, 1862.

   1857 Massacre. William Wood, Joshua Stewart, George Wood, Willie Thomas, two children of Joshua Stewart

   1862 Massacre. Ole Fohre, Mikkel Olson, Brita Langeland, Aagaata Langeland, Johanes Axe, Lars Furness, Anna Langeland, Nickolai Langeland, Knud Langeland, Knud Middssad and wife, Lars Gjornevik and wife. 1909

### 103.  MINNESOTA: A HISTORIC MEATPACKING POWERHOUSE
*Located on I-90 (east bound) in Clear Lake rest area*

By the late nineteenth century, Minnesota had established itself as a leader in the nation's thriving meatpacking industry. Founded by entrepreneurs with now-familiar names such as Armour Morrell, Swift, and Wilson, the industry was at first based in Chicago, a great railway center where farmers from surrounding states sent their livestock. Then enterprising developers transformed South St. Paul, near Minnesota's capital, into a regional railway hub that became home to one of the largest stockyards in the country. Packinghouses sprang up nearby to process the meat.

Interior of a cooler at Superior Packing, St. Paul, about 1940

With the advent of paved roads, trucks and mechanical refrigeration in the 1920s and 1930s, the meatpacking industry spread out. The towns of Albert Lea and Austin along Minnesota's southern border grew into important markets for Iowa's many hog farmers.

Young businessman George Hormel was the first to see the region's potential as a meatpacking center. In 1891 in Austin, he founded Geo. A. Hormel & Co., which soon came to dominate that city's economy. Thanks to the marketing genius of his son and successor, Jay C., the Hormel name gained worldwide fame. One of the company's many innovations, a canned luncheon meat called SPAM, introduced in 1937, became a food staple for the Allied troops during World War II.

Hormel also claims the country's first packinghouse labor union, part of a nationwide movement of the

1930s to organize America's workers. When the meat-packing industry experienced upheaval in the 1980s and unions went into decline, there were strikes over wages and plant closings across the country, including a bitter strike in Austin in 1985–86 that divided the community.

In recent decades, successful meat-processing companies like Hormel have reinvented themselves to keep up with changing consumer trends. Over just two generations, Minnesota's meatpacking industry grew from a specialized operation into a diversified food products business. Some companies have failed, new ones have been established and new areas of operations have evolved, as shown by the growing turkey and chicken processing plants. 2000

## 104. GOVERNMENT DITCHES: THE DRAINING OF MINNESOTA
*Located on I-90 (west bound) in Des Moines River rest area*

Drainage of surface water is vital to all aspects of development, from townsites to agricultural cropland. Its importance, impact, and consequences cannot be overstated. With the western expansion of the United States, swamplands, as they were called, or vegetated wetlands were found to cover over 215 million acres of land. In Minnesota this approximated one-fifth of the land available for use.

Traveling across Minnesota, it is not uncommon to see V shaped ditches along the roadside. These are man-made ditches, dug to drain excess water from the land. It was not until 1893 that the first such ditches were dug in the Red River Valley, with the formation of the Red River Drainage Commission. Initially the ditches were constructed by the State and the counties were required to maintain and repair them. Between 1900 and 1915 numerous drainage ditches were constructed; the demand for such projects lessened, however, as a result of World War I and the depression. By the late 1930s, demand for new ditches and repairs to existing ones was on the rise. Legislative changes in the 40s authorized district courts, hence came the common name "Judicial Ditches," and county boards to establish the drainage systems, and the State and township authority was removed.

The impact and extensive use of ditches and drain tile in Minnesota that followed can be illustrated in the Minnesota River Basin where only 58.3% of the land is considered well drained; however, by use of ditches and tiling, an additional 1,925,672 acres (20.2%) has been made more productive.

Since the 1950s, there has been increased emphasis on the environmental and conservation effects of drainage projects. This is reflected in recent State and Federal legislation. This concern must be balanced against the three categories of drainage projects: new systems, repairs, and improvements. One can easily understand the complexity and the controversy associated with ditches. 1999

Ditching machine and ditch diggers, about 1915

# KANDIYOHI COUNTY

### 105.  GEOLOGY OF THE WILLMAR REGION  △
*Located off U.S. highway 71 in north Willmar*
*at a wayside rest on the south shore of Foot Lake*
*near Ella Avenue N.W.*

The agricultural land of the Willmar region has a history that dates back 60 million years, when an inland sea covered the Great Plains from the Gulf of Mexico to the Arctic Ocean. As the adjacent land eroded and life in the sea flourished, sediments for sandstone, shale, and limestone were deposited on the sea floor and eventually became rock. Later, when the sea level dropped, these sedimentary rocks were exposed on dry land.

About 14,000 years ago, during the end of the Ice Age of the last two million years, glaciers advancing southward from Canada scraped up and carried great quantities of those sedimentary marine rocks from Manitoba and northwestern Minnesota. When the ice melted, rock fragments, crushed by the moving ice, were left as a layer of glacial drift across the state. This drift was rich in lime, magnesia, and potash, so became a great natural resource as the parent material for fertile soils over much of the state.

Earlier glaciers also advanced across Minnesota from the north-northeast about 25,000 years ago. This ice eroded the igneous bedrock in Ontario and the Lake Superior region and deposited a reddish, more sandy and rocky drift. Soils that developed from this parent material are not as fertile.

Most of the surface material in the Willmar region is the rich, fertile sediment deposited by the more recent glaciers from the northwest. The belt of hilly topography and abundant lakes northwest of Willmar, however, once marked the edge of a glacial lobe from the north-northeast. The margin of that ice left piles of sediment there at its farthest advance, forming a glacial deposit called a terminal moraine. While this moraine is buried under the more recent drift from the northwest, its effect on the topography is still very evident.

Erected by the Geological Society of Minnesota in partnership with the Minnesota Department of Transportation and the Minnesota Geological Survey. 1998

### 106. GURI ENDRESEN-ROSSELAND, VIKOR LUTHERAN CHURCH, SOLOMON LAKE
*Located off county road 5 on Little Crow Trail, 4 miles north of Willmar at East and West Solomon Lakes*

This monument has been placed to honor Guri Endresen-Rosseland and other early settlers of the Solomon Lake community. The settlers were predominately immigrants from Hardanger, Norway. Among the special characteristics of these pioneers were their courage and faith in Almighty God.

No one of them exemplified these characteristics more than Guri Endresen-Rosseland whose heroic deeds have resulted in her being acclaimed one of the most outstanding heroines of the nation. The State of Minnesota has recognized her heroism by erecting a monument alongside her grave. This monument is located in this cemetery.

During the Sioux Indian Uprising of 1862, a band of Indians attacked the Endresen cabin, killing the husband, Lars, and a son, Endre. Guri Endresen escaped with her infant daughter, Anna, by hiding in the cellar. After the Indians left, she hitched the family oxen to a cart and set out with her child for refuge at Forest City, some thirty miles away. En route she stopped at the homes of other settlers, attending to the needs of those wounded in the massacre. Some she took with her. All travel was by darkness.

Following the submission of Chief Little Crow and his warriors, Guri returned to the family homestead to rebuild her home. The cabin and graves are preserved in the Guri Endresen Cabin Site, located two miles west of the church at the end of the marked trail.

The Vikor Lutheran Congregation was organized at the Endresen cabin in 1871. It was named after the Vikor Church in Norway which was built by Lars Endresen.

This plaque has been placed in this centennial year of the Sioux Uprising in the State of Minnesota by the Vikor Memorial Association and the Council of Bygdelags, June, 1962.

### 107. BROBERG-LUNDBORG STATE MONUMENT 🏛

*Located on state highway 9, in Lebanon Swedish Lutheran Church Cemetery, at New London*

[North side] This Monument is erected by the State of Minnesota in memory of Anders Petter Lundborg born Mar. 23, 1837. Gustof Lundborg, born Apr. 30, 1839. Lars Lundborg, born Dec. 22, 1840. Anders Petter Broberg, born Sep. 16, 1819. His wife Christina, born Aug. 31, 1826. Their son Johannes, born Jan. 23, 1849. Their son Andreas, born Jan. 27, 1852. Their daughter Christina, born May 31, 1855. Their relative Johannes Nilson. Daniel Petter Broberg, born Jan. 8, 1824. His wife Annastina, born Mar. 31, 1832. Their son Alfred, born Mar. 31, 1858. Their son Johon Albert, born Oct. 22, 1861.

[West side] Anders and Lars Lundborg left Vårgorda, Westergötland, Sweden, May 8, 1858, landing at Boston, Mass., June 4, 1858, arrived at West Lake, Minn., in the spring of 1860.

Anders Petter Broberg and his brother, Daniel Petter Broberg, with their families left Vårgorda, Westergötland, Sweden, Apr. 28, 1861; landed at Quebec, Canada, June 19, 1861, and arrived at West Lake Minn., July 15, 1861.

All of these persons were massacred by the Sioux Indians Aug. 20, 1862, while on their way home from a religious meeting held at the house of Andrias Lundborg, in T. 121, R. 36, Kandiyohi Co., and conducted by Rev. Andrew Jackson, all being members of the Swedish Lutheran church.

The names of the parties massacred being kept on file in the records of the Nest Lake Lutheran Church of New London, Kandiyohi Co., Minn.

[South side] This monument was erected August 20, 1891, by a special act of the Legislature of Minn. in 1891.

John Lundborg, John Peterson and Erick Paulson, were appointed by the Governor, a committee to select and erect this memorial.

[East side] The massacre of these persons was the commencement of the Indian War of 1862.

"Derför varen ock I redo; ty den stund I icke menen kommer Menniskosonen, Luc. 12:40."

The remains of the massacred were removed from West Lake, Minn., June 19, 1891, and now rest where this memorial is erected. [Approved by 1891 legislature; dedicated August 20, 1891.]

**108.  GURI ENDRESEN ROSSELAND STATE MONUMENT** 🏛
*Located on county road 5 in Vikor Lutheran Church Cemetery, 4 miles north of U.S. highway 12*

Guri Endresen, 1813–1881. Erected by the State in memory of her heroic deeds during Indian Massacre 1862. Rosseland. 1907

# LAC QUI PARLE COUNTY

**109.  CAMP RELEASE STATE MONUMENT** 🏛
*Located off U.S. highway 212, 1.5 miles southwest of Montevideo*

Erected in 1894 by the State of Minnesota in accordance with an act of the Legislature approved April 11, 1893 and under the supervision of the committee therein named. C. C. Andrews, H. E. Hoard, W. H. Grant, Wm. M. Mills, and A. H. Reed—Committee.

To Commemorate The surrender here of a large body of Indians and the release of 269 captives mostly women and children September 26 1862. The result mainly of the signal victory over the hostile Sioux at Wood Lake by Minnesota troops under the command of General Henry H. Sibley. All being incidents of the Great Sioux Indian Massacre.

Battles: Redwood, Aug 18, 1862, Fort Ridgely, Aug 20–22, New Ulm, Aug 23–24, Birch Coulee, Sept 2, Fort Abercrombie, Sept 6, Wood Lake, Sept 23.

[Approved by 1889 and 1893 legislatures; dedicated July 4, 1894.]

## 110. CAMP RELEASE
*Located on U.S. highway 212 in a wayside west of Montevideo*

On September 26, 1862, 91 whites and about 150 mixed-blood captives, some of whom had been prisoners of the Dakota Indians for more than a month, were returned to Colonel Henry H. Sibley's military camp, later joyfully known as Camp Release. In the next few days, additional captives were freed, bringing the total to 107 whites and 162 mixed-bloods—269 in all.

When the 1862 U.S.-Dakota conflict moved into its final weeks in mid-September, attention on both sides had focused in the captives, mostly women and children, held by the Dakota. Sibley, holding a largely volunteer army, demanded that the captives be released before peace negotiations could begin. But the Dakota warriors led by Little Crow moved up the Minnesota River valley, still holding their prisoners.

Many Dakota who had not supported the war took great risks to help keep the captives alive. By late September Dakota peace factions led by Wabasha, Taopi, Red Iron, Mazomani, Standing Buffalo, and others were camped only half a mile from the war faction near the mouth of the Chippewa River. While Little Crow's men were fighting the battle of Wood Lake, the peace supporters took control of the captives, expecting to have to fight the returning war party if it were victorious against the white army. But Little Crow's men did not win at Wood Lake. The war leaders and many of their followers fled Minnesota, and the Dakota peace group sent a message to Sibley to arrange the prisoner release three days later. Many of the peace faction who surrendered to Sibley's army at Camp Release were among the Dakota exiled from Minnesota the following year. 1989

# LE SUEUR COUNTY

### 111. LE SUEUR
*Located near the junction of U.S. highway 169 and state highway 112 at the north edge of Le Sueur*

Named for Pierre Charles Le Sueur, French explorer who passed the site in 1700, this town on the old Red River trail includes two towns, Le Sueur and Le Sueur City which were laid out in 1852–53 on Prairie Le Fleche about a mile apart. Consolidation and incorporation occurred by legislative act in 1867. 1940

### 112. DR. WILLIAM W. MAYO HOUSE 🏛
*Minnesota Historical Society Historic Site*
*Located at 118 North Main Street in Le Sueur*

The accomplishments of the Mayo family in the field of medicine have brought fame both to its members and to Minnesota, for it was Dr. William W. Mayo and his two sons, William J. and Charles H., who founded the Mayo Clinic in Rochester, Minnesota, in 1903.

This little house was built by William W. Mayo in 1859. It is intimately associated with the Mayo family's early years in Minnesota, for here on June 29, 1861, the Mayos' first son, William J., was born.

His father had emigrated to the United States from England in 1845. By 1854 the doctor was living with his wife in Indiana. He left the family there when he departed suddenly in search of relief from the effects of malaria, saying to his startled wife, "Good-bye, Louise. I'm going to keep on driving until I get well or die."

Dr. Mayo's travels took him to St. Paul, the rude capital of Minnesota Territory, where he settled with his family. In 1859 he moved to Le Sueur, where he built this house with the help of his brother James. In 1863 he again moved, this time to Rochester, where in 1889 he was asked to become the medical director of St. Mary's Hospital, the nucleus of the future Mayo Clinic. 1968

### 113. THE JOLLY GREEN GIANT
*Located at the corner of Dakota Street and Commerce Street (state highway 112) in Le Sueur*

In 1903, fourteen of Le Sueur's leading businessmen met in the back of the Cosgrove Harness Shop to start a canning factory. They called it the Minnesota Valley Canning Company. Sixty-seven shares of stock at one hundred dollars per share were sold that evening. The sale provided enough money to buy one kettle, seed, sugar, salt and cans. Corn was brought in from the fields with horse-drawn wagons. Women husked the corn by hand for three cents per bushel.

Canning peas at Green Giant, about 1968

Eleven thousand seven hundred cans of white cream style corn were sold that first year. The profit from this was enough to buy two more kettles. The company continued to grow, and in 1907 it began canning peas under the Blue and Gold label. In 1925, the Green Giant brand of peas was added. Vacuum packed Niblet brand yellow whole kernel corn was introduced in 1929. Though the company continued to expand, packing a variety of vegetables and opening canning facilities throughout the United States, only corn and peas were ever canned in Le Sueur.

In the early 1940s, during World War II, many of the local men went into the military service. That left a shortage of help. Laborers from Mexico and Jamaica and German prisoners of war were assigned to help harvest the vital food crops needed.

In 1950, the Minnesota Valley Canning Company changed its name to the Green Giant Company. In 1978, one year before the company was acquired by Pillsbury, its national sales were over $485 million, and its net earnings were over $10 million.

Over the years, the canning company had a direct impact on the positive growth and development of the County of Le Sueur. The Le Sueur plant closed in 1995. Today its history remains, and if you listen carefully, the gentle laughter of the Jolly Green Giant can still be heard echoing through his valley. Erected by the Minnesota Historical Society and the Pillsbury Company. 1998

### 114. THE MINNESOTA RIVER VALLEY
*Located on U.S. highway 169 in the rest area north of Le Sueur*

Geologically young when compared with ancient rivers such as the Nile or the Amazon, the Minnesota River is only about 12,000 years old. It occupies a channel that was cut by the Glacial River Warren, when it drained Glacial Lake Agassiz, the largest lake to have ever existed. This all occurred at the end of the last glacial age, when the glaciers covering Minnesota, in some cases to a depth of over a mile, melted away.

Starting at the South Dakota border, at Browns Valley, the Minnesota River is the state's second largest river. It joins the Mississippi at the foot of Historic Fort Snelling, after traveling a distance of some 355 miles. By geological definition the Minnesota is an "underfit river," the term applied when a river occupies the channel of an earlier river. While the ancient valley is up to two hundred and fifty feet deep and in places 5 miles wide, the Minnesota is just a shallow, meandering river. During flood stages it swells beyond its banks, due to runoff from its extensive drainage basin.

History is abundant along its banks. Exposed by the waters are rocks that are more than 3.8 billion years old, attesting to the age of the earth. Ruins stand today as reminders of former homes, villages, military posts and sanitoriums that once served the residents of the area. Indian villages and crossing sites that predate the European settlement of the region, are also found along its course. Hundreds of steamboats once slowly traveled the river. Their use ceased with the coming of the railroads.

While the water flows by in an endless trip to the sea, and the life style changes with each passing year, the past will always be present here in the Minnesota Valley. 1997

### 115. BIG WOODS AND GELDNER SAW MILL
*Located on county road 15 at Bear Dam 4 miles south of Cleveland*

[Front] This historic sawmill played an important role in the settlement, clearing, and development of the countryside in which it stands. The machinery was manufactured in the late 1860s by Halbert and Paige of Painesville, Ohio, and by D. Lane and Company of Montpelier, Vermont. It was shipped to Le Sueur County by steamboat and placed in operation on upper Lake

Jefferson, then moved in 1870 to this location where it has remained for more than a century.

Because of frequent financial panics between 1870 and 1900, the mill passed through the hands of a number of owners before Leonard Geldner purchased it from the McCabe brothers. Geldner had worked as a millhand for several previous owners before becoming the proprietor of the mill in 1906.

Leo Geldner, from whom LeSueur County purchased the mill in 1978, is of the second generation of his family to have worked much of his life at the Geldner Mill.

From 1978 through 1982 the mill was restored as a historic site by the county with local funds and the help of grants from the United States Department of Interior and the Minnesota Historical Society.

**The Big Woods**
[Back] When Minnesota's borders were fixed prior to statehood in 1858, they encompassed a rich variety of vegetation. The northeastern half of the state was covered with coniferous forests mixed with a few types of deciduous trees. In the southwest and in the Red River Valley the land was a grassy prairie, sprinkled with patches of timber along lake shores and on the banks of streams and rivers.

Between these two areas lay a belt of deciduous hardwood timber varying in width from 20 to 60 miles and known as the Big Woods. It was remarkable for the abruptness with which it rose from the prairie grassland on its southwest side and for the clear demarcation line that separated it from the evergreen-dominated northeastern forest.

The Big Woods was made up primarily of hard and soft maple, basswood, oak, elm, ash, hackberry, box elder, and various nut trees. Pine and red cedar were its principal evergreen species.

Erected by the Cleveland chapter of the Le Sueur County Historical Society. 1984

# LINCOLN COUNTY

## 116. GEOLOGY OF THE LAKE BENTON REGION △

*Located on U.S. highway 75 near the junction with U.S. highway 14 in Lake Benton in a wayside by the lake*

The second highest point in southwestern Minnesota is about one kilometer north of here on the Bemis moraine, locally known as Buffalo Ridge. This ridge marks a drainage divide separating the watersheds of the Mississippi and Missouri Rivers. Lake Benton drains east to the Mississippi River, and the Flandreau River drains west to the Missouri River.

The ridge is a moraine, a pile of sediment (silt, sand, gravel, and boulders), that was left at the edge of a glacier. The Bemis moraine was formed on the western side of an ice lobe that originated in Canada and extended south into Iowa 14,000 years ago.

Here at Lake Benton there is a break in the moraine about one to two kilometers wide. There are similar but less spectacular breaks in the moraine at Lake Hendricks and Lake Shaokatan to the north. In all these cases, a straight wide channel, now occupied by a long lake such as Lake Benton, lies on the east side of a break in the moraine. These channels, called tunnel valleys, were formed by water flowing forcefully beneath the melting glacier.

On the west side of the Bemis moraine, beyond the former ice margin, rivers occupy sinuous channels that vary in width. These meandering stream valleys were carved by glacial meltwater that flowed out from the tunnel valleys that cut through the moraine.

The change in character of the valleys from one side of the moraine to the other is due to a change in pressure. Water that flowed under the ice was under great pressure from the weight of the ice above. Under such high pressure, the water could flow uphill—the floor of the tunnel valley actually slopes uphill toward the moraine. Once the water flowed out from under the glacier, the pressure was released and the stream was free to meander.

Erected by the Geological Society of Minnesota in partnership with the Minnesota Department of Transportation and the Minnesota Geological Survey. 1998

# LYON COUNTY

### 117.  THE FIRST SETTLEMENT OF ICELANDERS IN MINNESOTA

*Located off state highway 68 in Minneota*

Nearly nine centuries after Leif Ericsson established the first settlement of Europeans in North America, several hundred of his Icelandic countrymen left their native land to make their homes in the Minneota area. First of the Icelanders to arrive was Gunnlaugur Péturs-son, who, on July 4, 1875, established a homestead in Lyon County on the Yellow Medicine River. Later, 800 Icelanders settled in Lyon, Lincoln, and Yellow Medicine counties.

The Icelanders who came to Minnesota brought with

St. Paul's Icelandic Church in Minneota, about 1973

them little of this world's goods. Perhaps their most precious possessions were their sincere interest in public affairs and their traditional love of learning. Here they established schools, churches, libraries, reading societies, and the only Icelandic-language periodical in the United States. They also founded numerous farms and commercial enterprises including one of Minnesota's earliest consumer co-operatives, the Verzlunarfelag Islendinga—a general merchandise retail store.

Erected by the Minnesota Historical Society with the co-operation of the Minnesota Bicentennial Commission. 1976

### 118. WESTERHEIM PIONEER CEMETERY
*Located on county road 10, 8 miles northeast of Minneota*

On July 4th, 1875, the first Icelandic settler in Minnesota, Gunnlaugur Petursson, established a homestead on the Yellow Medicine River a mile south and a half-mile east of this marker. The homestead was originally named in honor of Gunnlaugur's ancestral home in northeastern Iceland but in more recent years has been known as "Riverside Farm."

Later, some 800 Icelanders settled in Lyon, Lincoln, and Yellow Medicine Counties. The largest single group arrived in the town of Minneota from northeastern Iceland in the summer of 1879. Many of these pioneers lie buried in this cemetery.

The Icelanders who came to Minnesota brought with them little of this world's goods. Perhaps their most precious possessions were their sincere interest in public affairs and their traditional love of learning. Here they established schools, churches, libraries, reading societies, and the only Icelandic-language newspaper in the United States, *Vinland*. They also founded numerous farms and commercial enterprises including one of Minnesota's earliest consumer cooperatives—Verzlunarfelag Islendinga—a general merchandise retail store, in 1886. It was housed in the "Big Store," listed in the National Register of Historic Places, in Minneota.

The Minnesota Historical Society placed this marker in the Westerheim or Western Home Cemetery to commemorate the 100th anniversary of the arrival of the first Icelandic family in Minnesota. 1977

# MARTIN COUNTY

### 119. FORT FAIRMOUNT
*Located at 201 Lake Avenue in front of the county courthouse in Fairmont*

Fort Fairmount, known also as Chain of Lakes post, was a substantial log stockade on the present Martin County court house grounds.

It was built in September 1862 for defense against the Sioux and was garrisoned by volunteers and troops of the 25th Wisconsin. A tablet marks the site.

This boulder marks the site of Fort Fairmount built during the Sioux Indian Uprising 1862 by Co. A 25th Wisconsin Volunteers under Major Jeremiah M. Rusk

Dedicated to the Pioneers who faced the dangers of pioneer life to establish homes in Martin County

Placed by Fairmont Chapter Daughters of the American Revolution. 1926

# McLEOD COUNTY

### 120. GLENCOE FORT
*Located off U.S. highway 212 at the east edge of Glencoe*

This town, laid out in June 1855, by Martin McLeod, Colonel John H. Stevens, and others, became the county seat of McLeod County. During the Sioux Outbreak of 1862 the town was heavily fortified and garrisoned, as many as four companies being stationed there during the winter of 1862–63. 1940

### 121.  HUTCHINSON STOCKADE
*Located on state highway 15 at the public square in
Hutchinson*

This tablet marks the site of a stockade built by the settlers of Hutchinson and vicinity for protection against
the Sioux Indians. Sept. 4, 1862, Chief Little Crow's
band attacked the stockade and was repulsed. Erected
October 4, 1905

### 122.  CHIEF LITTLE CROW
*Located on county road 18, .5 mile west of state
highway 15*

Chief Little Crow, leader of the Sioux Indian Outbreak
in 1862 was shot and killed about 330 feet south of this
point by Nathan Lamson and his son Chauncey, July 8,
1863. 1940

Little Crow (Taoyateduta) in 1862

# MEEKER COUNTY

### 123.  G. A. R. HALL
*Located at 320 North Marshall Avenue in Litchfield*

The Grand Army of the Republic was an organization established in 1866 by Union veterans of the Civil War to preserve friendships, honor fallen comrades, and aid widows and the handicapped. It also wielded great political influence in the years just after the war. The G.A.R. last met in 1949 for its 83rd encampment; today there are no survivors of this organization.

One of the finest examples of the architecture inspired by this movement is Litchfield's Frank Daggett Post, No. 35, organized in 1883 and named to honor the founder of the G.A.R. association in Meeker County. Dedicated on Memorial Day, 1885, the Memorial Hall was designed to resemble a fort and included a public library and reading and museum rooms. A "neat tin box" placed in the building's cornerstone contains a Bible, the names of post members and community leaders, and such memorabilia as postage stamps, coins, and battlefield relics. An addition built in 1961 houses the Meeker County Historical Society Museum. 1970

### 124.  NESS LUTHERAN CHURCH AND NESS MEMORIAL CEMETERY
*Follow county road 11 west from Litchfield to county road 1, south about 4 miles to county road 23, west about 1 mile, and north .75 mile on gravel road*

The first pioneers to settle in this area arrived by July, 1856, three months after their oxen-drawn prairie schooners left Rock County, Wisconsin. They were the families of Henrik H. Thoen, Ole H. Ness, Nels H. Colberg and bachelors Ole H. Thoen, Gunder Olson and Amos N. Fosen. They organized this community cemetery about one year later, with the first interment record in March, 1858.

In late summer 1858, circuit minister William Fredrickson of Goodhue County organized the St. Johannes Lutheran Congregation of Meeker and surrounding counties at the home of Ole H. Ness. Three years later, in 1861, the twenty-five member congregation was reorganized as the Ness Norwegian Lutheran Church of Meeker County.

One of Minnesota's oldest monuments, dedicated September 13, 1878, marks the common grave of the first five white settlers killed in the 1862 Sioux Indian War, which began about six miles to the west. Also interred here is Andreas Olson, killed by the Indians in September, 1862.

In 1864 the Ness Congregation purchased forty acres of land, which included the cemetery, for one hundred dollars. In need of a church, since services had been held in a barn, a granary, and homes, they constructed the present church building in 1874 at a cost of $798.57. The church still contains many of its original furnishings. The baptismal font, hand-hewn from a basswood log by Ellef Olson, dates from 1875. Also placed in the church that year were glass candleholders, now lavender with age.

Over the years, the Ness Lutheran Church has helped to establish more than twenty other churches. At the last Sunday service in 1968, the 110 year old congregation disbanded, leaving the church and its contents to the Ness Memorial Cemetery Association to be kept as a memorial to its members and the early pioneers. 1970

### 125. NESS LUTHERAN CEMETERY STATE MONUMENT 📖
*Follow county road 11 west from Litchfield to county road 1, south about 4 miles to county road 23, west about 1 mile, and north .75 mile on gravel road*

[North side] Erected by the State in 1878 under the direction of Meeker County Old Settlers Association.

[South side] In memory of the first five victims of the great Indian massacre of August 1862, and buried here in one grave.

[West side] Robinson Jones, Viranus Webster, Howard Baker, Ann Baker [Jones], Clara D. Wilson.

[East side] First blood [Approved by 1878 legislature; dedicated September 13, 1878.]

### 126. ACTON STATE MONUMENT 📑

*Located on state highway 4 about 3.25 miles southwest of Grove City on the site of the Howard Baker cabin at Acton*

[East side] This marks the spot where the first blood was shed in the Sioux Indian outbreak Aug. 17, 1862

[South side] Erected by the state of Minnesota on 47th anniversary, Aug. 17, 1909

[West side] Victims: Robinson Jones, Ann Baker-Jones, Howard Baker, Viranus Webster, Clara D. Wilson

[North side] Bodies of these victims are buried in Ness Cemetery. [Approved by 1909 legislature; dedicated August 22, 1909.]

### 127. THE ACTON INCIDENT

*Located on state highway 4 near the Acton Monument, 3 miles southwest of Grove City*

On a bright Sunday afternoon, August 17, 1862, four young Sioux hunters, on a spur-of-the-moment dare, decided to prove their bravery by shooting Robinson Jones, the postmaster and storekeeper at Acton in western Meeker County. Stopping at his cabin, they requested liquor and were refused. Then Jones, followed by the seemingly friendly Indians, went to the neighboring Howard Baker cabin, which stood on this site.

Here the whites and the Indians engaged in a target-shooting contest. Suddenly, the Indians turned on the settlers and without warning shot Baker; Viranus Webster, another settler; and Mr. and Mrs. Jones. Mrs.

Baker, Mrs. Webster and several children escaped by hiding. Then the Indians rode off, shooting Jones's adopted daughter, Clara D. Wilson, as they passed the Jones cabin.

The Indians fled south to their village forty miles away on the Minnesota River. There they reported what they had done, and the Sioux chiefs decided to wage an all-out war against the white man. Thus the unplanned shooting of five settlers here at Acton triggered the bloody Sioux Uprising of 1862.

The bodies of the settlers were buried in a single grave in the Ness Lutheran Cemetery, near present-day Litchfield. In 1878 the state of Minnesota erected a granite monument there. This site, where the Baker cabin stood, was similarly marked in 1909. 1968

# MURRAY COUNTY

### 128. AVOCA
*Located on U.S. highway 59 in Avoca*

This town begun in 1878 and named for a river in Ireland became a key point for the sale of 50,000 acres of railroad lands to Catholic colonists in Murray County through the activities of Archbishop [John] Ireland and the Catholic Colonization Bureau.

Early erection of a church, immigrant house and other public buildings, greatly facilitated settlement. 1940

### 129. LAKE SHETEK STATE MONUMENT 🏛
*Located at the entrance to Lake Shetek State Park, 3 miles north of Currie*

[South side] Patriotism
Erected A.D. 1924 by the State of Minnesota and dedicated to the memory of those who were slain in the Lake Shetek Indian massacre of Aug 20, 1862 and

to commemorate the privations and hardships and the heroic deeds of the surviving pioneer settlers of Murray County and vicinity.

[North side] Humanity

Almira Hatch Everett, wife of William Everett, Willie Everett age 5, Charlie Everett age 2, Sophia Walters Ireland, wife of Thomas Ireland, Sarah Jane Ireland age 5, Julianne Ireland age 3, Sophia Smith wife of Henry W. Smith, John Voigt, Andrew Kock, John Eastlick age 29, Frederick Eastlick age 4, Giles Eastlick age 2, Wm. J. Duley Jr. age 10, Belle Duley age 6

[East side] Courage

Shetek

[West side] Fidelity

Monument Commission. J. E. Baxter, Henry Paal, C. A. Portmann

[Approved by 1905, 1907, 1921, and 1923 legislatures; dedicated August 3, 1925.]

# NICOLLET COUNTY

### 130.  FORT RIDGELY ⓜ
*Minnesota Historical Society Historic Site*
*Located on state highway 4 at the entrance to Fort Ridgely State Park, 7 miles south of Fairfax*

Fort Ridgely, Minnesota's third military post, was established in 1853 to defend the frontier and watch over the Sioux who had been moved to the Minnesota Valley two years earlier. When it was completed in 1855, the fort consisted of a large parade ground surrounded by stone and wood buildings.

From 1853–1862 the post was garrisoned first by regular U.S. army troops and then, after the outbreak of the Civil War, by volunteer regiments. When the Sioux Uprising began in 1862, Fort Ridgely assumed great importance as the only military post in the valley and a vital defense point against the Indians. Hundreds of

settlers flocked here for safety, only to encounter two
Sioux offensives; these attacks were repelled mainly by
the skillful use of artillery by the fort's defenders.

After the withdrawal of the military in 1872, most
of the buildings deteriorated or were converted to other
uses by settlers. In 1896 the state of Minnesota erected
a monument commemorating the battles fought near
the old parade ground; in 1911 the legislature created
Fort Ridgely Memorial State Park. Archaeological exca-
vations in 1935 uncovered the foundations of eight
building sites, all now marked. The commissary, the
only stone building from the old fort to be preserved,
has been restored for use as a visitor's center. 1971

### 131. BATTLE OF FORT RIDGELY

*Located off state highway 4 near the visitors center in Fort
Ridgely State Park, 7 miles south of Fairfax*

Wednesday, August 20, 1862, 500 warriors assemble to
capture the fort. At 1 P.M. Chief Little Crow calls out to
the soldiers for a conference, but he is seated on his
horse to the west of the fort and remains just out of
range of the picket's guns. Suddenly the braves charge
up out of the wooded ravine to the N.E. Sgt. McGrew
brings his cannon out into the open to drive them back
while Lt. Gere and his men route the warriors from the
log buildings. Rifle fire from the barracks windows keeps
the Indians on the run. The cannon fire is new to the
Indians and proves to be too much for them to face. It
keeps them confused and disorganizes their attack.

Little Crow and the other chiefs can not organize
the warriors to get a well co-ordinated attack going. Finally at 3 P.M., one group charges out of the ravine to
the S.W., but again the fire power of the cannon throws
the warriors into a retreat. This cannon is in charge of
Sgt. Jones and has infantry support from the Renville
Rangers, a newly organized company of volunteers
from the Upper Indian Agency near Granite Falls.

An ink-wash drawing of Fort Ridgely in 1862

At 4 P.M. another group comes charging out of the ravine to the south, but here Sgt. Bishop's gun crew shooting across the open ground stops them before they reach the buildings.

The day ended with the young braves arguing with their chiefs over the strategy of the battle. The chiefs wanted to make a mass attack and take the fort, thus "opening the door to the Minnesota River valley," but the warriors wanted to go back to the easier task of driving the settlers from the farms and from New Ulm. The cannons at the four corners of the fort were more than they wanted to face, so off to New Ulm they rode.

Friday, August 22, 1862, 1200 warriors gather to take the fort, but most are reluctant to start the attack. A co-ordinated attack is agreed on, but at 1 P.M. only the group in the wooded ravine attack. The cannon fire from McGrew and Whipple again turn them back.

At 1:30 P.M. a large group from the west take the sutler's store and barn, but Sgt. Jones fires red hot shells into the barn setting it afire.

Another group comes out of the ravine to the S.W. and takes the barn. As the Indians build up their forces in the barn for a quick dash into the fort, Sgt. Jones maneuvers one of his cannons into position so that he can fire another red hot shell into the barn, thereby setting it on fire. This ends the threat for the time being.

By 4 P.M. the Indians seem to be getting organized for an all-out attack. A large group is gathering in the

ravine to the S.W. when Sgt. Jones fires several rounds
from the cannon into the ravine. Women and children
are also in the ravine so now the braves are furious and
an attack starts anew from the wooded ravine. At the
same time the Indians fire from a long distance N.W. of
the fort and lighted fire arrows are shot into the roofs
to set the buildings on fire. Everybody within the fort is
now busy putting out fires, making bullets or firing the
cannons. The attack sputters, and suddenly the Indians
withdraw.

For the next four days the Indians kept the fort surrounded, but did not make any mass attacks. On Aug.
27th the relief troops under Gen. H. H. Sibley arrived to
lift the siege. The Indians withdrew to the west never to
again threaten the fort, but they attacked a company of
these soldiers at Birch Coulee, some 18 miles west of
here, and nearly succeeded in wiping out the entire party.

Erected by Twin Cities Civil War Round Table. 1962

## 132.   JOHN S. MARSH STATE MONUMENT 🏛

*Located off state highway 4 in Fort Ridgely State Park,
7 miles south of Fairfax*

In memory of Capt. John S. Marsh; First Serg't. Russell
H. Findley, Serg't. Solon A. Trescott, Corp'l Joseph S.
Besse, Private Charles R. Bell, Edwin F. Cole, Charles E.
French, John Gardner, Jacob A. Gehring, John Holmes,
Henry A. Shepherd, Nathan Steward, Charles W. Smith,
Company B, died August 18, 1862, Private Mark M.
Greer, Company C, died August 22, 1862, Fifth Regi-
ment Minnesota Volunteer Infantry, Peter Quinn, U.S.
Interpreter, killed at Redwood Ferry Aug 18, 1862;
Christian Joerger, Durs Kanzig, James H. Kerr, Wenzel
Kusda, Henry McAllister, Wenzel Norton, Moses P.
Parks, John W. Parks, John Parsley, Harrison Phillips,
Nathaniel Pitcher

Erected by the State of Minnesota [Approved by the
1873 legislature].

### 133.  MRS. ELIZA MULLER STATE MONUMENT 🛡
*Located off state highway 4 in Fort Ridgely State Park,
7 miles south of Fairfax*

The State of Minnesota to the memory of Mrs. Eliza
Muller, 1877. Her valor and her devotion to the care of
the sick and wounded soldiers and refugees during and
after the Sioux Indian outbreak of 1862 will forever be
cherished in the hearts of a grateful people.

Mrs. Eliza Muller wife of Dr. Alfred Muller, born in
Berne Switzerland Apr 21, 1831 died Sep. 26, 1876

Thy Mission on earth was unbounded Charity, Thy
Reward is eternal Peace. [Approved by 1877 legislature.]

### 134.  FORT RIDGELY STATE MONUMENT 🛡
*Located off state highway 4 in Fort Ridgely State Park,
7 miles south of Fairfax*

In memory of the fallen; in recognition of the living;
and for the emulation of future generations.

Erected A.D. 1896, by the State of Minnesota, to
preserve the site of Ft. Ridgely, a United States military
post established in 1853, and especially to perpetuate
the names and commemorate the heroism of the soldiers and citizens of the State, who successfully defended
the Fort during nine days of siege and investment, August
18–27, 1862, and who gallantly resisted two formidable
and protracted assaults upon it, made August 20 and
22, 1862, by a vastly superior force of Sioux Indians
under command of Little Crow and other noted Indian
leaders and warriors.

August 18, 1862, the Sioux Indians of the Upper
Minnesota River, in violation of their treaties, broke
into open rebellion, and within a few days thereafter,
massacred about one thousand citizens in the south
western part of the State, and destroyed property of the
value of millions of dollars. Many men, women and
children fled to Fort Ridgely and were under its protec-

tion during the siege. The successful defense of the Fort by its garrison, consisting of parts of Companies B and C, Fifth Regiment, Minnesota Volunteer Infantry, the "Renville Rangers," and citizens and refugees, was very largely instrumental in saving other portions of Minnesota from ravage and devastation, and greatly contributed to the ultimate defeat of the Indians and their expulsion from the State.

During the entire siege of Fort Ridgely, the garrison was skillfully commanded by Lieut. Timothy J. Sheehan of Co. C, 5th Regiment, Minnesota Infantry. He was ably assisted by Lieut. Norman K. Culver, Co. B, of the same regiment, Acting Post Quartermaster and Commissary in charge of detachments; Lieut. Thos. P. Gere, Co. B, 5th Minnesota Infantry, in command of the portion of his company present, (Capt. John F. Marsh and 23 men of that company, and Peter Quinn. U.S. Interpreter, having been killed by the Indians at Redwood Ferry, August 18, 1862); Lieut. James Gorman, in command of the Renville Rangers; Hon. Benj. H. Randall, in charge of armed citizens; Ordnance Sergeant John Jones, of the Regular Army, in general charge of the artillery, with Sergt. James G. McGrew, Co. B., 5th Minnesota Infantry, and Mr. John C. Whipple, each in charge of a gun. Dr. Alfred Müller, Post Surgeon. The names of the other defenders of the fort appear elsewhere on this monument.

Renville Rangers. 1st Lieut. James Gorman, commanding (wounded)

Sergts. Theophile Richer, John McCole, Warren Cary.

Corpls. Louis Arner, Dieudonne Sylvestre, Roufer Burger.

Privates.

Urgel Amiot, Joseph Auge, Geo. Bakerman, Rocque Berthiaume, Ed. Bibeau, John Bourcier, Pierre Boyer, Samuel Brunnelle, David Carpenter, Antoine Chose, Geo. Dagenais, Fred. Denzer, Henry Denzer, Alexis Demerce, Francois Demerce, Carlton Dickinson, James

Delaney, Louis Demeule, B. H. Goodell, R. L. Hoback, Geo. La Batte, Fred. La Croix, Joseph La Tour, Cyprian LeClaire, (w'd), Medard Lucier, Moses Mireau, Theophile Morin, A. B. Murch, Ernest Paul, Henry Pflaume, Henry Pierce, Joseph Pereau, Thos. T. Quinn, Magloire Robidoux, Chas. Robert, Joseph Robinette, (w'd), Francois Stay.

Armed Citizens, B. H. Randall, Commanding.

Wm. Anderson, Robt. Baker, (killed), Werner Boesch, Louis Brisbois, Wm. Butler, Clement Cardinal, M. A. Dailey, J. W. De Camp, Frank Diepolder, Henry Diepolder, Alfred Dufrene, J. C. Fenske, (w'd), Jo. Jack Frazer, T. J. Galbraith, E. A. C. Hatch, Patrick Heffron, Geo. P. Hicks, Keran Horan, John Hose, Joseph Koehler, Louis La Croix, James B. Magner, John Magner, Oliver Martelle, Pierre Martelle, John Moyer, John Nairn, Dennis O'Shea, Joseph Overbaugh, B. F. Pratt, J. C. Ramsey, John Resoft, Adam Rieke, August Rieke, Geo. Rieke, Heinrich Rieke, (died), Victor Rieke, Louis Robert, Louis Sharon, Chris. Schlumberger, Gustav Stafford, Joshua Sweet, Louis Thiele, Nikolas Thinnes, Onisime Vanesse, (killed), A. J. Van Voorhes, John Walter, J. C. Whipple, C. G. Wykoff, Xavier Zolner.

A number of women cheerfully and bravely assisted in the defense of the Fort.

The following named rendered especially valuable services:

Anna Boesch, Kenney Bradford, Elizabeth M. Dunn, Margaret King Hern, Mary A. Heffron, Eliza Müller, Juliette McAllister, Mary D. Overbaugh, Agnes Overbaugh, Julia Peterson, Mrs. E. Picard, Mrs. E. Pereau, Wilhemina Randall, Valencia J. Reynolds, Mary Rieke, Mrs. R. Schmahl, Mrs. Spencer, Julia Sweet, Elizabeth West.

Ezekial Rose, Co. B. 5th Reg. Minn. Vols., was wounded when Capt. Marsh and 23 men of his company were ambushed and killed.

Sergt. J. F. Bishop, Co. B. 5th Minn. Vols., was in charge of a reserve gun during the siege.

The following citizens also rendered valuable services. Rev. S. D. Hinman, Alfred Valliant, John Robinson, James B. Robinson, Wm. R. La Framboise, John Loeffelmacher, Henry Elfkamp, Peter Glaser, Patrick Murname, Wm. Haley, Wm. Smith, John Smith, and Miss Elizabeth West.

Co. C. 5th Minn. Infty., 1st Lieut. T. J. Sheehan, commanding.

Sergts. John P. Hicks, F. A. Blackmer, (w'd) John C. Ross.

Corpls. M. A. Chamberlain, Z. C. Butler, Wm. Young, Dennis Porter (w'd).

Privates.

S. P. Beighley, E. D. Brooks, J. M. Brown, J. L. Bullock, Chas. E. Chapel, Zachariah Chute, Sidney Cook, L. H. Decker, Chas. Dills, Chas. H. Dills, Daniel Dills, S. W. Dogan, L. A. Eggleston, Halvor Elefson, Martin Ellingson, C. J. Grandy, Mark M. Greer, (killed), J. P. Green, A. K. Grout, Andrew Gulbranson, Peter E. Harris, (w'd) Philo Henry, James Honan, D. N. Hunt, L. C. Jones, N. I. Lowthian, A. J. Luther, (w'd), John Malachy, John Mc Call, Orlando McFall, F. M. McReynolds, J. H. Mead, J. B. Miller, Dennis Morean, Peter Nisson, Andrew Peterson, J. M. Rice, Chas. A. Rose, B. F., Ross, Edward Roth, C. O. Russell, W. S. Russell, Isaac Shortledge, (w'd), Josiah Weakley, G. H. Wiggins, J. M. Ybright, James Young.

Co. B. 5th Minn. Infy. 1st Lieut. N. K. Culver, Post Quartermaster and Commissary.

2nd Lieut. Thos. P. Gere, Commanding.

Sergts. Jas. G. McGrew, A. C. Ellis, Jno. F. Bishop.

Corpls. W. E. Winslow, T. D. Huntley, C. H. Hawley, Michael Pfremer, Arthur McAllister, Allen Smith, J. C. McLean.

Drummer, Chas. M. Culver. Wagoner, Elias Hoyt.

Privates.

Geo. M. Annis, Jas. M. Atkins, Chas. H. Baker, Chas. Beecher, Wm. H. Blodgett, Christ. Boyer, John

Brennan, L. M. Carr, W. H. H. Chase, James Dunn,
Caleb Elphee, A. J. Fauver, J. W. Foster, Columbia
French, Ambrose Gardner, Wm. Good, (w'd), W. B.
Hutchinson, L. W. Ives, J. W. Lester, Isaac Lindsey,
Henry Martin, J. L. McGill, (w'd), John McGowan, J. M.
Munday, Jas. Murray, E. F. Nehrhood, Thos. Parsley,
W. J. Perrington, H. F. Pray, Antoin Rebenski, Heber
Robinson, Andrew Rufridge, (w'd), Lauren Scripture,
John Serfling, R. J. Spornitz, (w'd), Saml. Steward, Wm.
J. Sturgis, Wm. A. Sutherland, Ole Svendson, M. J.
Tanner, J. F. Taylor, J. A. Underwood, Stephen Van
Buren, Eli Wait, O. G. Wall, A. W. Williamson, M. H.
Wilson. [Approved by 1895 legislature; dedicated
August 20, 1896.]

### 135.  CHIEF MOUZOOMAUNEE STATE MONUMENT 🏛
*Located off state highway 4 in Fort Ridgely State Park, 7
miles south of Fairfax*

Erected by the State of Minnesota in recognition of,
and to commemorate the loyal and efficient services
rendered to the State by Chief Mou-Zoo-Mau-Nee and
the Chippewa Indians during the Sioux Outbreak and
the Civil War [Approved by 1913 legislature; dedicated
August 20, 1914.]

### 136.  WATER AND ICE SHAPE THE LANDSCAPE ⛰
*Located off state highway 4 and county road 29 in Fort
Ridgely State Park*

The Minnesota River valley, which lies before you, is
uncommonly wide and deep. A colossal river, called
Glacial River Warren, carved it near the end of the last
glacial period. Between 11,700 and 9,500 years ago,
there were two separate spans of time during which
this immense river flowed for a total of about 1,000
years. With its headwaters near the site of Browns Valley, it was the main outlet for Glacial Lake Agassiz, an

enormous glacial meltwater lake. At its maximum, this lake covered the combined areas of the Red River valley, northwestern Minnesota, and much of Canada southwest of Hudson Bay. The tremendous power of Glacial River Warren cut down through layers of glacial sediment (clay, silt, sand, gravel, and boulders deposited by glaciers) and clay-rich deposits of weathered bedrock to expose hard granite and gneiss bedrock in places on this valley floor. No bedrock is exposed in Fort Ridgley Park.

Possibly twice, the glacial ice receded northward enough to open lower outlets to the Great Lakes via Lake Nipigon in Ontario, and Glacial Lake Agassiz drained. Since then, the huge channel that Glacial River Warren left behind has been filling in with sediment from the much smaller Minnesota River and its tributaries. The tributaries are cutting down their beds to match the riverbed slope. In the northern part of the park, one can see that Fort Ridgely Creek has cut deeply into banks of white kaolin clay, but only four kilometers upstream, it is a shallow upland stream. Erosion in the tributaries and sediment deposit in the channel will continue until the entire watercourse slope is uniform.

The white kaolin clay revealed by Fort Ridgely Creek is a layer of gneiss decomposed by weathering. About 100 million years ago, when Minnesota's climate was subtropical, weathering caused minerals in the gneiss to break down and form mostly clay minerals of the kaolin group.

In most places, the kaolin deposits are buried by tens of meters of glacial sediment, deposited during the Ice Age of the last two million years. Glacial sediment can be seen along the walls of the Minnesota River valley, and the modern river exposes more in the bottom of the valley.

Erected by the Geological Society of Minnesota in partnership with the Minnesota Department of Transportation, the Minnesota Geological Survey, and the Minnesota Department of Natural Resources. 2003

### 137. **TRAVERSE DES SIOUX** M

*Minnesota Historical Society Historic Site*
*Located on east side of U.S. highway 169 at Traverse des*
*Sioux Historic Site, one mile north of St. Peter*

This ancient fording place, the "Crossing of the Sioux," was on the heavily traveled trail from St. Paul and Fort Snelling to the upper Minnesota and Red River valleys.

Here, on June 30, 1851, Governor Alexander Ramsey, Commissioner of Indian Affairs Luke Lea, Delegate to Congress Henry H. Sibley, and other government officials established a camp on a height overlooking the small trading post and mission on the riverbank. They had gathered to negotiate an important treaty with representatives of the Sisseton and Wahpeton Sioux for almost twenty-four million acres called the Suland.

This vast tract comprised most of Minnesota west of the Mississippi and south of the line between present-day St. Cloud and Moorhead, as well as portions of South Dakota and northern Iowa.

News of the signing of the Treaty of Traverse des Sioux on July 23, 1851, started a great land rush, which brought swarms of settlers to the fertile lands acquired by the United States from the Sioux. 1968

Frank Blackwell Mayer, *Treaty of Traverse des Sioux* (1885, detail)

### 138. SITE OF TRAVERSE DES SIOUX TREATY 🔲
*Located off west side of U.S. highway 169 at the Traverse des Sioux wayside, one mile north of St. Peter*

Marking the site of the treaty of Traverse des Sioux, July 28, 1851

Erected by Captain Richard Somers Chapter, Daughters of the American Revolution, Saint Peter, Minnesota. 1913


### 139. OLD FRENCH CEMETERY
*Located off west side of U.S. highway 169 at the Traverse des Sioux wayside, one mile north of St. Peter*

The Old French Cemetery was located south of this ravine. The earliest settlers and a few Indians were buried there until about 1850.

Erected by Traverse des Sioux Chapter, D.A.R. 1939


### 140. E. ST. JULIEN COX HOUSE
*Located at 500 North Washington Avenue in St. Peter*

In 1871, Eugene St. Julien Cox, a man of eccentric tastes and "great vigor of mind" built this picturesque neo-Gothic Italianate house noted for its towered cupola, small balconies, and carved eaves.

Cox began his law career in 1857 and built a thriving practice in the frontier village of St. Peter. After brief service as a Union officer in the Civil War, Cox enrolled fifty men into the "Frontier Avengers" and led this unit in the defense of New Ulm during the Dakota War of 1862.

After the wars, the "affable and genial and always daintily dressed" Cox was elected St. Peter's first mayor. This was followed by his election to the Minnesota Legislature, first as a representative, later as a senator. In 1877, he was elected judge of the ninth judicial district. Within four years the Minnesota House impeached Judge Cox and the Senate organized a high court for trial pur-

E. St. Julien Cox, about 1865

poses. He was mainly charged with intoxication "caused by the voluntary and immoderate use of intoxicating liquors, which disqualified him for discharge of his official duties." In 1882, after a sensational five-month trail which included seventeen hundred pages of testimony and a petition for acquittal signed by four thousand people, Judge Cox was convicted and removed from his office as district judge by a bare two-thirds vote of the Minnesota Senate. Nine years later, the legislature passed a resolution "vacating, annulling, and expunging all the proceedings of the impeachment and trial." Nevertheless, a few years later, E. St. Julien Cox left Minnesota and died in Los Angeles on November 2, 1898.

The house remained in the Cox family until 1969, when it was donated to the Nicollet County Historical Society for preservation and restoration. In 1969, this property received the first grant awarded by the Minnesota Historical Society, as a part of the newly created State Grants In-Aid program, created for the preservation and restoration of Minnesota's historical sites. 1999

## 141.  FIRST MINNESOTA HOSPITAL FOR INSANE
*Located off U.S. highway 169 at St. Peter Regional Treatment Center*

Established by Legislative act, March 2, 1866. Located here, July 1, 1866, on 210 acres given to the State by St. Peter citizens. Kirkbride Building plan adopted, excavation began, July 22, 1867. Centre building and stone portico, finished 1874. Buildings completed, 1878, presenting a frontage of more than 800 feet with two 3 story wings for female patients on south side of Centre, same on the north for male patients. North Wing, destroyed by fire, November 15, 1880, rebuilt and occupied 1882. North and south wings razed in mid-1960's. Centre, only portion of original hospital buildings extant. Hospital's museum located 2nd floor Centre, 1975.

This historical marker erected in memory of Caroline Collins.


## 142.  MANKATO REGION  ⚠
*Located at an overlook on Lookout Drive in North Mankato*

This marker is located near the big bend of the Minnesota River directly opposite the mouth of the Blue Earth River. The abandoned channel east of it is the former course of the LeSueur before it joined the Blue Earth. Most of the broad valley of the Minnesota was carved out of bedrock prior to the last glacier which came from the northwest and partially filled the valley with debris. After the glacier melted, the river re-established itself in the old valley. The name "Glacial River Warren" is applied to the stage when it carried enormous volumes of meltwater from Glacial Lake Agassiz which for a long time occupied the Red River Valley region.

The rocks exposed in this road cut are from bottom to top—Jordan sandstone, Blue Earth siltstone, Oneota dolomite (Mankato quarry rock) and glacial drift of two ages. The lowest rock is about 500 million years old and the upper drift at least 10,000 years.

Erected by the Geological Society of Minnesota in
memory of Alger R. Syme, past president and mentor in
cooperation with the Department of Highways State of
Minnesota. 1950

# NOBLES COUNTY

### 143.  GEOLOGY OF THE ADRIAN AREA  △

*Located on I-90 (west bound) in Adrian rest area*

The landscape along Interstate 90 between Austin and
Adrian varies from a flat to a gently rolling plain. This
topography was shaped beneath a thick lobe of glacial
ice. About 14,000 years ago, glacial ice advancing
through the Manitoba region followed the lowlands of
the Red River valley and the Minnesota River valley
and reached south into central Iowa. At its maximum,
the ice lobe's western margin deposited glacial sediment (clay, silt, sand, gravel, and boulders) as it melted,
producing a broad belt of low hills called a moraine,
which extends to the northwest and upon which this
rest stop was built. Streams to the east of this moraine
drain into the Mississippi River system, whereas streams
to the west, like Kanaranzi Creek just south of here,
drain into the Missouri River system. Thus, the moraine
is now a drainage divide.

Farther westward and just north of Luverne, there
is a bedrock upland called Blue Mound. Blue Mound
can appear bluish from a distance, but it is actually
composed of a reddish-pink-to-whitish rock called
quartzite. The bluish appearance may be caused, in
part, by the lichens that cover the quartzite outcrops.
This quartzite formed from a quartz sand whose grains,
over time, were cemented by silica and partially recrys-
tallized, making a solid, hard rock that is resistant to
erosion. The color shades of the quartzite are due to
iron oxides that exist as thin films around and between

the quartz grains. The quartzite of Blue Mound has probably been a high point on the landscape for much of the time since its formation 1.7 billion years ago. It was an island when shallow seas covered this area 97 million years ago. The surrounding rocks contain fossils of animals that lived in these waters: sharks, turtles, sponges, and even mosasaurs—large fish-eating lizards related to the modern monitor lizard.

The area west of here was also glaciated, but much earlier—at least a half million years ago. Blue Mound was not high enough to escape the great thickness of ice that covered this region at that time. The hard quartzite bears the scratches left by those passing glaciers.

Erected by the Geological Society of Minnesota in partnership with the Minnesota Department of Transportation and the Minnesota Geological Survey. 2003

### 144.  A SEA OF GRASS
*Located on I-90 (west bound) in Adrian rest area*

When the wind blew it looked like waves upon the sea. This was the sight that greeted the explorers and then later settlers to southwestern Minnesota. Home for centuries to American Indians, this was a unique sight to people from the forested eastern United States. Stretching from Illinois to the Rocky Mountains was grass growing up to six feet high, broken with scattered trees near lakes and streams, this land lay waiting to be tilled.

Called the prairie, which is a French word for meadow, this expanse is duplicated in few other parts of the world, including the pampas of Argentina and the Black Earth Belt of Russia. There are three types of prairie, the short grass, the mixed grass and the tall grass prairie. It was the tall grass prairie that covered southwestern Minnesota where three grasses dominated. They were the Big Bluestem (Andropogon gerardi), Indian Grass (Sorghastrum nutans) and Switch Grass (Panicum virgatum).

Pollen records appear to indicate that prairies were established following the retreat of the Wisconsin Glacier some 18,000 years ago. The pattern of grass was maintained over the following years by moisture or lack thereof, fires, and the fact that once a prairie sod is established it is hard for other seedlings to compete. Today the prairie remains only in small patches in reserves or untillable areas. Most of the trees you see were planted as shelter belts by the homesteaders and later farmers. Although the prairie disappeared after nourishing the buffalo (bison) for years, it still continues to nourish. The rich farmlands of the corn belt that help feed the nation are the direct result of thousands of years of rotted grass roots. 1995

### 145. MILITARY HIGHWAYS
*Located on I-90 (east bound) in Adrian rest area*

As the state was explored and settled by Euroamericans, it became necessary to connect one place of settlement to another. The Native Americans had numerous trails that they used, some of which had developed from animal paths. The fur traders and the oxcarts that traveled between Winnipeg and St. Paul created other networks of trails, but as settlement increased there was a need for better maintained roadways.

Early roads established by the federal government were built to "facilitate the business of government." Establishing routes between military posts was the first order of business. In 1820 efforts were made to establish a road between Fort Snelling and Camp Missouri (located near present day Omaha, Nebraska), but surveys did not find a good route. In 1836 the U.S. Congress appropriated $100,000 to fund a road to connect the Red River of the North with Arkansas. Captain Nathan Boone arrived at Fort Snelling to begin the survey work in 1838, but it was never completed.

Not until the 1850s were the first military roads

built. A law requiring the Secretary of War to construct certain roads in the Territory of Minnesota was passed on July 18, 1850. They were as follows: the Mendota-Wabasha Road, the Point Douglas-St. Louis River Road, the Point Douglas-Fort Ripley Road and the Red River Addition, the Swan River-Long Prairie Road and the Mendota-Big Sioux River Road. The last, which would have connected Fort Snelling to Fort Leavenworth, Kansas, was only completed to Mankato. Of the original 560 miles of military roads only small portions are still in use, as county and township roads. But those five roads formed the framework of the statewide network of roads that followed. 1997

### 146.  THE MINNESOTA-IOWA BOUNDARY
*Located on state highway 60 in Bigelow*

Today the borders between states in the American union seem firmly fixed, but in the 19th century setting boundaries was an important part of the statehood process. Most of Minnesota's boundaries were eventually defined by rivers and lakes, but its southern border is a straight line determined entirely for political reasons in the United States Congress.

After 1838 the area now known as Minnesota was a part of two territories—Wisconsin Territory east of the Mississippi River and Iowa Territory between the Mississippi and Missouri rivers. When Iowa prepared to join the union in 1844, its constitutional convention voted to set the new state's northern boundary along the line shown above [map on marker], including the confluence of the Minnesota and Mississippi rivers. But Congress had other ideas. The admission of new states into the Union in pairs, one free and one slave, had by this time become an unwritten rule. In order to keep the balance, Congress favored a smaller state of Iowa to allow for the formation of at least two more free states from the former territory. Iowa's northern border was

thus fixed on the latitude of 43.30, and when Iowa became a state Minnesota's southern boundary was set
even before the Minnesota Territory was organized. The
important river confluence area, which would later be
settled as St. Paul and Minneapolis, remained well north
of the boundary line. 1992

# OLMSTED COUNTY

### 147.  GEOLOGY OF MINNESOTA △
*Located off U.S. highway 63 in Silver Lake Park
in Rochester*

The diversified scenery of Minnesota—of which the
Rochester area is one phase—is due to the location of
the state in the approximate center of the continent.
Situated midway between the Atlantic and Pacific
oceans, Hudson Bay and the Gulf of Mexico, the state
has within its boundaries three principal divides in the
watersheds of North America. Minnesota lacks the
rugged topography and high elevations found in most
continental divides. Its highest elevation, 2,300 feet on
the Mesabi Range, is in close proximity to its lowest,
the surface of Lake Superior, 602 feet above the sea.

The general surface of the state slopes from the
north-central portion near Itasca Park, in four directions
toward its distant and opposite corners.

The 10,000 lakes of Minnesota cover 5,600 square
miles, an average of 1 square mile of water for every 15
of land. This unprecedented supply of water, which has
a surface exceeding the water area of any other state,
finds its way to the ocean through Hudson Bay, the
Great Lakes and the Gulf of Mexico.

Erected by the Geological Society of Minnesota and
the Department of Parks, City of Rochester aided by a
grant from the Louis W. and Maud Hill Family Foundation. 1954

## 148.  ORONOCO GOLD RUSH

*Located on county road 12 in Oronoco, .5 mile east of*
*U.S. highway 52*

During the summer of 1858 gold was discovered in the
bed of the Zumbro River at Rochester and near Oronoco.
The news created a local sensation. On July 1, 1858,
the *Rochester Democrat* reported: "The excitement in
reference to the gold discoveries in and near Rochester
and near Oronoco is unabated. The diggings at Oronoco
are yielding two to six dollars a day, per man . . . Some
ninety to one hundred men are at work in the diggins."
While little came of the boom in Rochester, the Oronoco
Mining Company invested over $1,000 in sluices and a
water wheel erected about five miles below Oronoco. The
following spring, floods unceremoniously carried away
the miners' handiwork. Driven on by a frenzied desire
to "get rich quick," the prospectors rebuilt the installa-
tions and extracted enough gold to keep their appetites
whetted. A few months later, in July, 1859, another
flood demolished their works a second time. This catas-
trophe and the hard times lingering from the great
panic of 1857 exhausted the men's determination and
resources, and the boom died overnight. Perhaps some-
day gold will again be discovered in the river here, and
Oronoco will relive its all too short moment of glory.

Placed by the Olmsted County Park and Recreation
Commission. 1968

## 149.  MAYOWOOD

*Located at 3720 Mayowood Road S.W. in Rochester*

A great love of nature led Dr. Charles Horace Mayo, co-
founder of the Mayo Clinic, and his wife Edith (Gra-
ham) Mayo to purchase a small red brick house and
340 acres in 1907. Their growing family and desire to
preserve the natural beauty of the surrounding woodlands led to the construction of two more houses and
the accumulation of 3,300 acres. Ivy Lodge was built in

Mayowood, about 1972

1908, and in 1910 "Dr. Charlie" himself designed and
built the Big House on the hillside.

Unique in construction, the Big House reflects a variety of architectural styles and ideas gathered by the
Mayos in their world travels. It is built of poured rein-
forced concrete, with outside walls over a foot thick en-
closing an air space of hollow insulating tiles.
Nevertheless it remains homelike rather than monumental. Antiques and art treasures blend in an atmosphere of informality and hospitality. Ease of circulation
and ample lighting through long rows of windows and
large bays are among the additions made by Dr. and
Mrs. Charles William Mayo, the second occupants. Many
notables, including President Franklin D. Roosevelt,
Emperor Haile Salassie of Ethiopia, and the King and
Queen of Nepal, have been entertained here. In addition
to its houses, the estate has a summer teahouse, a green-
house, stables, and barns. 1968

### 150.  MEDICAL PIONEERS OF MINNESOTA
*Located on I-90 (west bound) in Marion rest area*

Minnesota's doctors and the institutions they built have
played a distinguished role in the medical revolution of

the past 150 years. Both the Mayo Clinic and the University of Minnesota Medical School have pioneered treatment techniques that have brought patients and students from around the world to their doors.

Dr. William W. Mayo and his two sons, William J. (Dr. Will) and Charles H. (Dr. Charlie) Mayo, working at St. Mary's Hospital in Rochester, achieved notable success in their new field of surgery during the 1890s. As the sons' skills grew, their practice expanded, until by 1904 the two doctors were operating on over 3,000 patients each year. New laboratories, improved medical record keeping, advanced training for physicians in many specialties, and quality medical diagnosis and care in well-equipped modern hospitals followed, bringing the Mayo Clinic a worldwide and still growing reputation.

Benefiting from cooperation and competition with the Clinic, the University of Minnesota Medical School in Minneapolis earned its own national reputation. Dr. Charles N. Hewitt, of Red Wing, who led early efforts to conquer typhoid, smallpox, and other deadly infectious diseases by means of vaccination and sanitation regulations, was a regular public health lecturer at the University. In the 1930s Dr. Owen H. Wangensteen revolutionized abdominal surgery with the invention of gastric suction procedures. The medical school also pioneered in open heart surgery, introducing the heart pacemaker

Dr. Charles H. Mayo operating at the Mayo Clinic in 1913

and artificial heart valves. In recent years it has played a major role in organ transplantation. These and other contributions have given rise to a concentration of fine hospitals and clinics and a sophisticated electronics industry producing pacemakers, valves, and other devices to heal the sick and prolong life. 1993

# PIPESTONE COUNTY

### 151. NICOLLET EXPEDITION

*Located off state highway 23 at Pipestone National Monument on the north end of Pipestone*

The J. N. Nicollet Expedition of 1838 rested here three days: John C. Fremont, Charles A. Geyer, Joseph Lafromboise, J. E. Flandin, Joseph Renville

Erected by Catlinite Chapter, Daughters of the American Revolution. 1925

# REDWOOD COUNTY

### 152. GEOLOGY OF THE MINNESOTA RIVER VALLEY △

*Located on state highway 19 in the Tiger Lake rest area 2.5 miles west of Morton*

Near the end of the last glacial period, this site overlooked a colossal river called Glacial River Warren. Between 11,700 and 9,500 years ago, there were two separate spans of time during which this immense river flowed for a total of about 1,000 years. With its headwaters near the site of Browns Valley, it was the main outlet for Glacial Lake Agassiz, an enormous glacial meltwater lake. At its maximum, this lake covered the combined areas of the Red River valley, northwestern Minnesota, and much of Canada southwest of Hudson Bay. The tremendous power of Glacial River Warren cut through layers of glacial sediment (clay, silt, sand, gravel, and boulders deposited by glaciers) and clay-rich deposits of weathered bedrock all the way down to scour some of the oldest bedrock in North America.

Some of the bedrock exposed on the valley floor is as old as 3.6 billion years. It is called Morton Gneiss (pronounced "nice"), and it formed deep in the earth's crust, where extreme heat and pressure changed, or metamorphosed, an earlier kind of rock. The extreme conditions may have resulted from small continental masses colliding and combining, the process that built the early North American protocontinent. The beautiful and distinctive banding of colorful minerals within the Morton Gneiss makes it an attractive building stone, which is used around the world.

Above the Morton Gneiss and visible in places along the valley walls is a layer up to 45 meters thick of gneiss decomposed by weathering. This deep and intense weathering occurred about 100 million years ago when Minnesota's climate was subtropical. Prolonged exposure to a warm atmosphere and acidic rainwater caused minerals in the gneiss to break down and form mostly clay minerals of the kaolin group. These white kaolin clays are mined throughout the river valley and are used for cement, bricks, and ceramics.

In most places, the kaolin deposits are buried by tens of meters of glacial sediment, deposited during the Ice Age of the last two million years. Glacial sediment can be seen along the valley walls, and the modern Minnesota River exposes more in the valley bottom.

Erected by the Geological Society of Minnesota in partnership with the Minnesota Department of Transportation and the Minnesota Geological Survey. 2003

## 153.   GEOLOGY OF THE REDWOOD FALLS REGION  △

*Located off U.S. highway 71 and state highway 19 in Alexander Ramsey Park in Redwood Falls in the picnic area*

Exposed in the rocky hillocks of the Minnesota River valley between Montevideo and Morton are some of the oldest rocks on earth. The pink-and-black-banded rock used for the pedestal of this tablet is a metamorphic rock called gneiss (pronounced "nice"). This gneiss formed when great and prolonged heat and pressure deep in the earth was applied to and altered earlier rocks. Because the change or metamorphism was so intense, the character and age of the original rocks have been obscured.

This metamorphism occurred about 3.6 billion years ago, probably during the creation of an early continental mass. Small pieces of continental crust, such as that containing the original rock of this gneiss, collided and stuck together to form protocontinents. As the continental pieces collided, their margins were compressed, producing the heat and pressure that caused the metamorphism. This process operated for billions of years, building larger continental masses like those we see today.

Technically, this rock is named Morton Gneiss, after the village of Morton where it is well exposed. Commercially, it is known as Rainbow or Tapestry granite. Gneisses have made popular building and monument stones throughout the world.

North of this tablet, across the Redwood River, a bank of residual clay 23 meters high is all that remains of some gneiss that completely decomposed. This type of deep and intense decomposition is characteristic of weathering in tropical climates. Such a climate existed here about 100 million years ago when the North American continent, during its very slow drift across the surface of the earth, was located at subtropical latitudes (30°–60° N). Continental drift is part of the dynamic global process of plate tectonics and has probably operated throughout most of earth's history.

Erected by the Geological Society of Minnesota in partnership with the Minnesota Department of Transportation and the Minnesota Geological Survey. 1998

## 154. MDEWAKANTON REPATRIATION BURIAL SITE
*Located off county road 2, 1 mile south of U.S. highway 71, at Lower Sioux Community Cemetery*

[Front] Near here are buried the repatriated remains of Mdewakanton Dakota. Many Dakota cooperatively worked for years with the State of Minnesota, the Bureau of Indian Affairs, and the Minnesota Indian Affairs Council to repatriate these remains. Used in an American Indian context, to repatriate means to return to the place of one's ancestry. The Lower Sioux Mdewakanton Community has returned the remains of more than 80 of their ancestors to their homeland through multiple repatriations.

The U.S.-Dakota War of 1862, a six week struggle, resulted from many years of uneasy interaction between Dakota, Euro-americans and the U.S. government. A devastating result of the War was that the majority of Dakota either left their traditional homelands or were forcibly exiled to areas farther west. When these Dakota died, they were buried in the area of their most recent residence rather than in their ancestral homelands in Minnesota.

Most of the Dakota whose remains are buried here resided in South Dakota or Nebraska at the time of their death. The remains of Chief Marpiya Oki Najin (Cut Nose) are of special concern to the Dakota. Chief Marpiya Oki Najin was one of thirty-eight Dakota men hanged at Mankato on December 26, 1862, for alleged crimes they committed during the War. After the hanging, doctors from Mankato and nearby towns stole the bodies of the dead Dakota men. For many years, the bodies were used for medical research and anatomical studies. Chief Marpiya Oki Najin's and those of two others are the only known remains of the thirty-eight Dakota hanged in Mankato to be recovered and properly buried.

While the remains of many Dakota have been repatriated to their ancestral homelands, the remains of many more are still awaiting repatriation and burial in a respectful manner with proper Dakota ceremonies. 2000

**Mdewakanton Ehdakupi Wanaǧi Makoće**
[Back] De oyanke ed Mdwakanton Dakota wićantanćan
ehdakupi kin hena wićaȟapi.
Hena 1862 U.S.-Dakota Okićize iyohakab tamakoće
etan wićakaȟapi.

Dena oyate wićatanćan ehdakupi he, he Dakota
tona waniyetu ota, Minisota Makobaśpe Oitanćan
Yankapi ka nakun Minisota Ikćewićaśta Ateyapi hena ko
ahtanipi onken hena ahtanipi un dehan he woyuśtan.
Tona akihde ehdakupi un, Ćanśayapi Mdewakanton Oyanke wićantanćan wikćemna śahdogan sampa
hunka wićayapi tamakoće ta wićahdohdipi okihipi.

1862 U.S.-Dakota Okicize he oko śakpe woteȟi, he
ećin he waniyetu ota Dakota ka Waśićun Oyate Tokeca
ka Tunkaśidayapi hena kokićipa unpi.
Okićize etanhan taku teȟiya ićaǧe kinhe dakota
wićota ehanna tamakoće etanhan iyayekiyapi kaiś
sampa wiyoȟpeyata kiya wićakaȟapapi.
Dena Dakota kin unśika tapi kinhan hena tuktek-
ted ounyanpi eda wićaȟapi. E'eś Minisota ehanna
tamakoće tawapi etu śni.
Tona ded wićaȟapi kin hena Dakotapi. Hena South
Dakota ka Nebraska hećiya tipi ka hećiya tapi.
Tka wićatanćan wanji he okidutatunpi kinhe,
Itanćan Maȟpiya Oki Najin (Stands in the Midst of
Clouds) (Cut Nose) he ee. Ćankapopawi wikćemna
num śakpe, omaka 1862 he, Makato ed, Dakota wićaśta
wikćemna yamni sahdoǧan otkewićayapi kinhe Itanćan
Maȟpiya Oki Najin wanji ee. Hena Okićize ićunhan
taku wośiće ecunpi iyawićaunpapi ka wicayaćopi.
Otke wićayapi iyokaham, pejuta wićaśta Makato ka
otunwe kiyeda wanke kin hena etanhanpi, Dakota
wićaśta tanćan kin hena manupi ka waniyetu ota hena
wićatanćan wounspekiya ka pejuta woiyukćan ed
wićahnakapi.
De Dakota wikćemna yamni śahdoǧan otke
wićayapi he etan Itanćan Maȟpiya Oki Najin he ee ka
nakun wićatanćan num he ehdakupi ka yuonihanyan
wićaȟapi.

Dehan Dakota wićatanćan ota hunka tamakoćeta ehdakupi. Tka hinań wićatanćan ota ehdakupi ka yuonihanyan, wakan wićohan ohna wićahapi kta akipapi.

### 155.  WOWINAPE OR THOMAS WAKEMAN (1846–1886)
*Located off North Redwood Road in Redwood Falls Cemetery in Redwood Falls*

Near this spot lie the remains of Wowinape (Place of Refuge), a survivor of the Dakota War of 1862. Wowinape was the son of Taoyateduta (His Red Nation), known to whites as Little Crow, spokesman and leader of the Dakota in that tragic war. In July, 1863 Wowinape was with his father when he was killed. He fled to Dakota Territory but was captured, tried and sentenced to hang. Reprieved and in a prison camp, he became literate in the Dakota language, a Christian convert, and took the name Thomas Wakeman.

Wowinape (Thomas Wakeman) in 1864

Pardoned in 1866, he went to the Santee Reservation and later homesteaded with other Dakota at the bend of the Big Sioux River in Dakota Territory. Thomas Wakeman married Judith Minnetonka in January, 1874. He farmed and carried the U.S. mail. Impressed by the Y.M.C.A., he worked with friends to found the first Indian chapter at Flandreau, Dakota Territory, on April 27, 1879.

Ill with tuberculosis, he returned to boyhood scenes and died at Redwood Falls, Minnesota on January 13,

1886. In his lifetime, he made a path between the Dakota Indian and Euroamerican worlds. 1992

### 156. ST. CORNELIA'S CHURCH
*Located off county highway 2 at Lower Sioux Agency*

A center of Mdewakanton Dakota community life for several generations, St. Cornelia's Episcopal Church is a symbol of Dakota continuity in the homeland from which they once were exiles. In 1987 the remains of 31 Dakota who died in an Iowa prison following the U.S.-Dakota Conflict of 1862 were returned to rest here among their own people.

Forced to sign away most of their traditional lands, the Dakota by the 1850s lived on a reservation along the Minnesota River. The U.S. government at the Lower Sioux Agency was slow to provide the schools it had promised. Finally, in 1860, hereditary chief Wabasha and leaders Good Thunder and Taopi asked Episcopal Bishop Henry B. Whipple to start a church and a reservation school.

Whipple sent 21-year-old Samuel D. Hinman to work with the Dakota people. Soon Hinman's school had 50 pupils, and by 1862 a church building, its cornerstone selected by Wabasha and laid by Whipple, was nearing completion. The church was destroyed in the 1862 conflict, and the Dakota were driven from the state.

After more than 20 years in exile, some Dakota people returned to their former home in the 1880s. By 1889 a new church was under construction. The same cornerstone used in the 1862 church was now installed in a new location on land donated by Good Thunder. Named for the wife of Bishop Whipple, St. Cornelia's was consecrated in 1891.

Among those Dakota who led the congregation after Hinman's death in 1890 were Napoleon Wabasha, the Rev. Henry Whipple St. Clair, George Crooks, and Sam Wells. Members of almost every Dakota family in the area provided support, and many of their children attended the mission school until it closed in 1920.

St. Cornelia's Church was placed on the National Register of Historic Places in 1979.

Erected by the Minnesota Historical Society in cooperation with the Lower Sioux Indian Community. 1988

# RENVILLE COUNTY

### 157.  REDWOOD FERRY
*Located on state highway 19, about 2 miles east of Morton*

On a summer day in 1862 the Redwood Ferry landing on the Minnesota River below this point was the scene of the first attack against military troops in one of America's most tragic Indian wars.

Early in the morning of August 18, 1862, a large party of Dakota (Sioux) warriors, enraged by delayed annuity payments and near-starvation conditions on their reservation, attacked the nearby Lower Sioux Agency. Surviving agency employees crossed the river on the Redwood Ferry and fled to Fort Ridgely some 13 miles downstream.

Discounting warnings of the Indians' strength and determination, the fort's commandant, John S. Marsh, set out toward the agency with interpreter Peter Quinn and 46 soldiers of the Fifth Minnesota Infantry. They found the Dakota waiting in ambush at the ferry. In the ensuing fight, Quinn and 23 soldiers were killed and Marsh was drowned while trying to escape by swimming across the river. The remaining men eventually made their way back to Fort Ridgely, which was itself attacked on August 20 and 22.

The war in the Minnesota River Valley claimed the lives of at least 450 whites and an unknown number of Dakota before it came to an end at Camp Release on September 26, 1862. 1985

**158.   BIRCH COULEE STATE MONUMENT** 🏛

*Located off state highway 19, .5 mile northeast of Morton*

[North side] Erected by the State of Minnesota in grateful remembrance of the Heroism of those gallant soldiers and citizens who fought the battle of Birch Coulee and to perpetuate their names. Captain Hiram P. Grant. Co. A. 6th Minnesota Vol. Inf. Commanding. J. W. Daniels surgeon. Sargent. W. Irvine, J. C. Cooledge, Corp. W. Coob, T. C. W. Beneken, Corp. S. Carbuckle, G. W. Eagles, E. Brown, E. S. Place, S. Fielding, S. Clark, G. Colter, C. F. Coyle, C. L. King, Co. G.—B. S. Terry, Co. A. Wounded—A. Hayford, D. G. House, C. Mayall, D. H. McCauley, Co. G—T. Barnes, H. Rolleau, H. Whetsler, F. C. Shanley, W. Vayhinger, S. J. Weiting, W. Russell, W. A. Newcomb, C. W. Smith, B. Viles.

[East side] 2nd Lt. G. W. Turnbull, Sargent. L. S. Elliot, Corp. J. C. Hooper, J. F. Farley, A. B. Dunn, W. Carlowe, David Caruther, Corp. J. Coursole, F. C. Griswold, F. G. Connely, C. A. Earl, G. Weaver, T. E. Byrne, J. Gailbrath, W. Hart, M. Nelson, J. Osia, W. H. Grant, H. Kreuger, F. Patch, H. Smith, J. Shoska, W. Forman; Citizens—J. W. Decamp, J. R. Brown, D. Blair, T. J. Galbraith, A. Fairbault, G. H. Fairbault, J. J. Trazee, Killed—D. Halbrook, Wounded—G. D. Redfield, F. Rose, J. E. Sherwin

Erected 1894.

C. D. Gilfillan, A. G. Stoddard, R. B. Hinton, J. Patton, J. W. Daniels, S. G. Arbuckles, W. H. Grant, Comm.

[West side] Sept 2nd and 3rd. 1862.

Co. D and E.

S. Swargert, Co. F.—R. K. Boyd, E. Braman, Co. A. Capt. H. P. Grant, 1st. Lt. H. J. Gillham, 2nd. Lt. J. E. Baldwin, Sargent, W. Pratt, G. Brennen, A. P. Connelly, Corp. S. Walters, W. F. Barness, J. Staples, M. B. Fields, R. Olson, B. F. Arbuckle, J. Auge, L. Klinkblower, Co. I.—J. S. J. Bean, H. M. L. T. Brown, Co. A—W. W. Balton, C. Bryant, W. H. Bowers, P. H. Burnes, L. Brunelle,

P. Brunelle, W. H. Gaine, A. M. Danills, B. Derosie, E. A.
Erickson, P. Felix, D. Felix, P. H. Freaney, C. B. Gardner,
H. Grunle, G. W. Hard, W. Havens, J. G. Hillberge, J.
Howard, F. Jarvis, M. Johnson, John R. King, A. Kil-
patrick, J. S. Leyda, H. C. Marsden.

[South side] S. Lindstrom, L. Malo, J. Madson, M.
Mencker, T. Miller, D. Murphy, M. Nesley, G. Memo, H.
Olson, J. Quinn, W. H. Rossman, W. Schurer, M. Seaman,
D. Sweaney, D. F. Teswilleger, P. H. Thielan, F. Trepan, B.
Webber, J. Right, T. S. Wirt, J. Young, Co. B.[—] A.
Thompson, J. Loftens, Co. D.—J. N. Richardson, Co. E.
Lewis Thiele.

Lt. J. H. Swan Co. I. 3rd Regt. Minn. Vol., Capt.
Anderson's Co. Killed. R. Baxter, Capt. J. Anderson, P.
Burkman, E. W. Earle, J. Martin, 1st Lt. J. Brown, T. Free-
man, Wounded—T. Barton, J. Cunningham, H. Fandle,
D. M. Smith, G. W. Brown, R. Gibbens, A. H. Bunker, G.
Dashney, C. Holmes, C. P. Troxel, J. J. Egan. [Approved
by 1893 legislature; dedicated September 3, 1894.]

### 159.  BATTLE OF BIRCH COULEE  🅜
*Minnesota Historical Society Historic Site*
*Located off U.S. highway 71, about 3 miles north of*
*Morton, at junction with county roads 18 and 2*

On the prairie half a mile east of this point, a party of
about 160 troops was attacked by Sioux at dawn, Sept.
2, 1862.

During the battle, the force was surrounded for
thirty hours, losing over a third of its number in killed
and wounded.

### 160.  SCHWANDT STATE MONUMENT  🄼
*Located on county road 15 near North Redwood,*
*12 miles south of Renville*

Erected by State of Minnesota 1915 in memory of mar-
tyrs for civilization: Johann Schwandt, Christina

Schwandt, & their children, Fredrik & Christian, John Walz, Karolina Schwandt, Walz & John Frass, Murdered by Sioux Indians Aug. 18, 1862. [Approved by 1915 legislature; dedicated August 18, 1915.]

### 161.   SIOUX INDIAN STATE MONUMENT 📖
*Located off state highway 19, .5 mile northeast of Morton*

Patriotism, Courage, Fidelity, Humanity

Erected A. D. 1899 by the Minnesota Valley Historical Society to commemorate the brave, faithful, and humane conduct of the loyal Indians who saved the lives of white people and were true to their obligations throughout the Sioux War in Minnesota of 1862 and especially to honor the services of those here named.

Other Day—Ampatutokicha, Paul—Mahzakute-manne, Lorenzo Lawrence—Towanetaton, Simon—Anahwangmanne, Mary Crooks—Mahkahta Heiya-win, Maggie Brass—Snana-win

Snana (Maggie Brass), about 1880

## 162.   FARTHER AND GAY CASTLE

*Located 6 miles south of Sacred Heart on county road 9 and 1 mile east on county road 15 in Joseph R. Brown State Wayside*

Memorial: Hans M. Strand 1929, Nels M. Strand 1929, Euphemia Strand 1929, Donors of this 3 acre memorial park in1937 [1968]

These ruins are all that remain of a large stone house built in 1861 by Joseph R. Brown, frontier fur trader, Indian agent, politician, journalist, and inventor.

The house, known as Farther and Gay Castle, was a center of hospitality and happy family life for the short time that Brown, his mixed-blood Sioux wife, and their twelve children lived in it.

On August 19, 1862, during the Sioux Uprising, the Browns were forced to flee their home, which was looted and burned by the attacking Indians. 1958

# RICE COUNTY

## 163.   ALEXANDER FARIBAULT HOUSE

*Located at 12 N.E. First Avenue in Faribault*

Alexander Faribault, for whom the city of Faribault was named, was the son of fur trader Jean Baptiste Faribault and his wife, Pelagie. Alexander first entered the area in 1826 to establish a trading post for the American Fur Company on Cannon Lake. He moved the post a few miles east in 1835 and in 1844 finally established it at the present site of the city of Faribault.

Like many of the traders, Faribault wielded great influence over the local Dakota Indians with whom he did business. He played a part in persuading them to sign treaties in 1851, opening most of their land in Minnesota to white settlement and assigning some of their treaty money toward the payment of fur trade debts.

With his fur trade and treaty profits, Alexander Faribault built this house in 1853. One of the first frame houses in the newly opened land, it served for many years as a community center, chapel, polling place, and meeting hall. It is now owned and interpreted by the Rice County Historical Society. 1978

### 164.  SEABURY DIVINITY SCHOOL (EPISCOPAL)— FOUNDED 1858

*Located at First Street S.E. and State Avenue S.E. in Faribault*

The Seabury Divinity School was one of several schools comprising the Bishop Seabury Mission founded in the frontier community of Faribault in 1858 by the Rev. James Lloyd Breck. Both the mission and seminary were named in honor of Samuel Seabury, America's first Episcopal bishop. Establishment of the mission in Faribault was a key factor in the community's designation in 1860 as See of the Diocese of Minnesota by Bishop Henry Whipple. The Faribault schools flourished under Whipple's direction from 1860 to 1901, educating area children and training clergy for missionary work in the West. The Divinity School shared a common campus with the Shattuck Grammar School until 1873, when the continued growth of both schools brought a decision to move the seminary to this site on the outskirts of town.

The seminary remained a vital component of the Diocese's educational work in Faribault until 1933, when it merged with Western Theological Seminary of Chicago to form Seabury-Western Theological Seminary located in Evanston, Illinois.

Johnston Hall, the only surviving structure on the seminary campus, was erected as a library-classroom facility in 1888 with funds bequeathed by Mrs. Augusta Johnston Shumway of Chicago. The structure, which has served as a nurses' training school since 1960 when Rice County District No. 1 Hospital was established on the campus site, is listed on the National Register of Historic Places.

Dedicated this 16th Day of April, 1983 during the 125th Anniversary year of the school's founding by the Episcopal Dioceses of Minnesota and Chicago.

## 165.  SHATTUCK–ST. MARY'S SCHOOLS
*Located off state highway 60 in Faribault off*
*Shumway Avenue*

Shattuck–St. Mary's Schools date from 1858 when the
Reverend James Lloyd Breck founded the Bishop
Seabury Mission and a coeducational day school in the
frontier community of Faribault.

Breck's "Bishop Seabury University" never material-
ized, but four schools did—Seabury Divinity School
(1858), Shattuck (1864) for boys, St. Mary's Hall (1866)
for girls, and St. James (1901) for younger boys.

When Minnesota's first bishop, Henry Whipple,
arrived in 1860, he found a flourishing day school and
seminary and designated Faribault as See of the Episcopal Diocese. On Breck's foundations, Whipple and his
wife Cornelia built strong endowed institutions. By
1900, Faribault had become a recognized center for
private secondary education.

Following a period of independence, Seabury
merged with Western Seminary of Chicago in 1933 and
relocated to Evanston, Illinois. In 1972, the three preparatory schools were coordinated into what is known
today as Shattuck–St. Mary's Schools. The Shattuck
campus and St. Mary's Hall are listed on the National
Register of Historic Places.

Dedicated this 16th day of April, 1983 during the
125th anniversary year.


## 166.  CATHEDRAL OF OUR MERCIFUL SAVIOUR
*Located at 515 Second Avenue N.W. in Faribault*

One of the earliest missionary centers of the Episcopal
Church in Minnesota and believed to be the first Epis-
copal cathedral built in the United States, the Cathedral
of Our Merciful Saviour is also a monument to Henry
Benjamin Whipple. Elected first bishop of the Episcopal
Diocese of Minnesota in 1858 at the age of thirty-seven,
Whipple soon became known as "Straight Tongue" by
the Dakota and Ojibway Indians whose rights he worked

to secure through the reform of U.S. Indian policies and an active Indian mission program. Speaking almost alone, it was Whipple who persuaded Abraham Lincoln to commute most of the sentences of Dakota men condemned to death after the conflict of 1862.

The cathedral developed out of work begun in 1858 by James Lloyd Breck. The cornerstone was laid on July 16, 1862. James Renwick, architect of St. Patrick's Cathedral in New York City is credited with the design. Envisioned as a gathering place for the Parish of the Good Shepherd, Seabury Divinity School, Shattuck, and St. Mary's Hall, the Faribault Cathedral was consecrated on June 24, 1869. The tower, designed by Ralph Adams Cram, architect of St. John the Divine in New York City, was added as a memorial to Bishop Whipple after his death in 1901. Whipple is buried in a crypt beneath the chancel.

In 1941, St. Mark's in Minneapolis became the diocesan cathedral. However, the "Bishop's Church in Faribault" remains the home of an active congregation and a place of pilgrimage in southern Minnesota. 1987

## 167.  A FLOUR MILLING REVOLUTION

*Located on I-35 (south bound) in Northfield rest area*

In the 1870s and 1880s, important changes took place inside several small flour mills in southeastern Minnesota. Those changes laid the groundwork for a technological revolution that made Minnesota's milling industry the largest in the world.

The changes grew out of a desire by millers to improve the quality of their flour. Most Minnesota farmers raised hard spring wheat, which had a reputation for producing speckled flour. Drawing on European technology, Minnesota millers developed a method of refining their flour by sending it through a purifier that removed the specks, or middlings, and by grinding the flour several times. Called the New Process, this method produced a whiter, purer flour that was soon in demand by consumers.

One of the first to experiment with this new technique was Northfield miller Jesse Ames, who used a purifier as early as 1865. Within a few years, purifiers were found at the Archibald mill in Dundas, the Mowbray mill in Stockton, the Gardner mill in Hastings, and the Faribault mill.

As the changes swept the milling industry in the 1870s, millers concluded that the traditional millstone, which required frequent redressing, was no longer efficient. They turned instead to rollers, already used in some parts of Europe. One of the earliest American attempts at roller milling occurred in 1872–73 at the Mowbray mill, where four-foot marble rollers were installed. Soon most Minnesota millers had replaced their old millstones, opting for more efficient porcelain-covered or iron rollers. 1995

### 168. ARCHIBALD MILL
*Located off county road 1 in Mill Park in Dundas*

Mill Park was established through the combined efforts of the City of Dundas, the State of Minnesota, and the National Park Service. Individual contributions and volunteer work were essential to complete the three year project. The ruins of the Archibald Mill lie just to the north of the park. Constructed in 1857, the Archibald Mill developed a flour milling process that was later introduced in the Minneapolis mills. The footbridge at the south end of the park spans 201 feet across the Cannon River linking Mill Park and Memorial Park. 1995

### 169. THOMAS ANDERSON VEBLEN AND KARI BUNDE VEBLEN FARMSTEAD
*Located off state highway 246 at the east side of Nerstrand*

[Front] From 1866 to 1893 this farmstead was the home of the Veblen family, one of the most prominent Norwegian immigrant families of the nineteenth century.

The most distinguished trait of the Veblen family

Thorstein Veblen at age 23

was its emphasis in education. Of the nine children who lived to adulthood, all but one finished secondary school, several studied on the college level, and three graduated from Carleton College. Both Andrew and Thorstein completed the Carleton curriculum in three years and then pursued postgraduate studies. Emily was reputedly the first daughter of Norwegian immigrants ever to graduate from an American college. Many of the Veblen children were teachers during at least part of their careers.

The most famous of them was Thorstein Bunde Veblen (1857–1929), the internationally recognized economist and social critic. He became a national literary and intellectual figure after the 1899 publication of his first book, *The Theory of the Leisure Class.* This book, still widely read, coined a number of new concepts, of which "conspicuous consumption" is best known.

The farm house marks a transition from the old world to the new. The exterior is in the Greek Revival style typical in the United States during much of the nineteenth century, but the full-length porch and exterior stairs derive from building traditions in the Valdres district in Norway, from which Thomas and Kari emigrated. The interior layout and decoration are predominantly Norwegian. The high level of craftsmanship evident throughout the house and barn are due primarily to Thomas, a skilled carpenter and cabinetmaker who brought his tools and talents to the new world.

### History of the Veblen Farmstead

[Back] The Veblens lived in Wisconsin from their arrival in 1847 until 1865, when they moved to Minnesota. They were attracted to this area by the good farmland and the presence of several relatives nearby.

In 1864 Thomas Veblen bought 200 acres of unimproved land surrounding this site. In 1865 he purchased another 90 acres of partly cultivated land just east of what is now Nerstrand Woods State Park. The family lived in a house on the smaller farm following their arrival in July 1865.

Work soon began on the new house. Foundation stones were quarried in what is now Nerstrand Woods State Park and hauled to this site during the winter. By the fall of 1866 the foundation walls had been completed and covered with a temporary roof. The family moved in late that year. The shell of the house was probably erected in 1867 and the house assumed its final form about 1870. The barn was erected around 1872.

The site operated as a farm until 1970. The homestead was placed on the National Register of Historic Places in 1975 and designated a National Historic Landmark in 1981. The survival of the farm buildings is due principally to the efforts of the Veblen Preservation Project, which raised funds to purchase the abandoned buildings and surrounding ten acres in 1982 and which made critical repairs. In 1992 a private individual purchased the property and assumed responsibility for its restoration. Thanks to the dedication and cooperative efforts of many individuals and groups, the home of Minnesota's "disturbing genius" and this remarkable family has been preserved and meticulously restored as a reminder of Norwegian-American immigrant life in the last half of the nineteenth century. 1996

# ROCK COUNTY

### 170. SIOUX QUARTZITE AND PIPESTONE

*Located on I-90 at the tourist information center in*
*Beaver Creek*

Scattered throughout the rich farmland of southwestern Minnesota are large outcroppings of a hard red-to-pink rock known as Sioux quartzite. These rocks were formed from sand, silt, and shells deposited by shifting seas that advanced and retreated over this land more than a billion and a half years ago. In a few locations, the ripple marks of ancient shorelines are still clearly visible in the rocks themselves.

Within the quartzite deposits are smaller layers of a dark red stone known as pipestone or Catlinite, named for the well-known nineteenth century artist George Catlin. For centuries Indians from many different tribes quarried the soft red stone at what is now Pipestone National Monument. From the precious rock they fashioned beautiful pipes and other ceremonial objects.

On many of the quartzite surfaces in this region are carved drawings of buffalo, turtles, thunderbirds, weapons, and human stick figures. Some of these mysterious works of art, called petroglyphs, are believed to be more than 5,000 years old and probably played a part in ceremonies to assure good hunting. 1985

# SIBLEY COUNTY

### 171. JOSEPH R. BROWN STATE MONUMENT 🖳

*Located off state highway 19 in Brown Cemetery at the west*
*end of Henderson*

Joseph R. Brown, Pioneer. Statesman. Soldier.
1805–1870. Founder of Henderson.
[Approved by 1909 legislature; dedicated September 27, 1910.]

# STEELE COUNTY

### 172.  GEOLOGY OF THE RICE LAKE AREA △
*Located on county road 19 in Rice Lake State Park*

The water in Rice Lake must have a difficult time decid-
ing: its two outlet streams flow in opposite directions!
Maple Creek, which is on the west side of the lake,
flows westward, while the South Branch, which is on
the east side of the lake, flows eastward. Although lakes
often have multiple inlets, only rarely do they have
more than one outlet, especially ones that flow in opposite directions. This unusual drainage exists because
the lake straddles a rise on a glacial deposit that was
created and modified by separate glacial advances.

About 14,000 years ago, glacial ice advancing
through the Manitoba region followed the lowlands of
the Red River valley and the Minnesota River valley
and reached south into central Iowa. The eastern edge
of this ice lobe reached to about two kilometers west of
Rice Lake. Along this melting margin, glacial sediment
(clay, silt, sand, gravel, and boulders) was deposited,
forming a broad line of low hills oriented north to
south, called the Bemis moraine.

The presence of gently rolling knob-and-kettle terrain east of the Bemis moraine indicates that, at some
earlier time, another ice lobe similarly reached eastward, but farther, to just past Rice Lake. As this earlier
ice melted, powerful streams under the ice carved elongated depressions in the land, called tunnel valleys. Because of the great pressure from the ice above, the
meltwater actually flowed uphill slightly, over moraine
sediments, until it reached the edge of the glacier.
There the pressure was released, and the meltwater
coursed eastward into what is now the Zumbro River.

Today, modern streams flow in former glacial
stream valleys. Maple Creek occupies one of these tunnel valleys, but now the water flows west, down its
slope, contrary to its glacial predecessor. Rice Lake oc-

cupies a shallow dip within this tunnel valley. The shallow water of the lake creates an ideal habitat for wild rice, which grows naturally in abundance and was first harvested by Native Americans.

Erected by the Geological Society of Minnesota in partnership with the Minnesota Department of Transportation, the Minnesota Geological Survey, and the Minnesota Department of Natural Resources. 2003

Classroom at the Owatonna State School, about 1900

### 173. MINNESOTA STATE SCHOOLS
*Located on I-35 (north bound) in Straight River rest area*

During its first session in 1858 the Minnesota State Legislature established the first of several schools for the training and care of citizens who suffered mental and physical disabilities and for children who were unable to care for themselves. The first school opened in Faribault in 1863, after five years of delay due to lack of funds. Called an "Asylum," later an "Institute," and now an "Academy," its students were those who were blind and deaf. Separate schools were later established here for the blind, the deaf and the mentally deficient.

In 1885, a State School for Dependent and Neglected Children opened in Owatonna. While it closed in 1970, the Faribault schools continue to function.

The schools are similar in both style and plan to buildings found at Minnesota state hospitals and correctional facilities. A typical complex included separate buildings for admission, classrooms, gymnasium, a hospital, dormitories, and service facilities such as a power plant, a laundry, and farm buildings. The farms allowed the schools to be partially self-sufficient. The schools were established by law to provide the students with activities and training, while protecting them from the "slights and rebuffs" of the outside world.

The first clinical psychologist to be employed in a mental retardation institute in the United States was at the Faribault State School. A.R.T. Wylie was that pioneer in the field of mental health research.

Several of the school buildings in Faribault and Owatonna are listed in the National Register of Historic Places. The school complex at Owatonna continues to serve the public. The buildings are used by the city, providing space for administrative offices, an art center, a museum interpreting the state school, and other uses. 1997

## 174. MINNESOTA CANNERIES
*Located on I-35 (south bound) in Straight River rest area*

Early settlers grew bumper wheat crops in southern Minnesota's fertile prairies, land that today supplies produce for a thriving 270-million-dollar-a-year canning industry.

Sweet corn canneries opened in Austin and Mankato in the early 1880s, followed soon after by similar factories in Faribault, Owatonna, and Le Sueur. Soon Minnesota's canners were experimenting with new technologies and new products, and in 1903 the automated Big Stone Cannery Company founded by F. W. Douthitt changed the industry nationwide. Douthitt's plant in Ortonville had a conveyor system, mechanical corn husking machines, and a power driven cutter that produced the first whole kernel canned corn. The Green Giant Company, also founded in1903 as the Minnesota Valley Canning Company, introduced golden cream-style corn in 1924 and the first vacuum packed corn in 1929.

Corn is still the major canning crop in Minnesota. The state's more than thirty plants also freeze and can peas, beans, carrots, tomatoes, pork, beef, chicken products, and such unusual items as rutabagas. Mankato was the site of the nation's first carp cannery in 1946. 1987

### 175. NATIONAL FARMERS' BANK OF OWATONNA
*Located in the city park across from 110 North Cedar Street in Owatonna*

Banker Carl Bennett wanted more than a prominent new building to house his family's business. He wanted a work of art. Bennett's search for an architect led him in 1906 to Louis Sullivan, one of the country's most inventive designers. Together they created a magnificent home for the National Farmers' Bank in the heart of downtown Owatonna. This brilliant collaboration of patron and architect produced what many consider the finest small-town bank in America.

After helping to make Chicago the country's architectural capital in the 1890s, Sullivan came through with a bank design for Owatonna unlike any other. Believing that function and form of a building should complement one another, he conceived a structure resembling a treasure chest, a fitting image for a bank that housed people's savings.

Sullivan chose for his bank a theme he used often—an arch within a square—then attached to it a rectangular office building. He combined those simple, monumental shapes with complex ornamental details that bring the building to life. Set in sandstone-and-brick walls are two huge stained-glass windows, each framed by a wide band of terra cotta—a hard, molded clay—accented by a narrow band of glass mosaic.

The architect did not create this masterpiece alone. His sketches were completed by his draftsman, George Elmslie, who designed much of the ornamentation and went on to become a noted Minnesota architect. Joining them were a team of skilled craftsmen who created the ornate interior—a "color symphony" of painted plaster, stained glass, and huge cast-iron chandeliers. The finished bank was dedicated in 1908.

Remodelings have altered some of the interior features. But much of the original splendor of Louis Sullivan's bank remains. In 1976 it was designated a National Historic Landmark. 1999

# TRAVERSE COUNTY

### 176. BROWNS VALLEY MAN
*Located on state highway 28, about .5 mile east of Browns Valley*

On October 9, 1933, William H. Jensen, an amateur archaeologist, uncovered the badly broken skeleton of a man in a gravel pit on the plateau visible about 1/2 mile south of this marker. The plateau was formed as an island in the ancient River Warren, an outlet of Glacial Lake Agassiz.

From flint spear points of the parallel-flaked type found in the grave and from the surrounding geological evidence, University of Minnesota archaeologists estimated that the burial dated to about 6000 B.C.

The skull of Browns Valley Man, reconstructed and measured at the university, was that of an adult male between 25 and 40 years of age who possessed many of the physical characteristics of the North American Indian. No additional traces of his culture have been discovered in the immediate vicinity.

The skeleton disappeared some time after it was returned to Jensen, deepening the mystery surrounding

Browns Valley Man. It was rediscovered by the Jensen family in 1987. The radiocarbon dating method has now dated the skeleton to 9,000 years ago. This makes the skeleton one of the earliest ever found, to date, in the New World. 1992

### 177. CONTINENTAL DIVIDE

*Located on state highway 28 at west end of Browns Valley*

Elevation 977 [shown on map of Minnesota]
Flow to Gulf of Mexico [arrow pointing left]
Flow to Hudson Bay [arrow pointing right]

### 178. WADSWORTH TRAIL

*Located on state highway 28 at west end of
Browns Valley*

This tablet marks the Wadsworth Trail extending from St. Cloud, Minnesota to Ft. Wadsworth, now Ft. Sisseton, South Dakota, blazed by pioneers in 1864.
Dr. Samuel Prescott Chapter D.A.R. 1935

### 179. SAMUEL J. BROWN STATE MONUMENT 🏛

*Located off state highway 28 in Sam Brown Memorial Park
at the west end of Broadway in Browns Valley*

Samuel Jerome Brown, Born March 7, 1845, Long Hollow, Roberts Co., South Dakota. Died August 29, 1925, Browns Valley, Minnesota. The "Paul Revere" of the northwestern frontier, because of his intrepid exploit of April 19, 1866. He was known as a scholar and admired for his noble, kind-hearted character. His pluck in the face of adversity upheld the renown of an illustrious ancestry.
"Love for country and fellow men/Burns just as brightly now as then."
[Approved by 1929 legislature.]

Samuel J. Brown, about 1910

# WABASHA COUNTY

### 180.   GEOLOGY OF LAKE PEPIN  ⌂

*Located on U.S. highway 61, at Reads Landing Overlook,*
*about 3 miles northwest of Wabasha*

Lake Pepin, a widening of the Mississippi River, occupies the river valley north of here for a distance of 35 kilometers. The lake was created by the delta of Wisconsin's Chippewa River, which enters the Mississippi directly east of this site. The Chippewa, a relatively small river, has a much steeper gradient, or slope, than the Mississippi. This steeper slope causes a faster flow, which transports more sand and coarser gravel than the Mississippi can remove. Consequently, the sediments brought in by the Chippewa dam the Mississippi back in this gorge, thus forming Lake Pepin.

But this scene was not always so tranquil. About 10,000 years ago, near the end of the last glacial period, this site was submerged by a colossal river that spanned the gorge. The immense volume of water came from the combined discharge of Glacial River Warren draining Glacial Lake Agassiz, Glacial River St. Croix draining

Glacial Lake Duluth, and many smaller tributaries. That tremendous current eroded this gorge to its present width and flushed it clean of sediment, right down to the bedrock.

After the glacial meltwaters were gone and the Mississippi dwindled, sediment from the Chippewa dammed the main channel. At that time Lake Pepin extended for 100 kilometers—all the way back to where St. Paul is today. Where the Mississippi first entered the lake, its sediments deposited to form a delta. The delta has since advanced downstream by progressively filling in the head of the lake and thus reducing its length.

The top of the bluffs that line the shores of Lake Pepin are about 140 meters above the surface of the lake. The walls of the gorge are composed of sandstone, shale, and dolostone. These rocks were deposited as sediment in a warm, shallow sea that covered the area of southeastern Minnesota and much of North America about 500 million years ago. The rock-walled gorge extends 46 meters below the lake surface. It has been filled to the present lake bottom mostly with clays that have settled out of the still waters of the lake.

Erected by the Geological Society of Minnesota in partnership with the Minnesota Department of Transportation and the Minnesota Geological Survey. 2003

### 181. LAKE PEPIN

*Located on U.S. highway 61, 2.5 miles*
*northeast of Reads Landing*

"City dwellers need go no farther than this if they seek romantic solitude," wrote panorama artist Henry Lewis in 1848. "One cannot imagine a more lovely expanse of water than Lake Pepin in quiet, clear weather, and no wilder scene than when, whipped by storm, its waves bound against the rocky cliffs."

Between the towns of Red Wing and Wabasha most of the rugged valley of the Upper Mississippi is filled by this river widening known as Lake Pepin. Long before the European explorer Father Louis Hennepin "discovered" what he called the "Lake of Tears" in 1680, its served as a highway for Indian people of many cultures. Their burial mounds and earthworks can still be found along its shores.

After the Minnesota Territory was opened to settlement in 1849, Lake Pepin saw a brisk commercial traffic generated by lumbering and agriculture. Huge rafts of logs, some 1,200 feet long and 300 feet wide, were towed down the river. Steamboats brought in thousands of new settlers and carried out the wheat and flour produced on the rich land. The lake itself provided resources for commercial fishermen and for clammers, who sold the clam shells to be used in button making.

Today's "city dwellers" and others still seek "romance" and recreation in sailing, water skiing, and fishing on the beautiful lake that has welcomed generations of visitors to Minnesota. 1985

### 182.  MINNESOTA MAP
*Located on U.S. highway 61, 2.5 miles northeast of Reads Landing*

[Map of state of Minnesota] 1939

### 183.  HISTORIC LAKE PEPIN: BIRTHPLACE OF WATERSKIING
*Located on U.S. highway 61 near the Lake City pier on Lake Pepin*

"I decided that if you could ski on snow, you could ski on water." In 1922, after first trying barrel staves, then snow

Ralph Samuelson in 1925 with an early pair of skis

skis, eighteen year old Ralph W. Samuelson succeeded in waterskiing on eight foot long pine boards, steamed in boiling water to curve the tips. During the next fifteen years, Samuelson put on one-man waterskiing exhibitions, donating most of the admission charges to Lake City for the purchase of harbor and park land. Because of Samuelson's pioneering efforts in this popular sport, the American Water Ski Association in 1966 officially recognized Lake City as the birthplace of waterskiing. 1971

# WATONWAN COUNTY

### 184. ASHIPPUN POST OFFICE
*Located on state highway 60, 5.5 miles east of St. James*

In the spring of 1857, Halvor Knudsen Barland and his family halted their ox-driven covered wagon about one-quarter of a mile south of this site and began construction of a log house on their new homestead. The Barland cabin subsequently became Ashippun Post Office—the first U.S. post office in Watonwan County—and also served as a meeting place and church for Rosendale Township's early residents. Ashippun was a stopping place for stage coaches traveling the territorial road from Mendota to the Big Sioux River, a part of which now parallels the route of Minnesota Trunk Highway 60.

Like many immigrants, the Barland family arrived in the United States after a long and difficult voyage from their native Norway. They settled briefly in Wisconsin before continuing on to Minnesota Territory in 1857. Their new life here was not an easy one—on two occasions hostile Indians drove them from their cabin, and in one attack a neighbor boy named Ole Boxrud was killed. A marker commemorating Boxrud is located 1 1/2 miles northeast of this site.

John A. Helling, Barland's grandson, gave the log cabin to the Ruth Peabody Curtis chapter of the Daughters of the American Revolution, and it was moved to Madelia's Flanders Park in 1928. The Watonwan County Historical Society moved the structure to its new Historical Center in 1973.

Erected by the Watonwan County Historical Society. 1978

# WINONA COUNTY

### 185.   GREAT RIVER BLUFFS  △

*Located on U.S. highway 61 at the junction with county road 3, about 3 miles southeast of the county road 7 junction*

From Winona to La Crosse, the Mississippi River valley displays its greatest depth as it extends vertically through more than 240 meters of a sedimentary-rock plateau. Here, Highway 61 follows the narrow strip between the river and the steep bluffs that mark the valley's western wall. The valley walls are composed of sandstone and carbonate rock, which formed from sand and lime mud deposited about 500 million years ago in a warm, shallow sea that covered much of what is now North America. The lower, more sloping parts of the valley walls are composed mostly of weakly cemented sandstone, which erodes easily. On the upper parts of the walls, steep cliffs shape the bluffs. The cliffs are composed of dolostone, a chemically altered limestone that is resistant to erosion.

Bluffs are formed as the Mississippi or a tributary cuts into the soft sandstone, initiating sandstone rockfalls that undercut the dolostone. The dolostone then breaks along vertical joints, leaving steep cliffs. Two of the most prominent bluffs in the area, King's Bluff and Queen's Bluff, are visible southeast of this site on the west side of the valley. King's Bluff is the closer one. Both are within Great River Bluffs State Park and are designated Scientific and Natural Areas by the Minnesota Department of Natural Resources for their unusual geology and rare biological communities.

These bluffs are within the "Driftless Area," an area of deeply eroded stream valleys primarily east of the Mississippi River and covering southwestern Wisconsin. During the Ice Age of the last two million years, glacial ice never passed over and leveled this area, and no drift, or glacially carried sediment (clay, silt, sand, gravel, and boulders), was deposited here. However, the landscape before you was blanketed with a layer of loess—a wind-blown, tan-colored rock dust. This dust was carried by winds from floodplains still bare of vegetation, which were repeatedly loaded with very fine sediment by streams that drained melting glaciers. Today, a distinctive and fertile soil has developed in the top of the loess, which helps to give rise to the diverse and sometimes unique plant communities found on these bluffs.

Erected by the Geological Society of Minnesota in partnership with the Minnesota Department of Transportation and the Minnesota Geological Survey. 2002

### 186.  MISSISSIPPI RIVER  △

*Located on U.S. highway 61 in an overlook about 10 miles north of Winona at U.S. Lock and Dam #5*

In its traverse of 2400 miles from Lake Itasca to the Gulf of Mexico, the Mississippi River falls 1475 feet, nearly two-thirds of which is within or along the eastern side of Minnesota. For 300 miles from Minneapolis, its course lies between rocky bluffs bounding a valley from one to six miles in width. The gorge has existed throughout the Pleistocene period of geologic time, during which it has served as a drainage channel for meltwaters from the glaciers of the Great Ice Ages.

The melting of the ice at the end of each glacial epoch produced torrential floods which scoured the valley 200 feet below the present river surface. During the inter-glacial stages, after the ice had melted, the river, greatly reduced in volume and no longer able to transport sand and gravel, filled its valley to the present level.

The history of the Mississippi River during the last million years, while Minnesota and Wisconsin were undergoing repeated glaciation, is characterized by corresponding cycles of erosion and channel filling, the latter being the phase in which it is now engaged.

Erected by the Geological Society of Minnesota in cooperation with the Department of Highways State of Minnesota. 1960

### 187. SUGAR LOAF BLUFF

*Located off U.S. Highways 14 and 61 on Parks Avenue in Winona*

"The crown of the majestic Sugar Loaf Bluff is disappearing before the strokes of the utilitarian quarryman," editorialized the Winona Daily Republican in 1886. "In a very few years that widely known landmark will be but a homely reminiscence of its former beauty and grandeur."

The quarrying operation that resulted in the unusual formation at the top of Sugar Loaf provided limestone to build Winona's sidewalks and trim for many brick buildings before work was discontinued before World War I.

Rising over 450 feet above Winona, the peak in its original configuration as a rounded dome with a fringe of evergreen on the crown was well known to early explorers, traders, tourists, and river boat pilots. An often repeated legend says that the mountain was Chief Wabasha's red cap, originally presented to him by a British officer. The site is called "Wabasha's cap" in early narratives. 1989

### 188. WHITEWATER STATE PARK ⌂

*Located off state highway 74 in Whitewater State Park*

The bold and picturesque bluffs of the Whitewater

Valley, from the Jordan sandstone below to the massive Oneota dolomite at the top, represent deposition during a hundred million years. Much of the erosion of these marine sedimentary rocks occurred later, during the great ice ages, caused by meltwater from the glaciers descending rapidly from the highlands into the flooded valley of the Mississippi River.

During the glacial high-water stages in the Mississippi Valley the velocity of the water in the Whitewater Valley was retarded. In consequence the sediments brought to the Whitewater River by its tributaries could not be carried any farther and were deposited on the valley floor.

Later, as the water level in the Mississippi Valley was lowered, the Whitewater River gained velocity and eroded downward into the accumulated sediments to the level of its present channel, leaving high on the valley walls alluvial terraces of sand and gravel to mark its elevation when the Whitewater River stood at a higher level.

Erected by the Geological Society of Minnesota and the Department of Conservation, State of Minnesota aided by a grant from the Louis W. and Maud Hill Family Foundation. 1955

### 189. MINNESOTA'S "FASHIONABLE TOUR"
*Located on I-90 at the tourist information center in Dresbach*

In the years between 1835 and 1860, steamboats from St. Louis and the Illinois river towns of Rock Island and Galena carried hundreds of tourists up the Mississippi River past "a thousand bluffs which tower in countless fascinating forms." Their destinations were the frontier town of St. Paul and the famous Falls of St. Anthony in what is now Minneapolis.

Made popular in the east by panorama painters, writers, and lecturers, the "Fashionable Tour" of the upper Mississippi River combined the scenic "grandeur and majesty" of the west, a chance to glimpse real Indian villages along the shores, and the luxury and fine food provided by the big excursion boats. By 1854 visitors could travel from New York City to Rock Island entirely by rail in about 48 hours, step onto a steamboat heading north, and experience the "tonic of wildness" in a comfortable four-day round trip to St. Paul, where boats docked at the rate of four or five a day during the summer months.

Today the steamboats of the "Fashionable Tour" are gone, but the drive along the Mississippi River bluffs and through the old river towns proud of their historic heritage is still one of Minnesota's most popular and scenic tourist attractions. 1985

## 190.  THE GEOLOGY OF SOUTHEASTERN MINNESOTA
*Located on I-90 (east bound) in Enterprise rest area*

The face of Minnesota has undergone many changes over the centuries as a result of the forces of nature. Its present appearance is the result of modification over four glacial periods that have created the landscape you see along the roadways. These glaciers were masses of moving ice and snow that covered the surface of Minnesota at various times during the past 2 million years. The last, called the Wisconsin, melted away some 10,000 years ago.

As you travel east and descend into the Mississippi River valley, you will notice that the terrain changes. This corner of the state is the driftless area, an area that was not covered by the last glacier. Here you will find no natural lakes, and the deep valleys and towering bluffs are the end result of the erosion caused by meltwaters of the glacier, located to the north and west. The extreme southeastern corner may never have been glaciated, just like the southwestern corner of Wisconsin.

As you travel through the valley you will notice in the roadcuts and bluffs, exposures of limestone, sandstone and dolomite. These rock formations were deposited by oceans which have covered the area several times in the past, the most recent being some 70 million years ago. These types of stone are easily eroded by groundwater, and there are numerous sinkholes and even caves to be found in the area. Fillmore County, south of here, has two extensive caves, Niagara and Mystery, which have been explored and are open to the public.

The rich soil and the natural beauty of the area attracted first settlers and later tourists. Numerous trails have been developed for use by both residents and visitors, allowing them the opportunity to enjoy and explore the geology of the area. 1997

# YELLOW MEDICINE COUNTY

### 191.  BATTLE OF WOOD LAKE SEPTEMBER 23, 1862
*Located off state highway 67 in Wood Lake State Wayside, 12 miles southeast of Granite Falls near Rock Valley Lutheran Church*

In the summer of 1862 the Dakota Indians were desperate and near starvation. Confined by treaties to a narrow strip of land on the south side of the Minnesota River, they waited for treaty money and food from the government and talked of war to regain their homeland.

On August 17, a group of young Dakota men killed five settlers in Meeker County. Many Dakota felt the die had now been cast: there was no alternative but to go to war. The next day the warring faction led by Little Crow attacked the Lower Sioux Indian Agency, and the war erupted over western Minnesota.

Settlers were killed or driven off their farms, but attacks on Fort Ridgely and New Ulm were unsuccessful. An army of volunteers was formed, led by Henry H. Sibley, who had been Minnesota's first state governor. Here, at Lone Tree Lake (mistaken for Wood Lake, three

and a half miles to the west), Sibley's men fought a decisive battle against the Dakota on September 23, 1862.
Three days later most of the Dakota surrendered. Little
Crow and his most ardent followers escaped to the
west and north.

White Minnesotans demanded revenge. A government tribunal sentenced more than 300 Dakota to
death. President Abraham Lincoln, at the urging of
Episcopal bishop Henry B. Whipple, greatly reduced
this number. Nevertheless, on December 26, 1862, 38
Dakota were hanged in Mankato, in what has been
called the largest mass execution in the United States.
Some 1,700 Dakota, most having not participated in the
war, were confined at Fort Snelling. Many died over the
winter; the survivors were shipped to a reservation in
what is now South Dakota. 1995

### 192.   WOOD LAKE STATE MONUMENT 🗐
*Located off state highway 67 in Wood Lake State Wayside,
12 miles southeast of Granite Falls near Rock Valley
Lutheran Church*

To the memory of the men who here lost their lives in
an engagement between Minnesota Volunteer Soldiers
and the Sioux Indians Sept. 23, 1862.

### Wood Lake Battlefield
Anthony C. Collins, Richard H. McElroy, Ernest
Paul, Charles F. Frink, Edwin E. Ross, De Grove Kimball
and Mathew Cantwell were killed and thirty-four men
were wounded in action.

Erected by the state in 1910 under the supervision
of Commissioners appointed by the Governor—Loren W.
Collins, Ezra T. Champlin and Mathias Holl participants
in the battle.

The soldiers were commanded by Col. Henry H.
Sibley, the Indians by Chief Little Crow.

[Approved by 1909 legislature; dedicated October
18, 1910.]

### 193.   UPPER (OR YELLOW MEDICINE) SIOUX AGENCY

*The following seven markers are located on state highway 67 in Upper Sioux Agency State Park, about 8 miles southeast of Granite Falls*

By the treaties of 1851 and 1858 the lands of the once mighty Sioux were reduced to shoestring reservations along the southern bank of the Minnesota River. The Sisseton and Wahpeton bands of Upper Sioux held the land from Lake Traverse to the Yellow Medicine River.

The Upper, or Yellow Medicine, Agency was established to serve as the government's headquarters for distributing annuity payments to the Sisseton and Wahpeton. It was also the center where schools were set up and where government employees attempted to teach the Indians to farm. The agency site, selected in July, 1854, by Agent Robert G. Murphy, was near the missions of Dr. Thomas S. Williamson and the Reverend Stephen R. Riggs.

Like the Lower Agency thirty miles downriver, the Upper boasted sturdy homes for its physician, carpenter, farm superintendent, blacksmiths, and other employees; a two-story brick warehouse and agent's residence; a school; stables; a brick kiln; and a jail. Nearby were four traders' stores and at least a hundred houses for farmer Indians.

Here at the Upper Agency, in August 1862, the initial rumblings of the Sioux Uprising were heard. The annuity payments were late, and the Sioux were starving and restless. Although there was food in the warehouse, the Indian agent at first refused to distribute it until the annuity money arrived. When the Indians threatened a fight, the agent yielded, and the situation temporarily quieted down.

Later that month the Sioux Uprising broke out, and the Indians looted and burned the Upper Agency. A leader of the peaceful faction of Upper Sioux, John Other Day, led many whites from the agency to safety. 1966

## 194.  AGENCY HOMES

Located here are cellar depressions of the employee homes erected at the Upper Sioux Agency. The Indian agent, assistant agent, warehouse clerk, and blacksmith were among those who lived here. How the frame and hewn-log homes looked is not known, but it appears that their cellars had wood floors, plastered walls and walkout entrances. A root cellar and a cistern also are visible. Halfway down the ravine is the spring which supplied water to the agency. 1970

## 195.  THE ANNUITY CENTER

The largest and most important building in the complex Upper Sioux Agency was the warehouse. Annuity goods were stored within it before being issued to the Indians. It also contained the offices of the agent, his assistants, and the doctor. The two-story brick structure measured 105' in length by 33' in width. Built in 1859, it was severely damaged by fire during the Sioux Uprising of 1862. Its ruined walls were finally torn down in the 1870s. 1970

## 196.  EMPLOYEES' DUPLEX NO.1

This brick structure was erected in 1859–60. One of the earliest duplexes constructed in Minnesota, it housed the head carpenter and the superintendent of farms with both their families in the agency period. During the Sioux Uprising it was gutted by fire. George Olds claimed the building in 1866, remodeled it, and used it as his family home. Initially, it contained six rooms, stood two stories high, and had a cedar shingle roof. The style of the original roof line can still be seen on the west ell. 1970

## 197.  EMPLOYEES' DUPLEX NO. 2

This structure was identical in appearances and function with Duplex No. 1. The bricks for this building and others were made at the agency brickyard, approximately one mile west of here. The timber used was cut locally and processed at the agency sawmill, located just to the south on the Yellow Medicine River. While it is not known which of the agency employees lived in this building from 1859 to 1862, it is known that U.S. troops were stationed at the agency in 1860 and that the officers were quartered here. In 1866, Joseph Fortier used part of the damaged structure as a trading post and store. 1970

### 198.  THE MANUAL LABOR SCHOOL

In an unsuccessful attempt to teach the Indians the three R's as well as agriculture, sewing, and carpentry, the government erected an impressive two-story school. The failure was largely due to untrained educators and frequent friction between the government policy and the mission schools in the area.

The first floor contained classrooms and a combined carpentry and blacksmith shop. The second floor served as living quarters for the teachers.

Erected in 1859, the building was used as a school only until 1861. Before its destruction in 1862, it briefly housed U.S. troops from Fort Ridgely. Constructed of brick, with three gabled ends, this building was listed in government records as the most expensive one erected at the agency. 1970

Employees' Duplex No. 1 in 1975

## 199. MAZOMANI

On this ridge is located the grave of Mazomani, a leader of the Wahpetonwan (Dwellers in the Leaves) Dakota, who died of injuries he received on September 23, 1862, at the battle of Wood Lake during the Dakota (Sioux) War.

Mazomani (Iron Walker) was among the Dakota leaders who went to Washington, D.C., in 1858 to negotiate a treaty selling half of the Minnesota River Valley reservation. Throughout the course of the tragic 1862 war, he tried repeatedly to make peace between Dakotas and whites and to protect those Dakota who had chosen to remain at peace from those who tried to force them to fight. According to Dakota oral traditions, he was wounded by white soldiers while carrying a flag of truce as he tried to enter their camp to arrange for the release of captives. His friends and followers carried him from the battlefield to a camp near here, where he died early the following morning after embracing his wife and daughter and telling them, "I love you very much, but I am going to leave you now."

Mazomani's daughter, Mazaokiyewin (Woman who Talks to Iron), was among the many Dakota forced into exile at Crow Creek on the Missouri River following the 1862 war. She eventually returned to this region where she was known as Isabel Roberts and was a leading member of the Dakota community. Many of her descendants still live in the area today.

Erected by the Minnesota Historical Society with the co-operation of the Upper Sioux Dakota Community. 1984

# NORTHEAST
# REGION

Northeast Region
Markers 200–265

# AITKIN COUNTY

### 200. SAVANNA PORTAGE CONTINENTAL DIVIDE ⚠

*Located on county road 36 in Savanna Portage State Park
at the trail junction of Wolf Lake Trail and Savanna
Portage Trail*

The Savanna Portage Trail crosses the continental divide
between the Mississippi River and Great Lakes watersheds. Streams and rivers draining to the south and
west flow into the Mississippi River and on to the Gulf
of Mexico. Those draining to the east flow into Lake
Superior and, eventually, into the Atlantic Ocean. The
Savanna Portage extended from West Savanna River
across the drainage divide to East Savanna River. Although this divide made for a laborious portage, it was
an important overland link between two rivers that
helped connect two vastly different geographical regions by water. Many generations of Native Americans
and, later, fur-trading voyageurs made this trail their
route of choice.

During the Ice Age of the last two million years,
many glaciers crossed this area, stripping off soil and
bedrock and grinding it up as they moved along. This
soil and rock debris was deposited along the margins of
the melting glaciers in belts of hills called moraines.
Meltwater streams that flowed under the glacial ice
washed sediment from the lower reaches of the ice and
deposited some of it along their subglacial courses.
When beyond a glacier's edge, these streams deposited
sediment as outwash plains or carried it into glacial
lakes, where it settled to the bottom.

About 14,000 years ago, a melting glacier deposited
a moraine along its margin in the Sandy Lake area. As
this glacial ice continued to melt, a subglacial stream
flowed southwest through the Sandy Lake moraine and
deposited a long ridge of sand and gravel. This ridge,
called an esker, runs along the southeast side of Big

Sandy Lake and extends through much of Savanna Portage State Park.

The meltwater from this glacier eventually collected, forming Glacial Lake Aitkin-Upham, which spread from Aitkin northeast to the Mesabi Iron Range. The Sandy Lake moraine was a peninsula into this lake. The lake had two outlets: one flowing southwest to the Mississippi River, and one flowing east to the St. Louis River. As the lake level lowered, higher ground in the middle was exposed, splitting the lake in two. That higher ground is now part of this continental divide.

Erected by the Geological Society of Minnesota in partnership with the Minnesota Department of Transportation, the Minnesota Geological Survey, and the Minnesota Department of Natural Resources. 2003

### 201.  SAVANNA PORTAGE
*Located on county road 36 in Savanna Portage State Park*

This rough swampy six-mile trail between the West and East Savanna rivers connected Sandy Lake and the Mississippi with the St. Louis River and Lake Superior.

From 1755 for more than a century this portage was heavily traveled by explorers, fur traders, and missionaries.

### 202.  SANDY LAKE POST
*Located off state highway 65 on Sandy Lake near Libby at the dam*

Sandy Lake Post of the American Fur Company was established near here about 1830 after an earlier location further south at the Northwest Company's station had been abandoned.

William A. Aitkin for many years was a leading trader in this region. Indian missions were also located here from 1832 to 1855.

### 203.   "TELL HIM I BLAME HIM FOR THE CHILDREN WE HAVE LOST . . . " AISH-KE-BO-GO-KO-ZHE (FLAT MOUTH), DECEMBER 3, 1850

*Located off state highway 65 about 8 miles north of McGregor at Sandy Lake*

[Front] In late 1850, some 400 Ojibwe Indians perished because of the government's attempt to relocate them from their homes in Wisconsin and Upper Michigan to Minnesota west of the Mississippi River. The tragedy unfolded at Sandy Lake where thousands of Ojibwe suffered from illness, hunger and exposure. It continued as the Lake Superior Ojibwe made a difficult journey home.

In the 1840's, Minnesota politicians began pressuring the U.S. government to remove Ojibwe people from lands the government claimed they had ceded, or given up, in 1837 and 1842 treaties. Territorial governor Alexander Ramsey and others claimed they were acting to "ensure the security and tranquility of white settlements." But their true motivation was economic. If Indians were moved from Wisconsin and Upper Michigan onto unceded lands in Minnesota, local traders could supply the annuity goods the government had promised to provide to the Ojibwe under the treaties, and they could trade with the Ojibwe themselves. Minnesotans could also build Indian agencies and schools in return for government funding and jobs.

Ojibwe mother and two children, about 1870

From the outset, the Lake Superior Ojibwe vigorously opposed removal. They pointed to promises made at the treaty negotiations that they could remain on ceded lands. Knowing that the Ojibwe would not consent to removal, government officials devised a plan to entice the Ojibwe to Sandy Lake, hoping that they would simply remain here and abandon their homelands in Wisconsin and Michigan.

In 1850, the Ojibwe were told to arrive at Sandy Lake no later than October 25th where their treaty annuities—cash, food and other goods promised in exchange for the land cessions—would be waiting for them. In prior years, these annuities for the Lake Superior Ojibwe had been distributed at La Pointe on Madeline Island in Lake Superior, a traditional hub of Ojibwe culture and a more accessible location.

By November 10th, some 4,000 Ojibwe had arrived. They were ill prepared for what they faced at Sandy Lake. The promised annuities were not waiting for them, and the last of the limited provisions that were available were not distributed until December 2nd after harsh winter conditions had set in. While they waited the nearly six weeks, they lacked adequate food and shelter. Over 150 died from dysentery caused by spoiled government provisions and from measles. Demonstrating their steadfast desire to remain in their homelands, the Ojibwe began an arduous winter's journey home on December 3rd. As many as 250 others died along the way. On the same day, Aish-ke-bo-go-ko-zhe, the Ojibwe leader also known as Flat Mouth, sent word to Ramsey that he held him personally at fault for the broken promises that resulted in suffering and death.

As word of the Sandy Lake disaster spread, so did opposition to the government's removal policy. Non-Indian settlers—including missionaries, newspaper editors, legislators, and local citizens—voiced their support for the Ojibwe. Ojibwe leaders traveled to Washington to secure guarantees that annuities would be distributed at La Pointe and that the Ojibwe could remain in their homelands. In 1852, Congress passed a law authorizing that future Ojibwe treaties would instead provide for permanent reservations in areas the Ojibwe traditionally occupied.

**The Ojibwes' Sandy Lake Journey**
[Back] [Map of journey] This map shows the locations of some of the villages of the 19 Ojibwe Bands whose treaty annuities were paid at Sandy Lake in 1850. Today, these 19 Bands are succeeded by the 12 federally recognized Bands whose present-day reservations also are shown. The Wisconsin and Upper Michigan Bands—who were required to come to Sandy Lake rather than go to La Pointe on Madeline Island for their treaty payments—traveled hundreds of miles. Some of the approximate distances and the likely canoe/foot routes involved were:

Red Cliff/La Pointe (Madeline Island) to
Sandy Lake via Lake Superior, St. Louis River
and Savanna Rivers/Savanna Portage .......... 220 miles

Bad River to Sandy Lake via Lake Superior,
St. Louis River and Savanna Rivers/Savanna
Portage ............................................... 250 miles

Lac du Flambeau to Sandy Lake via
Chippewa River and route traveled from
Lac Courte Oreilles ............................... 430 miles

Lac Courte Oreilles to Sandy Lake via
Namekagon River, St. Croix River, Bois
Brule River, Lake Superior, St. Louis River,
and Savanna Rivers/Savanna Portage .......... 260 miles

Lac Vieux Desert to Sandy Lake via
Ontonagon River, Lake Superior, St. Louis
River and Savanna Rivers/Savanna Portage ... 370 miles

Keweenaw Bay to Sandy Lake via Lake
Superior, St. Louis River and Savanna
Rivers/Savanna Portage ........................... 460 miles

Lac du Flambeau to Sandy Lake via
Chippewa River and route traveled from
Lac Courte Oreilles ............................... 430 miles

Lac Courte Oreilles to Sandy Lake via
Namekagon River, St. Croix River, Bois
Brule River, Lake Superior, St. Louis River
and Savanna Rivers/Savanna Portage .......... 260 miles

Lac Vieux Desert to Sandy Lake via
Ontonagon River, Lake Superior, St. Louis
River and Savanna Rivers/Savanna Portage .... 370 miles

Keweenaw Bay to Sandy Lake via Lake
Superior, St. Louis River and Savanna
Rivers/Savanna Portage .......................... 460 miles

2001

Delegation of Ojibwe men in Washington, D.C., either 1857 or 1862

# CARLTON COUNTY

### 204.   GEOLOGY OF THE ST. LOUIS RIVER ⛰

*Located on state highway 23, one mile north of junction
with county road 18 at a roadside veterans memorial*

Two kilometers northwest of here, the St. Louis River
flows on its way to Lake Superior. Its broad river valley,
visible from this point, is in a western extension of the
Lake Superior basin. Over the last two million years,
the Lake Superior basin was scoured out by kilometer-

thick glaciers repeatedly advancing along its length and eroding the soft sedimentary rocks that had filled it.

Near the end of the last glacial period, about 12,000 years ago, a tongue-shaped lobe of ice in the Lake Superior basin, called the Superior lobe, started to melt and recede northward into the basin. The southwestern end of the basin filled with its meltwater, forming Glacial Lake Duluth. The meltwater lake contained large amounts of red clay glacially eroded from the red sandstones and shales in the basin. Glacial Lake Duluth existed for centuries, and during that time more than 100 meters of lake sediment, comprised mostly of red clay, were deposited. That red clay is exposed down the slope from this overlook and forms the banks of the St. Louis River valley.

As the ice melted further northward into the basin, the primitive Lake Superior was able to drain by newly opened eastern outlets to the lower Great Lakes, and the lake level dropped about 60 meters below its present level. As the lake level fell, the meandering channel of the St. Louis River removed much of the red clay, creating the terrain you see.

Relieved of the great weight of the glacial ice, the earth's crust has been slowly rising. The rate of rebound is fastest where the load of ice has been most recently removed. Thus, the northeastern lake basin and its eastern outlet are rising faster, thereby tilting the basin toward the southwest and flooding the lower course of the St. Louis River from Fond du Lac to the Duluth harbor.

Erected by the Geological Society of Minnesota in partnership with the Minnesota Department of Transportation and the Minnesota Geological Survey. 1998

### 205.  MOOSE LAKE REGION  △

*Located on U.S. highway 61 in a wayside park at the south edge of Moose Lake*

Toward the end of the great ice ages about 10,000 years ago, the glacier, which had pushed its way along the trough of Lake Superior, retreated toward the northeast, and near Moose Lake crossed the divide between the Mississippi River and Lake Superior. When the lobe of ice was shrunken so that it lay wholly within the rim of the lake basin, Glacial Lake Nemadji was formed around the southwest margin of the ice.

The earliest outlet was at this, the western, end, when the lake stood 523 feet above the present level of Lake Superior and nearly reached the elevation of the State Hospital in the distance. During the centuries of drainage from here through the Moose River to the Mississippi, this channel was eroded downward to the present level. When lower outlets for the Lake Superior basin were opened, the Moose River Valley was abandoned as an outlet, and this part of the ancient watercourse became the basin of Moosehead Lake.

Erected by the Geological Society of Minnesota and the Department of Highways, State of Minnesota aided by a grant from the Louis W. and Maud Hill Family Foundation. 1955

### 206. MOOSE LAKE STATE MONUMENT 📖
*Located off county road 61 in Riverside Cemetery at the north edge of Moose Lake*

Erected to the memory of the men, women and children who perished in the forest fire of October 12, 1918. [Approved by 1929 legislature; dedicated October 12, 1929.]

### 207. JAY COOKE STATE PARK ⛰
*Located on state highway 210 in a rest area in Jay Cooke State Park*

This point overlooks the St. Louis River Valley. The steeply inclined rocks in the river channel upstream are alternating beds of slates and graywackes of the Thomson formation, thousands of feet thick.

Slates are rocks formed from original deposits of mud which are first compacted into shale and subsequently converted into slate by heat, pressure, and movement in the earth's crust. Graywackes originate as beds of sand with enough gray and black grains to produce the dark color.

These original sediments collected on the sea bottom about two billion years ago and subsequently, by deep-seated earth movements, were folded, fractured, and tilted to stand at varying angles.

Glacial ice, moving over this area, completely filled the Lake Superior basin and blocked the natural drainage through the St. Lawrence River. The meltwaters from the ice, unable to flow eastward, created a glacial lake standing 500 feet higher than Lake Superior. At this stage the water reached Jay Cooke Park and the red lake-clay sediments, found in the road cuts in the park and in the valley downstream from this location, were deposited.

Erected by the Geological Society of Minnesota and the Department of Conservation State of Minnesota. 1960

### 208. JOSIAH B. SCOVELL
*Located on state highway 210 in Jay Cooke State Park at wayside*

One half mile south of this point lie three islands, known as numbers 1, 2, & 3, in the St. Louis River, which were settled by Josiah Boardman Scovell, original U.S. patentee in 1881, who retained ownership for the balance of his life.

Islands donated as part of Jay Cooke State Park by Edith Scovell on Nov. 18, 1944 in memory of her father. 1957

### 209. J. RODNEY PAINE
*Located on state highway 210 in Jay Cooke State Park at wayside*

The State of Minnesota recognizes J. Rodney Paine, first superintendent of Jay Cooke State Park 1915–1931 for his contribution to the development of public parks.

### 210.   HENRY OLDENBURG
*Located on state highway 210 in Jay Cooke State Park
at wayside*

A tribute by the people of Carlton County to the
memory of Henry Oldenburg 1858–1926 whose loyalty
and love for this north country made possible Jay
Cooke Park. 1930

### 211.   HENRY C. HORNBY
*Located on state highway 210 in Jay Cooke State Park
at wayside*

540 acres of land southwest of this point, embracing
Silver Creek in Jay Cooke State Park are dedicated to
the memory of this pioneer civic leader who made
great contributions to the establishment and development of this park.

Lands donated by Mr. Hornby's daughters in January 1953 in memory of their father. 1957

### 212.   EVERGREEN MEMORIAL DRIVE
*Located on state highway 23, 2 miles south of Fond du Lac*

Dedicated October 5, 1947 in grateful memory of all
men and women from Carlton, Pine, and St. Louis
counties, who served in the armed forces of our country
during the World Wars.

### 213.   THE IRON RANGE
*Located on I-35 (north bound) in Culkin rest area*

One hundred miles north and west of Duluth lies the
Iron Range. North America's largest iron ore region
consists of three major iron ranges: the Vermilion, the
Mesabi, and the Cuyuna. The Vermilion was the first to
ship iron ore from Minnesota beginning in 1884 at
Tower-Soudan. Extending from Tower to Ely, the Vermilion ore was found in vertical deposits requiring the use

of underground mining techniques. The great Mesabi Range, extending for nearly one hundred miles from Grand Rapids to Babbitt, was discovered in 1890. Because the iron was located in shallow basins near the surface, the technique of open pit mining was used to extract the ore. The Cuyuna Range, located between Brainerd and Crosby-Ironton, shipped its first ore in 1911. Both open pit and underground mining occurred on the Cuyuna, which was noted for its high grade manganese ores.

More than 400 mines in Minnesota produced over three billion metric tons of ore that were shipped east on ore boats across the Great Lakes. The ore was used to make the steel that built America's industries, transportation systems and many things used in everyday life.

Many mines are now closed; only those on the Mesabi Range continue to operate, producing taconite, a less rich iron ore requiring processing prior to shipment. The Soudan Mine, where the first ore was mined, was established as a state park after the mine closed in 1962. Since 1963, visitors have descended over twenty-five hundred feet into the ground, as the miners once did, to learn how iron ore was extracted at such depths.

Steam shovel and crew at Biwabik Mine in 1895

The Iron Range offers many places where evidence of its past is plainly visible and well interpreted.

Immigrants from many parts of Europe forged a regional identity as they toiled in the mines and the boardinghouses, and frequently battled the mining companies. That fighting spirit remains in the people called "Rangers." 1997

# COOK COUNTY

### 214.   FATHER BARAGA'S CROSS
*Located on state highway 61 about a mile northeast of Schroeder*

Father Baraga 1846

### 215.   S. REX GREEN
*Located on state highway 61 about 7.5 miles southwest of Grand Marais*

In Honor of S. Rex Green, a man of foresight as engineer of lands and right of way, he helped establish this highway for the public's full enjoyment of the glories of forest stream, and lakes. 1960

### 216.   GOOD HARBOR BAY  ⛰
*Located on state highway 61 about 5 miles southwest of Grand Marais*

The rocks of the North Shore of Lake Superior record the last period of volcanic activity in Minnesota. This volcanism occurred 1.1 billion years ago when the North American continent began to rupture along a great rift valley, which extended from the Lake Superior region southwest to Kansas. As this rift valley opened, basaltic lavas erupted into it intermittently for about 20 million years, accumulating to a thickness of up to 20 kilometers in the Lake Superior region.

With each eruption, red-hot lavas fountained from kilometer-long fissures for up to decades at a time, flooding over large areas of a barren landscape. Flood basalt eruptions typically followed one another in geologically rapid succession, but at times there were significant intervals (thousands to millions of years) without volcanic activity. During such intervals, streams and rivers flowing over and eroding the volcanic terrain would deposit sediments into lakes in low-lying areas. When volcanic activity resumed, these sediments could in turn be buried, heated, and compacted by lava flows and transformed into sedimentary rocks.

An example of such a geological cycle of eruption, sedimentation, and renewed volcanism appears in the cliff face across the highway from this marker. Beneath a dark-gray basalt flow is a reddish, thinly bedded siltstone, sandstone and shale formation. Beneath these sedimentary rocks is another lava flow, which is exposed in the creek bed of Cut Face Creek just north and down the hill from this road cut. The full thickness of this sedimentary rock formation is about 40 meters. This thickness indicates a prolonged lull in volcanic activity, perhaps lasting several million years. The broken-up and mineralized character of the basalt at the left side of the cliff face resembles features observed when lavas explosively encounter standing water. This and the fine sediments beneath the lava suggest that a shallow lake may have existed in the area at the time of renewed volcanism.

Erected by the Geological Society of Minnesota in partnership with the Minnesota Department of Transportation and the Minnesota Geological Survey. 1998

### 217.  GRAND MARAIS  △

*Located on state highway 61 overlooking the bay at Grand Marais*

The harbor of Grand Marais is the result of unequal weathering or erosion of two types of rock. One of these, called diabase, resulted from the cooling of molten material which was forced between two earlier lava flows. The dark, massive diabase, being very hard and resistant to wave action, has become the outer barrier to the harbor, while the lava, which was much fractured and easily eroded, was worn away to form the harbor basin.

To the west of Grand Marais, the serrated crest of the Sawtooth Range, clearly visible from the harbor breakwater, is another example of unequal erosion. Here the relatively soft basalt and the more resistant diabase have, through the process of weathering, produced the notched profile of the hills along the coast.

To the east of Grand Marais rise the hills near the mouth of the Arrowhead River, while to the north, along the Gunflint Trail are older rocks. At Saganaga Lake, the Saganaga granite, one of the oldest granites in North America, marks a core of the ancient mountains of the Laurentian Highlands.

Erected by the Geological Society of Minnesota and the Department of Highways, State of Minnesota aided by a grant from the Louis W. and Maud Hill Family Foundation. 1955

### 218.  ST. FRANCIS XAVIER CHURCH
*Located on state highway 61 at east edge of Grand Marais*

Erected in 1895, Jesuit French architecture, Site of early Chippewa City, Morrison home used as mission before 1895.

### 219.  JUDGE C. R. MAGNEY STATE PARK
*Located on state highway 61 in Magney State Park*

"Our State Parks are Everyman's Country Estate."
—C. R. Magney. Judge C. R. Magney State Park. So named in honor of Clarence R. Magney (1883–1962), Lawyer, Mayor of Duluth, District Judge, Justice of Minnesota's Supreme Court, Student of Minnesota History,

Defender of Its Wilderness Areas, Champion of Their Preservation.

As a young man he walked the wilderness trails of the North Shore and came to know its trout streams, picturesque waterfalls, rockbound shores, and rich historic traditions.

Judge Magney secured large park preserves in Duluth, advocated a Fort Snelling State Park, performed an indispensable role in establishing Grand Portage National Monument, and dedicated half a century to adding a dozen state parks of natural scenic beauty along his beloved North Shore.

The Legislature in grateful recognition chose this— one of his favorites—to be named as a perpetual memorial to Judge C. R. Magney.

Dedicated 1964 by the Minnesota Council of State Parks, the Minnesota Historical Society and the Division of State Parks, State of Minnesota.

### 220.  THE GRAND PORTAGE
*Located off state highway 61 at Grand Portage National Monument*

Circumventing 21 miles of falls and rapids, this portage ran some nine miles from this vicinity to a point upstream on the Pigeon River. It was first mentioned in 1722, by a French trader named Jean Pachot. Following its use in 1732 by La Vérendrye, it replaced the Kaministiquia Route as the canoe route to the West. About 1767 the Grand Portage became a rendezvous for Canadian fur traders and, after 1778, the North West Company's inland headquarters. By the Treaty of Paris, 1783, the Portage fell within American territory. In 1803 the Company moved its headquarters to Fort Kaministiquia (Fort William), and the Pigeon River route was then abandoned.

Archaeological and Historic Sites Board of Ontario.

## 221.   MINNESOTA'S NORTHERN BORDER
*Located on state highway 61 at the international border
tourist information center*

Determining, surveying, and marking Minnesota's border with Canada took 142 years and left the state with
a tag end called the Northwest Angle standing isolated
and alone on the Canadian side of Lake of the Woods.

At the end of the American Revolution in 1783,
British and American negotiators agreed to separate
Canada and the United States by a line running from
the Atlantic Ocean to the Northwesternmost point of
Lake of the Woods in what is now western Ontario.
They based their work on the mistaken assumptions
that the Mississippi River would be the western border
of the U.S. and that a line drawn straight west of Lake
of the Woods would intersect with that river.

By the time the U.S. purchased the Louisiana Territory from France twenty years later, it was clear that
the western U.S. border would not be the Mississippi
River and that the river's source lay south, not northwest of Lake of the Woods. In 1818 British and American negotiators dropped the U.S.-Canadian boundary
line straight south from the northwesternmost point of

Drawing from 1855 of voyageurs in a birch-bark canoe

Lake of the Woods to the 49th parallel and then straight west along the parallel to the crest of the Rocky Mountains, leaving a chimney-like projection that included the Northwest Angle.

The eastern part of Minnesota's northern border lay along the old fur trade water routes beginning at the mouth of the Pigeon River near Grand Portage, now a national monument just a short distance from here. The routes connected Lake Superior and Lake of the Woods, but the boundary's exact demarcation had to wait until a survey in the 1920s. 1991

### 222.  EAGLE MOUNTAIN

*Located 25 miles northwest of Lutsen, a 2.5 mile hike from the north end of county road 4*

When Newton H. Winchell, Minnesota's state geologist, and Ulysses S. Grant II (the president's son) surveyed this area in the 1890s, they concluded that a peak in the Misquah Hills was the state's highest point. Using an aneroid barometer, they set its elevation at 2,230 feet. Later comers argued that Eagle Mountain, which Winchell and Grant did not measure and which can be seen from the Misquah Hills, was higher.

In 1961 a United States Department of the Interior Survey team remeasured, using aerial photographs and controlled bench marks. They found Eagle Mountain's elevation to be 2,301 feet, making it Minnesota's highest point. They also determined that the first Misquah Hills peak is surpassed by another unnamed summit 2,266 feet above sea level, located in section 19 of T63N, R1W, in the same western Cook County area. The state's lowest point is Lake Superior, which has an elevation of 602 feet.

The igneous rock composing Eagle Mountain is as old as the Duluth Gabbro, which geologists estimate at over a billion years in age. 1969

**223. HEIGHT OF LAND PORTAGE**
*Located off county road 12 on the Minnesota-Ontario border between North and South Lakes*

The Height of Land Portage is a part of the Laurentian Division of the Continental Divide. At this point, two of the three great river systems of the North are born. Streams rising east of the divide flow to the Atlantic via Lake Superior and the St. Lawrence River. Streams rising north of the divide flow ultimately into Hudson Bay. Together, these two river systems provide water communication across two-thirds of Canada.

The Height of Land was important to the fur trade as the transition point between difficult, "uphill" paddling, and easier "downhill" coasting. Crossing this portage also marked the transition from novice to "Nor'wester." Here, the novice was sprinkled with a pine bough dipped in water, and made to promise "never to kiss a Voyageur's wife without her permission, and never to allow any newcomer to pass without a similar initiation."

Superior National Forest, United States Department of Agriculture. [1968]

# ITASCA COUNTY

**224. GEOLOGY OF THE HILL ANNEX MINE** ⌂
*Located off U.S. highway 169, 2 miles north of Calumet, near the mine overlook next to the visitor center*

The lowest layer visible on the mine face is a thick exposure of reddish-brown sedimentary rock called the Biwabik Iron Formation. About 1.9 billion years ago, this rock layer formed underwater, near the shoreline of a shallow sea. In that marine environment, blue-green algae grew. Now classified as a type of bacteria, these ancient microbes were photosynthetic: they made their own food from water, carbon dioxide, and sunlight, and gave off oxygen as a by-product. At that time, the seas contained much dissolved iron, and when oxygen was introduced, it combined with the iron. The resulting iron oxide precipitated from the seawater, mixed with silica sediments on the seafloor, and eventually solidified into sedimentary rock. Much later, groundwater infiltrated the rock and circulated, especially along the faults and fractures. The water concentrated the iron by leaching out silica and caused further oxidation, producing an enriched ore containing 55 percent or more iron by weight.

About 95 million years ago, during the Cretaceous period, another shallow sea advanced over this area. The erosive action of rivers, waves, and weather broke down the surface of the Biwabik Iron Formation and produced a layer of boulders, cobbles, pebbles, and sand-sized particles on top of the iron formation. As the sea level rose, finer sediments were deposited on the seafloor. Fossilized clams, oysters, snails, fish teeth, turtle bones, crocodile bones, and plant debris are all found within these sediments, now called the Coleraine Formation. Most of this formation has been eroded or mined. Only a thin, patchy layer remains, and it is mostly hidden by vegetation. However, excellent exposures exist at the east end of the mine.

At the top of the mine face is a light-colored layer of glacial sediment (clay, silt, sand, gravel, and boulders), which was mixed and deposited by glaciers that repeatedly covered this area during the Ice Age of the last two million years. Meltwater streaming from the edge of a glacier has in some places sorted the glacial sediments by size. The glaciers last receded from this area about 11,000 years ago.

Erected by the Geological Society of Minnesota in partnership with the Minnesota Department of Transportation, the Minnesota Geological Survey, and the Minnesota Department of Natural Resources. 2003

# KOOCHICHING COUNTY

## 225. ROUTE OF THE VOYAGEURS
*Located off U.S. highway 71 and state highway 11 in International Falls*

From the late 1600s to about 1820 the chain of water-ways of which Minnesota's border lakes form a segment was the thoroughfare of a vast fur trading empire. At its longest, this water route stretched from Montreal to Lake Athabasca, and over it a treasure in furs from the North American wilderness reached the markets of Europe and Asia. A mainstay of this commerce were the rollicking, indomitable men who paddled the trader's canoes and packed his goods on their backs over portages. Mainly French-Canadians, they were called "voyageurs"—the French term meaning travelers.

Over these waters early each summer they paddled fur-laden canoes eastward to inland depots like Rainy Lake, Grand Portage, or Michilimackinac; each July they returned, carrying trade goods and supplies to the isolated wintering posts. They were a fiercely proud breed, who could paddle eighteen hours a day or carry a load of 450 pounds and yet retain a lusty joy in their work. Decked out in gay sashes and ostrich plumes, they strutted, quarreled, consorted with the Indians, and lightened their toil with French folk songs, gay and rhythmic or hauntingly sad. Today their route, scarcely touched by the modern world, remains open to all who seek adventure. 1969

## 226. STEAMBOATS ON THE RAINY RIVER
*Located on U.S. highway 53 in International Falls*

As a part of the fabled "Voyageurs Highway" of rivers and lakes, Rainy Lake and the Rainy River saw a traffic of fur trade canoes for nearly two centuries before the first steamer, the *Louise Thompson,* was put into service in 1875. Her mission was to help build a canal and locks at Koochiching Falls, connecting the lake and the river and encouraging the movement of Canadian homesteaders into the area around Fort Francis, Ontario. Work on the canal was soon abandoned, however, when the development of the Canadian Pacific Railroad bypassed Fort Francis and opened more desirable frontier areas further west.

Steamer traffic on the 90 miles of river "highway" from Fort Francis to Rat Portage (later Kenora) on Lake of the Woods boomed with the area's settlement in the 1890s. During 1894 a total of 27 steamers and 29 barges carried a total of 2,100 tons of freight and 20,086 passengers on the lake and river system.

The big boat news of 1897 was the maiden voyage of a new steel steamer, the *Kenora,* hailed as a "floating palace" with electric lights and accommodations for 200 passengers. The editor of the local newspaper confidently expected that such a "first class steamer would result in summer resorts" on both sides of the Rainy River.

Steamer traffic declined in the 1900s with the arrival of railroad service. By the time the expected summer resorts were a reality, the steamers that had carried excited passengers on delightful summer excursions were gone. 1991

One of the Rainy River steamboats, about 1915

# LAKE COUNTY

### 227. BUCHANAN
*Located on county road 61 at the mouth of the Knife River*

This town site, named after President Buchanan, was laid out in October, 1856. From September 1857 until May 1859 the place, though little less than a wilderness, was the seat of the U.S. land office for the northeastern district of Minnesota. After the removal of the land office the settlement disappeared. 1940

### 228. ARTHUR V. ROHWEDER MEMORIAL HIGHWAY
*Located on state highway 61 in Knife River wayside*

The Arthur V. Rohweder Memorial Highway so designated by the Minnesota State Legislature and enacted into State Law, April 20, 1961.

In recognition of the eminent leadership and outstanding contributions of Arthur V. Rohweder to the achievement by Minnesota of notable success and national prominence in all areas of accident prevention work.

Serving as Superintendent of Safety and Welfare for the Duluth, Missabi and Iron Range Railway Company for forty-two years; as one of the founders, and President of the Minnesota Safety Council for twenty-five years; as First National President of the Veterans of Safety in 1941; as Vice-President and member of the Board of Directors of the National Safety Council for twenty-five years; and as Safety Consultant to eight Governors of Minnesota, Arthur V. Rohweder was dedicated to the cause of saving lives and eliminating sorrow and suffering attendant upon all types of accidents, and he worked unselfishly and tirelessly toward that end.

This Highway is so named in his honor. Dedicated—August, 1965. Veterans of Safety, D.M.&I.R. Railway Company, Minnesota Safety Council

### 229. "3 SPOT"

*Located off state highway 61 at Lake County Museum in Two Harbors*

This locomotive arrived at Two Harbors on a scow July 1883 and was used in laying first rails between Two Harbors and Tower, Minnesota.

It was the first locomotive put in service by the Duluth and Iron Range Rail Road Company.

It was acquired by the Thirty Year Veterans' Association of the Duluth and Iron Range Rail Road Company to perpetuate its memory and placed in its present position in July 1923.

The tablet at rear of tender is the gift of the Baldwin Locomotive Works. Thereon appear the names and years of service of the veterans who made this memorial possible.

### 230. LAKE SUPERIOR AGATE △

*Located on the lake side of state highway 61, 2 miles northeast of Two Harbors*

As you walk the pebbled beaches of the North Shore, watch for translucent, color-banded, and reddish-brown stones called Lake Superior agate—Minnesota's state gemstone. The story of the Lake Superior agate begins 1.1 billion years ago, when basaltic lava repeatedly erupted here and flowed out over the landscape.

When basaltic lava flows over the earth's surface, the gases it contains form bubbles, which slowly rise in the viscous liquid. Rapid heat loss at the top surface of a flow causes the lava just below the surface to solidify quickly. This quick-hardening lava captures the bubbles within it, creating a zone of porous rock along the flow top.

Sometime after the lava flows in the Lake Superior region solidified, warm groundwater containing varying dissolved chemicals percolated through the basalt, especially through the porous zones, and lined the gas cavities with layers of different minerals until the cavities were filled. A common cavity-filling mineral is called chalcedony, which is a type of quartz with microscopic crystals shaped like fibers. When chalcedony is color-banded, it is known as agate. The colored bands are due to small amounts of impurities (such as iron, copper, and aluminum) that are precipitated cyclically in every other layer of the fibrous quartz. In the layers receiving impurities, the quartz fibers formed are thinner and twisted. The center of an agate is often filled with coarsely crystallized quartz.

Since the time that agates and their basalt hosts formed, this continent has drifted very slowly several times across tropical climate zones, by a global process called plate tectonics. Under tropical conditions, intense chemical weathering caused the basalt to break down, but not the more resistant agate.

By the time the Ice Age began, about two million years ago, basalt flows near the surface of the land were very weathered, weakened, and rich in hard agate nodules. As enormous glaciers advanced from the north and scoured the Lake Superior basin, they ground away the basalt and picked up the agates, transporting some as far away as Kansas. Many agates in Flood Bay may actually have been carried from areas in Ontario, where similar rocks are found.

Erected by the Geological Society of Minnesota in partnership with the Minnesota Department of Transportation, the Minnesota Geological Survey, and the Minnesota Department of Natural Resources. 2003

### 231.   GEOLOGY COMPLICATES BRIDGE FOUNDATION
*Located on state highway 61 at the Gooseberry Falls State Park bridge*

The classic steel arch bridge that spans this gorge is impressive for its simple beauty and elegance. Equally remarkable, but not as obvious to the onlooker, is the massive underground foundation that keeps this bridge sound and secure. To construct a foundation on rock is normally routine, but at this site, with its unusual geology and rugged terrain, nature created a considerable challenge for the builders.

Many years before construction began, a team of geologists and engineers began studying this site. They were searching for a subsurface material that would support the enormous forces exerted by the bridge and its traffic. Initially, it seemed as if the basalt rock exposed in the gorge would be sufficiently strong for this task. Lurking beneath the hard, resistant surface, however, lie weaker layers. Each lava flow contains a solid, strong middle section, with much weaker, porous zones above and below. These porous zones are the result of gases that were trapped in the rapidly cooling outer portions of each flow. Groundwater later percolated through these zones for a long time, and they weathered to a near-soil condition. Complicating matters further, sagging of the Lake Superior basin has caused the rock layers in this area to dip about ten degrees to the east. Together, these factors made the design of the 16 different footings that support the bridge an intriguing problem.

Subsurface core drilling and the detailed mapping of outcrop, or exposed rock, helped geologists predict the three-dimensional extent of the solid portions of the lava flows. This study was made more difficult by the inability to drill at some of the foundation locations, because of the adverse terrain and the team's desire to preserve the natural beauty of the area. After the solid and weak layers in the rock were carefully mapped, construction plans were drawn up and the bridge was built. Predictions of the subsurface layers proved reliable, and only minor adjustments were required during construction.

Erected by the Geological Society of Minnesota in partnership with the Minnesota Department of Transportation and the Minnesota Department of Natural Resources. 2003

The Roleff family camping at the mouth of the Gooseberry in 1922

## 232.   THE GEOLOGY BEHIND THE WATERFALLS △

*Located on state highway 61 in Gooseberry Falls State Park near the Middle Falls*

About 1.1 billion years ago, this continent began splitting apart along a rupture called the Midcontinent Rift, which extended from the Lake Superior region southwest to Kansas. During a period of about 20 million years, thousands of lava eruptions flowed out over a flat landscape. Layer upon layer of flows accumulated until the growing stack reached a thickness of up to 20 kilometers in the Lake Superior area. Most of these flows solidified into the dark volcanic rock called basalt.

The waterfalls of the Gooseberry River reveal the layering of these lava flows. When basaltic lava erupts at the earth's surface, the gases it contains form bubbles, which slowly rise in the viscous liquid. Rapid heat loss at the top surface of a flow causes the lava just below the surface to solidify quickly. This quick-hardening lava captures the bubbles within it, creating a zone of porous rock along the flow top. Because the interior of a lava flow stays liquid longer, its gases have time to escape, leaving a solid section. After the flows here accumulated, warm groundwater percolated through the layers for a long time, altering minerals and softening the porous flow tops more readily than the solid interiors. This process left each flow supported by the weakened porous top of the flow underneath it.

If you walk on the flows nearby, you will see some polygonal patterns of cracks in the basalt. The geometric shapes are actually the tops of rock columns that extend down into each flow. The columns formed parallel to the direction heat was lost when each lava flow cooled. Slow, uniform contraction of the rock during its cooling created the pattern of cracks, called columnar joints.

The columnar joints of a flow and the erosion of the weakened flow top underneath it work together to partition a flow into poorly secured columns. These columns are broken apart by weathering and frost, and the rushing water of the river removes the chunks from the downstream edge of the flow. Thus, the way in which these ancient lava flows erode produces waterfalls in the shape of giant stairsteps.

Erected by the Geological Society of Minnesota in partnership with the Minnesota Department of Transportation, the Minnesota Geological Survey, and the Minnesota Department of Natural Resources. 2003

### 233. GEOLOGY OF THE SPLIT ROCK REGION △ Ⓜ

*Minnesota Historical Society Historic Site*
*Located off state highway 61 at Split Rock Lighthouse*
*Historic Site at the visitor center*

The geology of the shoreline between Split Rock and Little Marais is the direct result of cataclysmic events that occurred many kilometers below the earth's surface. About 1.1 billion years ago, this continent began to split apart along a great rupture, called the Midcontinent Rift, which extended from the Lake Superior region southwest to Kansas. For about 20 million years, this crustal rupture was repeatedly injected with molten rock, or magma, which had been generated in the earth's mantle some 40 to 100 kilometers below the surface. Most of this magma erupted at the surface as volcanic lava flows, but some never reached the surface. Instead, it was forced into fractures and weaknesses in the crust and formed pools that slowly cooled to become igneous intrusions.

In the Split Rock area, successive lava flows accumulated, forming an extensive pile of great thickness. Magma also intruded into this growing stack and solidified to form sheets and irregular masses that created a group of intrusions called the Beaver Bay Complex. Some of the Beaver Bay intrusions contain huge chunks of a light-colored, coarse-grained rock called anorthosite. These chunks were fragments of the lower crust that were caught up in the magma as it rose from the mantle to the upper crust. A large, light-green anorthosite inclusion forms the top of the cliff supporting the base of Split Rock Lighthouse. The surface of this rock is whitish from weathering. The magma that carried this anorthosite inclusion solidified to become the dark intrusive rock called diabase.

The rugged topography of this part of the North Shore reflects the contrast in erosion rates between the many durable igneous intrusions and the more fractured and porous volcanic rocks into which the intrusions were forced. The erosion-resistant character of the diabase exposed from here to Beaver Bay makes this stretch of shoreline especially bold and rocky. The even greater erosional resistance of the massive anorthosite inclusions contained within the diabase enables the anorthosite to support prominent rounded hills along the shore from Split Rock to Grand Marais. Carlton Peak, near Tofte, is such a prominence.

Erected by the Geological Society of Minnesota in partnership with the Minnesota Department of Transportation, the Minnesota Geological Survey, and the Minnesota Historical Society. 2003

### 234. PALISADE HEAD

*Located on state highway 61 north of Silver Bay*

Rising from the waves of Lake Superior, this cliff face serves as an awesome reminder of Minnesota's geological past. Eruptions of molten lava over a billion years ago, followed by eons of weathering and glacier scouring, created the spectacular North Shore landmark so much admired and photographed.

Palisade Head, and Shovel Point to the northeast, sometimes called the Little Palisade, are rills of igneous rhyolite overlaying softer basalt and undercut by the eroding waves of North America's largest lake. Well known by the early lake travelers and surveyors, Palisade Head became a major scenic attraction when the North Shore highway, completed in 1924, brought tourists and campers in large numbers. Today the cliff's flat face is a challenge for rock climbers, and from its top visitors have a breathtaking view of the jagged Sawtooth Range. On a clear day the Apostle Islands, 30 miles distant, can sometimes be seen. 1989

# PINE COUNTY

### 235. CHENGWATANA

*Located on U.S. highway 61 at the north edge of Pine City in Pine County*

The area of land at the outlet of the Snake River from Cross Lake approximately one mile northeast of here has played an important part in the history of the region. Its name comes from an Ojibwe word, pronounced "Sheng-wha-tah-nah," which has been translated both as "Pine City," and as "the steep end of a spur of hills." Archeological evidence suggests that various peoples frequented the area from at least 6,000 B.C. Artifacts fashioned from native copper have been found in the valley, and early fur traders, geologists, and speculators heard rumors of copper deposits in the mid-1800s. But it was the construction of a logging dam at the Cross Lake outlet in 1950 that led to the first Euro-american settlement there.

In 1854 the Government Road under construction from Point Douglas (near Hastings) to Superior, Wisconsin, crossed the Snake River about one-half mile below the dam. The road attracted settlers, even though one traveler commented that there were enough mosquitoes to protect the country from extensive development. The townsite of Chengwatana, established in 1856, was named the county seat when Pine County was organized in 1857.

But the young community was born just in time for the national financial "panic" of 1857, which slowed its development. In the next few years several destructive fires and the railroad's bypass of the town spelled the end for Chengwatana. By the early 1870s most of the residents and businesses had moved to Pine City, which was now designated county seat. Despite a brief copper mining "boom" in 1899, the town disappeared early in the 20th century. A W.P.A. dam built in 1936 on the site of the original logging dam is all that remains today to mark Chengwatana's place in history. 1990

### 236.  PINE CITY
*Located on county road 61 at the north edge of Pine City*

Pine City, platted in 1869, was named from the Chippewa word "Chengwatana," City of Pines. It was a rough lumberjack town in the early days. From here, logs were floated down the Snake River into the St. Croix River to Stillwater. A rich deposit of copper was discovered here and a $250,000 company was formed which sank some 150-foot shafts. Today, the site of the old copper mine is an interesting drive for visitors and a place for the bass fisherman to try his skill along the river. On Lake Pokegama, three miles west, Rev. Frederick Ayer and others established a Protestant Mission and a school for Chippewas in 1836. 1950

### 237. THE HINCKLEY FIRE
*Located on county road 61 at the north edge of Hinckley*

Between three and five o'clock on the afternoon of September 1, 1894, a raging forest fire driven by strong southwest winds swept over the town of Hinckley, killing 248 residents. The conflagration burned over 480 square miles in parts of five counties, also consuming the surrounding towns of Brook Park, Mission Creek, Miller, Partridge, and Sandstone. At least 418 people died in the disaster.

Trains of the St. Paul and Duluth Railroad and the Eastern Minnesota Railroad carried nearly 500 people to safety through the burning countryside. More than 1,500 individuals lost their homes and possessions, with fire relief efforts receiving donations from as far away as London and even Turkey as news of the tragedy spread. The mass graves of the Hinckley townspeople who died in the fire are marked by a state monument in Lutheran Memorial Cemetery.

The Hinckley fire was among the worst of many that followed the end of large scale pine logging operations in northern Minnesota. As the virgin red and white pine was removed, a tinder-dry refuse of stumps, slashing, and brush provided ready fuel for several other disastrous fires, including those at Baudette in 1910 and at Cloquet in 1918. 1985

The locomotive that carried survivors from Hinckley, about 1895

## 238.   HINCKLEY FIRE STATE MONUMENT 🏛
*Located off state highway 48 in Hinckley Memorial Cemetery, 1 mile east of Hinckley*

[North side] In Memoriam: In the four Trenches North of this monument lie the remains of Two Hundred and Forty Eight Men, Women, and Children, Residents of Hinckley, who perished in the fire which this monument was erected to commemorate.

[South side] The Great Hinckley Fire

This monument is erected by The State of Minnesota under an Act of the Legislature

Approved April 7th. A.D. 1899

To the Memory of Four Hundred and Eighteen Men Women and Children Who perished in the Great Hinckley Forest Fire of September First A.D. 1894

[East side] September 1st A.D. 1894 On the First Day of September A.D. 1894 between the Hours of Three and Five O'Clock in the afternoon, a forest fire swept over Central Pine County devastating Four Hundred square miles of Country, Consuming the Villages of Hinckley, Sandstone, Mission Creek and Brook Park, and destroying more than Four Hundred and Eighteen human lives.

[West side] Dedicated September 1st A.D. 1900

This Monument is dedicated to the Pioneers of Civilization in the forests of Minnesota. [Approved by 1899 legislature; dedicated September 1, 1900.]

## 239.   BROOK PARK FIRE STATE MONUMENT 🏛
*Located on county road 126 west of Brook Park and about 1 mile south of state highway 23 in Brook Park Cemetery*

The Great Hinckley Fire

This monument is erected by the state of Minnesota to the memory of twenty-six men, women and children who perished in the great Hinckley forest fire of September A.D. 1894

Dedicated October 1st 1915 A.D.

This monument is dedicated to the pioneers of civilization in the forests of Minnesota

September 1st A.D. 1894 On the first day of September A.D. 1894 between the hours of three and five o'clock in the afternoon a forest fire swept over central Pine County devastating four hundred square miles of country, consuming the villages of Brook Park, Mission Creek, Hinckley and Sandstone and destroying more than four hundred and eighteen human lives.

In Memoriam

In the two trenches east of this monument lie the remains of twenty-three men, women and children, residents of Brook Park, who perished in the fire which this monument was erected to commemorate. [Approved by 1915 legislature.]

### 240. SANDSTONE FIRE
*Located on county road 61 at the south edge of Sandstone*

Along with Hinckley and other communities in the western part of Pine County this town was totally destroyed by the terrible forest fire of September 1, 1894.

More than 400 men, women, and children lost their lives in the area swept by the fire. 1940

### 241. CHRISTOPHER C. ANDREWS, CONSERVATION PIONEER
*Located on I-35 (south bound) in General Andrews rest area*

In the 1880's, when General Christopher C. Andrews began urging the state to consider the future of its forested lands, most Minnesotans could not believe that there might ever be a shortage of timber. But by the time of his death in 1922 the vast virgin pine forests were gone, lumber was being imported from the Pacific Northwest, and a series of devastating fires had claimed hundreds of lives and millions of acres.

Andrews served as captain, and colonel of the Third Minnesota Regiment of Volunteers during the Civil War, and finally as Brevet Major General United States

Volunteers, at the close of the war. He was appointed minister to the combined state of Sweden and Norway in 1869, and while living in Stockholm he became interested in reforestation. When he returned to Minnesota he began his efforts to save parts of the state's remaining forests, to encourage replanting, and to start a school of forestry. He implemented the Swedish idea of only cutting the annual growth of trees for lumber each year and as a result is considered by professional foresters to be the father of "sustained yield" in the United States. He met with little success until 1895, the year following the Hinkley fire that killed more than 400 people. The legislature then passed a bill written by General Andrews and calling for the "preservation of forests and the prevention and suppression of forest fires." Andrews was named the state's first chief fire warden.

Forest preservation was difficult in regions where there were still hundreds of logging camps, miles of railroads with uncleared rights of way, and acres of "slashing"—tree tops and branches left by the lumbermen. In spite of Andrews' efforts, carried out with almost no funding, terrible fires ripped through northern Minnesota in the early years of the 20th century.

In addition to his firefighting work, Andrews played a key role in the establishment of Superior and Chippewa national forests and the development of a forestry board to oversee the management of state forest reserves. He served the forest service for 26 years at an average salary of only $1,650, and his work, much admired today, was appreciated by only a farsighted few of his fellow citizens. 1991

## 242.  LUMBERING IN MINNESOTA
*Located on I-35 (north bound) in Kettle River rest area*

Lumbermen first arrived in this area in the 1830s, logging the white and red pine stands along the St. Croix River. Sawmills were few and much of the pine lumber was floated down the St. Croix to the Mississippi River

A loaded sled taking logs to the river in the 1890s

and on to other states. Logging camps, which supplied the timber, operated in the winter months with about 15 men and a few teams of oxen.

The industry grew quickly, however, and in 1840, lumbermen supplied the growing nation with 5 million board feet of lumber. Ten years later, 90 million board feet was harvested from the new Minnesota territory.

By the 1880s, the industry boomed with an influx of new wealth from lumbermen who had made fortunes in Michigan and Wisconsin and the new markets in the West. Sawmills powered by steam engines ripped through millions of logs annually as lumberjacks spilled into the forest of the north. Logging camps swelled to an average of 70 men, and horses replaced oxen. It wasn't long, however, before horses were replaced by steam-powered equipment. In 1900, the peak year of the pine log harvest, the state produced over one billion board feet of logs—enough timber to build a nine-foot wide boardwalk around the earth at the equator.

Production began to decline after 1905, as pine timber was depleted and timber companies shifted their interest towards new pine stands in the Pacific Northwest and the South. By 1930, the pine sawmill industry died with the closing of the last sawmill near Virginia,

Minnesota. After 100 years of logging most of the pine
was gone.

Minnesota's timber industry was rekindled in the
1970s; over a dozen new forest product plants were built
or expanded, producing paper, composite board, lami-
nates and other items. Harvest of all forest products in
the state in the 1990s matched harvest levels of 1900.
today the products of Minnesota's forests are marketed
throughout the world and are found in your home,
your car and even in the ice cream you eat. 1997

### 243.   KETTLE RIVER RAPIDS  ⛰

*Located on state highway 18, 2 miles east of I-35
in Banning State Park*

The light-brown sandstone that forms the cliffs along
this part of the Kettle River valley is called the Hinckley
Sandstone. This sandstone formed as a result of a major
geological event. About 1.1 billion years ago, this continent began to split apart along a rupture called the Midcontinent Rift, which extended from the Lake Superior
region southwest to Kansas. As this great rift valley
opened, volcanic eruptions filled it with thousands of
dense, basaltic lava flows. Then the rifting and volcanic
activity stopped. Over time, the weight of the dense
basalt caused the rift area to subside, or sag, forming a
long basin. Streams and wind brought in sand, which
accumulated in the basin. Eventually, deep underground, minerals carried by groundwater cemented the
buried sand grains, forming sandstone. The Hinckley
Sandstone, one of several sandstone units deposited, is
cemented with iron oxide and silica. The iron oxide
gives it its light-brown color, and the silica helps to
make it one of the strongest sandstones in Minnesota.

During the Ice Age of the last two million years,
glaciers repeatedly covered this area. About 10,000
years ago, as the last glacier here receded into the Lake
Superior basin, meltwater collected at its southwestern
edge, forming a great lake, called Glacial Lake Duluth.

Water from this lake found an outlet and increasingly poured southward through the present-day Kettle River valley. That ancient river would make today's turbulent Kettle River look tame by comparison. Torrents of water were channeled into fractures in the sandstone, which readily eroded down, leaving the blocky cliffs one sees along this stretch of the river.

Along the Hell's Gate Trail one can see kettles, or potholes, in the rock that in some places are 15 meters above the present river. These potholes are evidence that water once raged through this valley at levels much higher than today. Potholes commonly occur behind the base of a large boulder or other flow obstruction. They are made when turbulent water forms an eddy, or whirlpool, strong enough to swirl pebbles and cobbles around in one spot. There the swirling stones grind a cylindrical hole down into the bedrock.

Erected by the Geological Society of Minnesota in partnership with the Minnesota Department of Transportation, the Minnesota Geological Survey, and the Minnesota Department of Natural Resources. 2003

### 244. MILITARY ROAD
*Located on state highway 18, 2 miles east of I-35 in Banning State Park*

**Bad Roads and Railroads**
[Front] Although incomplete, the Point Douglas-Superior Military Road was a significant improvement over existing trails because it could accommodate wagon and stage traffic. As early as 1854, a Superior to St. Paul stage line carried mail and passengers over the finished sections of the road.

Despite its importance, the military road's condition deteriorated after federal support ended in 1858. State law placed the route under local control without providing for adequate funding. To maintain local roads, townships levied a tax, payable in either cash or labor. Inevitably, residents performed the minimum amount of labor necessary to work off their tax, but made little actual improvement.

In the late 1860s and 1870s, railroads replaced Minnesota's muddy, rutted highways. The Lake Superior and Mississippi Railroad opened between Duluth and St. Paul in 1870 and captured most of the traffic formerly carried by the Point Douglas-Superior Military Road. With attention shifted to rails, local roads received even less maintenance than before. Not until 1905 with the coming of the automobile, did the Minnesota Legislature establish a State Highway Commission to improve highway design, construction, and repair.

By 1875 the Point Douglas-Superior Military Road passed through what is now Sandstone, linking it with St. Paul and Superior. But the poorly maintained and incomplete route never improved travel enough to attract settlers to the area.

An alternative to the military road finally appeared in 1895, when William Henry Grant arranged for a spur of the Lake Superior and Mississippi Railroad to run to his new sandstone quarry on the Kettle River. The opportunities offered by the railroad and the quarry did attract residents, and the following year Grant platted the town of Sandstone.

### Petitioning for Roads

When Minnesota became a territory in 1849, only a few rough trails crossed its woodlands and prairies. The residents of the new territory were desperate for better roads to carry mail and commerce and to open the isolated north to settlement and lumbering.

In 1849 and 1850 Henry Hastings Sibley, Minnesota's territorial delegate, petitioned Congress to construct roads to help defend the territory. The military nature of the routes was largely a protest, because Congress would not fund a project which solely benefited local interests.

On July 18, 1850, Congress passed the Minnesota Road Act. With an additional act in 1855, the law appropriated money for roads radiating outward from the St. Paul area. Three roads ran through the southern third of the territory, linking the region's small farms and villages. The other routes penetrated into the sparsely settled north.

**Harriet E. Peet: An Early Traveler**
[Back] In the winter of 1855, Harriet and James Peet traveled from St. Paul over this road to Superior, Wisconsin, where they established a religious mission. It took nine days to complete the arduous overland trip, for the road had not been completed past the Snake River, 18 miles south of Sandstone, and the countryside was largely uninhabited. In a letter, James Peet later recalled that his wife was one of only "six or seven women" to have passed through this route.

Even until the twentieth century, overland travel was difficult because neither the state nor townships could afford to build and maintain good roads. The Peets were thus fortunate that this route existed. It was part of a network of military roads built by the federal government for the "defense" of the Minnesota Territory. This section of the old Point Douglas-Superior Military Road is now called "Government Road" in recognition of its origin.

Today's travelers still rely on many other sections of the old government roads. Although now substantially improved and virtually indistinguishable from later roads, these routes retain their significance as the first highways in the state. 1990

# ST. LOUIS COUNTY

### 245. FLOODWOOD
*Located on U.S. highway 2 at the east edge of Floodwood*

This village incorporated in 1899 is the site of an early Indian settlement and burial ground. The waters of the

Floodwood, St. Louis and East Savanna Rivers meet here and it was important as the junction of two great canoe routes used in the fur trade by North West Company and later by the American Fur Company. The Savanna route connected the Great Lakes and the Mississippi River, while the St. Louis route went northward to Lake Vermilion and the border lakes. From 1890 to 1925, Floodwood was the scene of large-scale lumbering operations.

Erected by the St. Louis County Historical Society in cooperation with the Minnesota Highway Department. 1956

## 246. MINNESOTA'S SEAPORT

*Located on I-35 in the Thompson Hill information center near Duluth*

More than three billion tons of iron ore, along with millions of tons of grain, timber, fish, and coal, have passed through the Duluth-Superior harbor since the beginning of Minnesota's Iron Age. The first ore from the rich Mesabi Range left the harbor for smelters on the lower lakes in 1892 and by 1916 yearly shipments had reached nearly 38 million tons. Huge loading docks, built first of wood and later of steel and concrete, could load four or five ore-carrying lake freights simultaneously from nearly 400 railroad cars. In 1953 an all-time yearly record 64 million tons of ore was shipped. As the rich hematite ore became scarce in the late 1950s, methods were developed to process and ship taconite, a plentiful lower grade ore.

The mouth of the St. Louis River forms a fine natural harbor with some 49 miles of serviceable frontage protected by one of the longest freshwater bay mouth bars in the world. The Duluth ship canal, originally a hand-dug cut through the bar, opened in 1870. Superior, Wisconsin, is located directly opposite the only natural harbor entrance.

For much of the twentieth century this harbor was second in total tonnage only to New York among U.S. ports, even though it is open to shipping only about eight months each year. Since the completion of the St. Lawrence Seaway in 1959, ocean-going vessels have carried the grain harvests of the northern plains and Montana soft coal from the Twin Ports to destinations around the globe. 1987

### 247. GEOLOGY OF DULUTH HARBOR △

*Located on I-35 in the Thompson Hill information center near Duluth*

Lake Superior is situated over the Midcontinent Rift, which is a rupture in the North American continent that formed a great rift valley from the Lake Superior region southwest to Kansas about 1.1 billion years ago. For about 20 million years as the rift valley opened, basaltic lavas erupted into it, accumulating to a thickness of up to 20 kilometers in the Lake Superior region. After the rifting and volcanic activity ended, the great thickness of dense basalt here depressed the crust into a trough-shaped basin. As the depression formed, it was filled in by sediment eroded and washed in from the surround-

Ore boats of Republic Steel Company in Duluth harbor in 1950

ing heights. Ultimately, the sedimentary deposits reached a thickness of many kilometers.

Over the past two million years, glaciers more than a kilometer thick have repeatedly advanced along the buried trough and scoured out much of the soft sedimentary rock that once filled it. The harder, erosion-resistant volcanic rocks along the margins of the trough now form the rocky coastline of much of Lake Superior.

Ten thousand years ago, as the glacial ice in the basin melted west to east, water ponded in front of the ice almost to the level of this marker to form Glacial Lake Duluth. Eventually, the ice melted out of the eastern lake basin and a drainage way opened to the lower Great Lakes. When the eastern outlet first formed, it was lower in elevation than today and drained the lake to 60 meters below its present level.

Relieved of the great weight of this glacial ice, the earth's crust has been slowly rising. The rate of rebound is fastest where the load of ice has been most recently removed. Thus, the northeastern lake basin and its eastern outlet are rising faster, thereby tilting the basin toward the southwest and flooding the mouth of the St. Louis River. Duluth harbor, which was formed by this submergence, has been enlarged by the formation of Minnesota Point, a baymouth bar sand deposit washed there by easterly waves and shore currents transporting beach sand from Wisconsin.

Erected by the Geological Society of Minnesota in partnership with the Minnesota Department of Transportation and the Minnesota Geological Survey. 1998

### 248.  FOND DU LAC

*Located on state highway 23 at Boyd and 93rd Avenues in Duluth*

Fond du Lac was incorporated in 1857 and became a part of the City of Duluth in 1895. This was the site of a major Chippewa Indian settlement from the sixteenth through the nineteenth centuries and is situated on the early canoe route along the St. Louis River from Lake Superior to Lake Vermilion and the Upper Mississippi. Daniel Greysolon, Sieur du Lhut, visited the site in 1679. The American Fur Company established a trading post in 1817. Lewis Cass camped here in 1820 while searching for the source of the Mississippi River, as did Henry R. Schoolcraft in 1826 [1832]. The Chippewa Indian Treaty, negotiated by Cass, was signed at Fond du Lac in 1826. A branch of the Superior–St. Paul Military Road was built to Fond du Lac about 1856, and the first railroad to reach Duluth—the Lake Superior and Mississippi—was constructed through the settlement in 1870.

Erected by the St. Louis County Historical Society in cooperation with the Minnesota Highway Department. 1956

### 249. MINNESOTA'S OLDEST CONCRETE PAVEMENT

*Located at the intersection of East 7th Street and 25th Avenue East in Duluth*

The streets of this Duluth neighborhood are the first concrete pavements constructed in Minnesota. They were built of portland cement concrete in 1909 and 1910 and ushered in the era of modern roads and streets in the state. A distinctive feature of these pioneer concrete pavements is the scored surface pattern of rectangular grooves. This indented design was used, according to the records of the day, to provide a firm and substantial footing for horses.

Dedicated in 1959 by the St. Louis County and Minnesota Historical Societies, Duluth Chamber of Commerce, and City of Duluth. [1959]

### 250. CLIFTON-FRENCH RIVER

*Located on state highway 61 at French River*

Clifton, first townsite surveyed in the United States section of the North Shore, was platted west of the mouth of the French River in 1855. This river was known to early explorers as Riviere de Francais. Rumors of nearby copper deposits resulted in widespread prospecting and townsite planning in the 1850s. Like many of the projected towns, Clifton never developed. From 1864 to 1866, the French River Mining Company and the North Shore Mining Company dug several exploratory shafts, but failed to locate profitable copper deposits. Extensive lumbering operations were carried on here in the 1880s.

Erected by the St. Louis County Historical Society in cooperation with the Minnesota Highway Department. 1959

## 251.  A THREE-WAY CONTINENTAL DIVIDE
*Located on U.S. highway 53 in Anchor Lake rest area*

A drop of rain water falling here in the Giants Range, a rare three-way continental divide, may flow either north into icy Hudson Bay, east into the Atlantic Ocean, or south into the warm waters of the Gulf of Mexico.

From the north slope of these very old granite ridges, streams flow into the Red River of the North, through Lake Winnipeg, and into Hudson Bay in northern Canada.

Creeks and rivers in the south slope flow into the St. Louis River, enter Lake Superior at Duluth and eventually reach the north Atlantic through the Great Lakes and the St. Lawrence River.

On a western spur of Giants Range the great watershed of the immense Mississippi River system gathers the flow from a maze of streams and swamps as the legendary river begins its winding course from Lake Itasca to the Gulf of Mexico, more than 2,500 miles away.

Lying as it does near the center of the North American continent, Minnesota marks the transition between eastern woodlands and western prairies and between northern coniferous forests and rich grain-growing lands of the mid-nation. It is a land of dramatic differences, tied to the world through three great waterways that originate in these rocks and streams. 1993

## 252. GEOLOGY OF THE MESABI REGION ◱

*Located off U.S. highway 169 on 13th Street at the west end of Bennett Park in Hibbing*

The dramatic history of the Mesabi Range dates back over 2.5 billion years to a period when a mountainous terrain, perhaps similar to the California Coast Ranges today, extended from Minnesota to Hudson Bay. The mountains slowly eroded down to their granite cores, and about two billion years ago the region was flooded by a sea that encroached from the south. Along the shallow margins of that sea, chemical sediments made of iron oxides and silica, which were precipitated out of the seawater, accumulated on the ocean floor to form the Biwabik Iron Formation. Evidence of primitive life forms (mostly algae) is preserved in the Biwabik and iron-formations of similar age around the world. It is believed that oxygen produced by the photosynthesizing algae modified the chemistry of the seawater and enabled iron and silica to precipitate from the ancient oceans.

Farther out to sea, fine sediments (mud, silt, and fine sand) accumulated to form the shales and siltstones of the Virginia Formation. As the sea level rose and submerged the eroded mountains, deeper water covered previously shallow environments where the iron-formation had been deposited. In the deeper water, fine sediments were also deposited over the iron-formation. As the iron-formation was buried under the younger sediments, the increasing pressure and temperature converted it to solid rock.

At some point after rock was formed, groundwater infiltrated and circulated through the Biwabik Formation, especially along its faults and fractures. The water effectively concentrated the iron by leaching out silica and caused further oxidation to produce the soft ores first mined on the Mesabi Range. With the gradual depletion of those enriched ores, most mining since the 1950s has instead extracted the magnetic mineral magnetite from unoxidized ore (taconite).

Erected by the Geological Society of Minnesota in partnership with the Minnesota Department of Transportation and the Minnesota Geological Survey. 1998

## 253. HULL-RUST-MAHONING MINE
*Located off Third Avenue East in Hibbing*

It has been called the "Grand Canyon of the North"— a fitting title for the world's largest open pit iron mine. The Hull-Rust-Mahoning pit actually began as separate mines, named for their owners, first dug in 1895, that gradually merged into one. Today this enormous pit measures 1.5 by 3.5 miles with a depth of 600 feet. Because of its size and the important developments that took place here, the Hull-Rust-Mahoning Mine played a key role in making Minnesota the leading iron-ore producer in the country.

Sitting in the midst of the Mesabi Range, the largest of Minnesota's three iron ranges, this mine owed its dominance to its particular iron formations. Here, vast stretches of high-grade, soft ore lay in shallow deposits that could be scooped up with giant steam shovels, machinery perfected at this site. Using the open pit method, mining companies removed huge quantities of iron ore quickly and economically, dumping it into rail cars that were moved out of the mine on tracks circling the slopes of the pit.

A steam shovel in the Hull-Rust Mine, about 1910

Large mining operations required extensive financial resources. Small local developers were soon driven out, and the wealthy ones with names like Rockefeller and Carnegie took over. In 1901 J. P. Morgan consolidated their mining and manufacturing operations as United States Steel, creating what was then the biggest corporation in the world.

The Hull-Rust-Mahoning Mine developed rapidly in the early 1900s, when demand was high for iron and steel to build railroads, bridges, and skyscrapers. In its peak production years during World Wars I and II, this pit supplied as much as one-fourth of all the iron ore mined in the United States. It was designated a National Historic Landmark in 1966. 1999

### 254. THE EMERGENCE OF MAN THROUGH STEEL
*Located on U.S. highway 169 across from Ironworld USA in Chisholm*

They toiled with purpose, those miners of ours . . . moving tons of iron for massive steel towers

This devotion to a nation, they adopted as one, makes the heritage of the iron range foremost 'neath the sun.

The legend lives. They were the "iron men" who dug the mines and contributed to the building and expansion of this country, during an industrial age. They helped to provide the iron needed when freedom was threatened.

Today, as the industrial age ebbs, and the technical age advances, the iron men are honored with a shrine that tells us they will never be forgotten. The magnificent sculpture evokes strength and embodies past history and ensures continued remembrance of the "iron men."

Look at the contentment in the chiseled face, and you will see the soul of all the iron men who ever were.

This statue, the third largest free-standing memorial in the United States, is a lasting tribute to the Mesabi,

Vermilion, Cuyuna and Gogoebic ranges' men of steel,
who carved out of a sylvan wilderness the iron ore that
made America the industrial giant of the world.
They shall live forever!
Yes, the iron man lives.
By Veda Ponikvar

### 255.   MESABI RANGE ORE DISCOVERY

*Located off U.S. highway 169 (Second Street) in
Mountain Iron*

The first iron ore was discovered on the Missabe [Mesabi]
Range at Mountain Iron, on November 16, 1890. It was
found three quarters of a mile north of this place by
Captain J. A. Nichols for the Merritt Brothers.

The first development work was done by Captain
A. P. Woods in 1891–1892.

A shaft was sunk in 1892 and the first ore was
taken from the mine for shipment.

The first car of ore was shipped from Mountain
Iron Oct. 17, 1892 and was sent to Duluth where it was
on exhibition. This shipment of 20 tons assaying 65 per
cent metallic iron, was sent in standard wooden ore car
No. 342.

4,245 tons of ore were shipped during the year 1892
from the Mountain Iron Mine.

This monument was erected to commemorate the
fortieth anniversary of the discovery of iron ore on the
Missabe Range.

Dedicated June 13, 1931. [Citizens of Mountain Iron]

### 256.   MOUNTAIN IRON MINE

*Located one block north of U.S. highway 169, near the
village hall in Mountain Iron*

Mountain Iron Mine has been designated a National
Historic Landmark

Under the provisions of the Historic Sites Act of
August 21, 1935, this site possesses exceptional value in

commemorating or illustrating the history of the
United States.

U.S. Department of the Interior National Park
Service. 1969

### 257.  THE FIRST TEST PIT ON THE MESABI
*Located off county road 21 at Babbitt*

This 28 ton piece of magnetic taconite was removed
from the Peter Mitchell Mine near the area where Peter
Mitchell, in 1871, put down the first recorded test pit
on the Mesabi Range. Pit location: 6,248 yards 40
degrees East of South from this point.

Erected by Minnesota Historical Society, St. Louis
County Historical Society, Village of Babbitt, Reserve
Mining Company [1958]

Dedicated August 27, 1980, to commemorate the
70th anniversary of the construction of the first concrete street paving in Minnesota, St. Louis County Historical Society.

### 258.  THE LAURENTIAN DIVIDE △
*Located on U.S. highway 53 about 5 miles north of
Virginia at the Laurentian Divide rest area*

The Laurentian Divide separates the watershed of
streams that flow north to the Arctic Ocean from the
watershed of streams that flow southeast through the
Great Lakes to the Atlantic Ocean. Where you are standing, the divide is formed by a prominent array of hills
known as the Giants Range. This ridge has been a highland for over two billion years!

The name "Laurentian" is used because the granites
forming the ridge are similar to, and were once thought
to be related to, granites of the Laurentide Mountains
in Quebec. Although this connection is no longer made,
the name has remained.

The Giants Range is made up mostly of several types
of granite that formed several kilometers deep in the

earth's crust about 2.7 billion years ago. Uplift and erosion slowly brought the granites to the surface; they have formed a highland throughout time because they are resistant to erosion. In the road cuts near the parking lot, crisscrossing bodies of darker and lighter granite record several successive intrusions of molten rock. Because of the complexity of the rocks, this site is known as "Confusion Hill" to local geologists.

About two billion years ago, the lower ground south of these highlands was covered by an ocean in which sediments were deposited. These sediments formed the rocks that include the world-famous Biwabik Iron Formation of the Mesabi Range. About 80 million years ago during the Cretaceous period, sediments were again deposited in an ocean that lay south of the Giants Range.

Between two million and 10,000 years ago, glaciers that advanced and receded across this terrain removed most of the Cretaceous sedimentary rocks and scoured the older, underlying bedrock surface. Deposits of silt, sand, gravel, and boulders left behind by these glaciers now cover most of the bedrock.

Erected by the Geological Society of Minnesota in partnership with the Minnesota Department of Transportation and the Minnesota Geological Survey. 1998

### 259.  LAURENTIAN DIVIDE, SUPERIOR NATIONAL FOREST
*Located on U.S. highway 53 about 5 miles north of Virginia at the Laurentian Divide rest area*

The Laurentian Divide is the ridge of low, rugged hills meandering through Northern Minnesota that separates the headwaters of streams which flow North and South. Streams which begin on the North slope of the Divide flow through Canada to Hudson Bay and the Arctic Ocean.

On the opposite side of the divide, streams flow South into Lake Superior, eventually reaching the Atlantic Ocean. The Laurentian Divide, at this location, is only a remnant of a once gigantic mountain range formed more than a billion years ago.

Forest Service, U.S. Department of Agriculture

C. M. Everet's place near Tower, about 1905

### 260.  TOWER
*Located on state highway 169 at the Tower-Soudan Historical Society Museum between Tower and Soudan*

Named for Charlemagne Tower, one of the developers of the Vermilion Range and the Duluth and Iron Range Railroad. It was incorporated as a village in 1884 and as a city in 1889. A saw mill was established here in 1882.

An Indian settlement was located on near-by Lake Vermilion at Pike Bay, and trading posts of the North West and American Fur Companies were established there in the 19th century. It was the terminus of the Vermilion Trail, built from Duluth in 1865 for gold rush prospectors pouring into the region. During its construction the first evidences of iron ore were found.

This ore crusher, used in search for gold, was one of the first pieces of mining equipment in the area. It was found underwater in Trout Creek in 1934 [1926?].

The first iron mine in Minnesota was opened near here at Soudan in 1884.

Erected by the St. Louis County Historical Society in cooperation with the Minnesota Highway Department. 1957

### 261. FIRST IRON MINE

*Located on state highway 169 at the Tower-Soudan Historical Society Museum between Tower and Soudan*

From the Breitung pit of the Soudan Mine just north of this town [Soudan] the first commercial shipment of Minnesota iron ore was made by the Minnesota Iron Company July 31, 1884, over the Duluth and Iron Range Railroad.

This line had just been built by Charlemagne Tower and associates to open up the Vermilion Range.

### 262. THE SOUDAN MINE

*Located off state highway 169 near the visitor center in Soudan Underground Mine State Park*

Minnesota's iron mining industry was born here in 1884, and the opening of this mine was one of the great commercial events of the nineteenth century.

The first ore was shipped from the Breitung pit of the Soudan Mine on July 31, 1884, beginning the development of the rich iron ore deposits of the oldest of Minnesota's three ranges, the Vermilion.

The Soudan was at first mined from seven open pits, but it soon became an underground operation. The mine, which operated from 1884 until 1962, is the deepest, as well as the oldest, in Minnesota. Its shaft extends to a depth of 2,500 feet with drifts or tunnels running three-fourths of a mile to the east and west. At the peak of its production in 1892 the Soudan shipped more than 568,000 long tons of high-grade ore and employed 1,800 men.

The mine was presented to the state of Minnesota in 1963 by the Oliver Iron Mining Division of the United States Steel Corporation. 1967

### 263.  SOUDAN MINE

*Located off state highway 169 near the visitor center in Soudan Underground Mine State Park*

The first shipment of iron ore from Minnesota came from the Soudan Mine in 1884; by 1900 Minnesota was the leading iron ore producer in the United States.

The Soudan Mine headframe sits atop the largest iron deposit in the Vermilion Range, one of three vast iron ranges in northern Minnesota. On the nearby Mesabi Range, where the ore was soft and close to the surface, it could be scooped up with steam shovels, giving rise to open pit mining. But on the Vermilion Range, ore deposits were embedded deep in hard rock that required drilling and blasting. These mining methods made the Soudan an underground operation, with a shaft that descended nearly 2,400 feet and tunnels that ran almost a mile from end to end.

Pennsylvania investor Charlemagne Tower and his son Charlemagne Junior were the first to develop the riches of the Vermilion Range. After buying more than 20,000 acres, they brought in experienced miners to work the new mine at Soudan and founded the town of Tower to serve the fast growing population. To ship the ore, they built the Duluth and Iron Range Railroad, linking their mine to the town of Two Harbors on Lake Superior, where they constructed an ore dock.

At its peak in the 1890s, the Soudan Mine employed 1,800 men and shipped more than half a million tons of ore a year. In 1901, years after Tower had sold it, the mine came under the control of the newly formed United States Steel Corporation.

The Soudan Mine remained in almost continuous operation until it closed in 1962, not because its resources were depleted but because changing economics and technology made underground mining too expensive. In 1963 U.S. Steel gave Minnesota's oldest and deepest mine to the state, which established it as a state park in 1965. Its name was changed in 1985 to the Soudan Underground Mine State Park. In 1966 the mine was designated a National Historic Landmark. 1999

A lower level of the Soudan Mine in 1963

### 264.   THE OLD VERMILION TRAIL AND WINSTON CITY
*Located on state highway 169 at the west end of county road 526, one mile west of Tower*

On October 28, 1865, geologist Henry E. Eames returned to St. Paul after initiating a survey of the mineral wealth present in the Lake Vermilion area only to find an abundance of rumors concerning a valuable gold strike on the shores of that lake. A number of gold mining companies were quickly organized, and a St. Paul newspaper dispatched a special correspondent to the Vermilion gold field. Hundreds of men, including recently discharged Civil War veterans, made their way to Duluth, where they purchased food and supplies for the trek north to the supposed gold fields.

During the winter of 1865–66, many of these men were employed by the mining companies to break open a road from Duluth to Pike Bay of Lake Vermilion. This road followed in part an old Indian trail from the Head of the Lakes. The improved trail stretched 85 miles to the north, and, in time, became known as the Old Vermilion Trail. At first only a winter road, it was improved in 1868–69 by George R. Stuntz, who directed a resurvey and construction project financed in part by government funds.

Three-quarters of a mile northeast of this marker the gold prospectors created a log cabin and shack community named Winston City. In 1866 it boasted several stores, a hotel, four saloons, and a post office. But gold was not found in quantities sufficient to cover the cost of mining. In 1867 the disappointed miners deserted their gold-diggings, and Winston City shortly became the first ghost town of the Vermilion Range.

Erected through the cooperation of—Minnesota Historical Society, St. Louis County Historical Society, Tower-Soudan Historical Society, Citizens of Vermilion Township, Minnesota State Highway Department. 1973

## 265.  ORIGIN OF McCARTHY BEACH  ⚊
*Located off county roads 5 and 65 in McCarthy Beach State Park*

The beautiful, sandy beaches of Sturgeon Lake are a gift from the glaciers. During the Ice Age of the last two million years, glacial ice advanced out of the Ontario region and repeatedly covered this area. As the ice advanced, it gouged the earth, scraped up and crushed the rock and soil, and carried these sediments along. About 12,000 years ago, when the last glacier in this area was receding to the northeast, it left piles of sediment along its edge, forming a ridge of hills called a moraine. These hills can be seen northeast of Sturgeon Lake, where the ridge they form has a northwest-to-southeast orientation.

The receding glacier also left some stranded blocks of ice in this area. Glacial meltwater that flowed down onto the lowlands on this side of the moraine was free to meander. Its slower velocity could not continue to carry the sand it washed out of the ice, so the sand was deposited. Over time, the sand accumulated creating a large outwash plain that buried the stranded blocks of ice. Slowly, the hidden ice blocks melted, forming a group of sandy, water-filled basins called kettle lakes.

Since the shores of the kettle lakes and the nearby land were composed entirely of sand, the shorelines eroded readily and the kettles grew until they joined to form Sturgeon Lake with its many bays. The lake has many wide, shallow margins because waves wash the beach sand into the lake, and as a result, the shoreline migrates outward, widening the shallows. Under the right conditions, one can see the wide zone of shallow water extending about 100 meters out from the shore near this marker. The place where the bottom drops off sharply, to a depth of more than two meters, is close to where the shoreline was when it started to migrate.

Erected by the Geological Society of Minnesota in partnership with the Minnesota Department of Transportation, the Minnesota Geological Survey, and the Minnesota Department of Natural Resources. 2003

# NORTH CENTRAL / WEST REGION

North Central/West Region
Markers 266–348

# BECKER COUNTY

### 266.  THE LAKES OF MINNESOTA  △
*Located on U.S. highway 10 about 1 mile southeast of*
*Detroit Lakes in a wayside park on the shore of Detroit Lake*

The great ice ages that began about one million years
ago, were characterized by the advance and recession of
huge ice sheets over vast areas of North America. These
continental glaciers, originating in Canada, moved
southward, scraping up mantle rock and soil which was
dropped in central and southern Minnesota to produce
plains and irregular belts of hills. Most of Minnesota's
10,000 lakes lie in such deposits and trace their origin
directly or indirectly to glaciation.

In the rugged surface that extends from Detroit
Lakes to Alexandria, where glacial action was particularly vigorous, the lakes are irregular in outline. Elsewhere they may be round, long, wide, narrow, big, little,
sun-warmed or ice-cold; shallow and sandy or rocky and
deep; mucky and weed-fringed or clear as crystal; with
or without islands, inlets, bays, sand bars, beaches, or
cliffs. Taken together they give Minnesota a water area
greater than that of any other state. Many exhibit landscapes of unusual beauty, but all, regardless of location
or character, add to Minnesota's most valuable mineral
resource—water.

Erected by the Geological Society of Minnesota in
cooperation with the Department of Highways, State of
Minnesota. 1960

### 267.  THE WOODS TRAIL
*Located on U.S. highway 10 by Detroit Lake in*
*Detroit Lakes*

Through woodland and prairie, along riverbanks and
through sloughs, the mixed-blood American and Canadian buffalo hunters called Metis blazed trails with
their oxen and squeaky-wheeled wooden carts. They

carried buffalo robes and pemmican from their homes
along the Red River of the North to market in St. Paul,
and then carried supplies back again. The heyday of the
complex network of Red River trails lasted from about
1820 to 1872, when the first railroad reached the Red
River at Moorhead.

The northernmost of the Red River trails ran
through forested stretches along a portion of the 400
mile route. It was known as the Woods Trail and passed
right through this location. This name was an exagger-
ation, since only the section from Detroit Lakes to
Crow Wing was wooded. South from Pembina the trail
crossed the Red and ran along the east bank through
low savannah dotted with willow and onto a high and
treeless prairie. It followed beach ridges of glacial Lake
Agassiz on the eastern border of the Red River Valley,
entering the forest at Detroit Lakes. The trail proceeded
along the Otter Tail and then the Leaf and Crow Wing
rivers to the east until it reached an important stopping
point, the village of Crow Wing, which also lent its name
to the trail. From there the Crow Wing Trail made its
way over sandy prairie on the east bank of the Mississippi to Sauk Rapids, where it merged with the Middle
Trail, which took a more southerly route toward the
Mississippi River, for the rest of the distance to St. Paul.

Erected by the Minnesota Historical Society and
the Becker County Historical Society. 1996

## 268.  ST. COLUMBA MISSION

*Located on the grounds of St. Columba's Episcopal Church
at White Earth*

The first Minnesota mission to be named for Saint
Columba was built by James Lloyd Breck in 1852 at
Gull lake near present-day Brainerd. It was the fourth
Episcopal church established in Minnesota.

The initial group of Chippewa Indians arrived here
from Gull Lake on June 14, 1868, to begin life on the
White Earth Reservation which had been created the

year before. In the fall of 1868 they were joined by John Johnson or Enmegahbowh, a Canadian Indian who had served at the former mission on Gull Lake. The first religious service in Becker County was conducted that fall by Enmegahbowh, who was ordained the following year. He is said to have been the first Indian to be ordained by the Episcopal church in the United States.

The second mission church of St. Columba, built of logs in 1868, stood several miles north of the present town of White Earth. It was replaced in 1871 by a frame church, located near the present site and consecrated by Bishop Henry B. Whipple in 1872. The present church was built in 1980. Enmegahbowh is buried in the nearby cemetery. 1985

### 269. CHIEF WHITE CLOUD STATE MONUMENT 🏛

*Located in Calvary Catholic Cemetery near St. Benedict's Mission, about 1 mile south of White Earth*

Erected by the State of Minnesota appreciating a helpful, kindhearted, brainy man of true worth, born 1828 died Oct. 7, 1898

Erected June 14, 1909 under the direction of D. A. Ball, Gus H. Beaulieu.

White Cloud, a leader of the Gull Lake Ojibwe, about 1865

## 270.   GEOLOGY OF BAD MEDICINE LAKE   △

*Located on state highway 113 in Bad Medicine Lake rest area at the Continental Divide*

Bad Medicine Lake is on the southwestern flank of a glacial highland called the Itasca moraine. The moraine is composed of glacial sediment (clay, silt, sand, gravel, and boulders) deposited by ice that advanced from the northeast about 25,000 years ago. The Itasca moraine is the highest land formation in northwestern Minnesota and stands 350 meters higher than the Red River valley, which is 100 kilometers to the west. More recent glacial advances from the northwest, north, and northeast eroded the Itasca moraine and deposited more glacial sediment, which created the very rough knob-and-kettle highland topography we see today.

Following a more recent glacial advance, meltwater was discharged at high pressure from beneath the glacial ice, and with great force it cut the picturesque narrow valley that contains Bad Medicine Lake. The lake is confined to a six-kilometer segment of the steep-walled valley and has a small drainage basin with no inlet or outlet stream. Fed by groundwater springs, Bad Medicine Lake is noted for its exceptional water quality and clarity. Groundwater also flows out of the lake through the surrounding sand and gravel.

A continental drainage divide called the Laurentian Divide is about six kilometers west of here. Locally, it is oriented northeast to southwest. Surface water west of the divide drains into the Red River of the North and, eventually, into Hudson Bay. Surface water on this side of the divide drains southeastward into the Mississippi River and on to the Gulf of Mexico. Surface water divides are different from groundwater drainage divides, which are formed by underground features. But in this case, the groundwater from Bad Medicine Lake also flows to the south and east.

Erected by the Geological Society of Minnesota in partnership with the Minnesota Department of Transportation and the Minnesota Geological Survey. 2003

### 271.  BAD MEDICINE LAKE

*Located on state highway 113 in Bad Medicine Lake rest area at the Continental Divide*

Bad Medicine Lake, also called the Lake of the Valley, was originally known to the Ojibway Indians as Ga-wimbadjiwegamag (Lake lying in a mountain depression). Among the many stories about the name's origin are legends of serpentine fish and monster pike that dwelt in the lake's blue-green depths.

Bad Medicine is one of the clearest and least polluted lakes in Minnesota. It is entirely spring fed and has no inlet or outlet. The Laurentian Divide separating the Hudson Bay and Mississippi River watersheds crosses Minnesota Highway 113 about one and a half miles west of this marker.

Between 1904 and 1918 the Nichols-Chisholm Lumber Company cut most of the majestic white and Norway pine stands that surrounded the lake. The pine logs were hauled to Commonwealth Landing on Elbow Lake, and from there they were carried in massive spring drives down the Otter Tail River to the company mill at Frazee. Old Headquarters logging camp, near Long Lost Lake, was the hub of an extensive network of standard gauge railroad lines used to haul the logs. The outlines of rotting ties still mark the locations of the railway beds in the surrounding forests. Blackened stumps and fire-scarred pines are mute reminders of the huge forest fires of 1918 which followed the logging operations.

Erected by the Residents of Bad Medicine Lake. 1985

# BELTRAMI COUNTY

### 272.  COUNT BELTRAMI STATE MONUMENT 🄴

*Located on county road 15 at Count Beltrami State Memorial Wayside on the southeast shore of Lake Julia*

At a point near this site, in 1823, Beltrami, an Italian explorer, ended his search for the source of the Missis-

sippi River. His long, difficult journey across wilderness
spaces terminated on the shore of the nearby lake,
which he named "Julia." His observations here con-
vinced him that this lake was the most northern or true
source of the river. Lake Itasca, now known to be the
true source of the Mississippi, Beltrami called the western source.

Erected by State of Minnesota Department of
Transportation August 22, 1948.

# BENTON COUNTY

### 273. BENTON COUNTY TAKES SHAPE
*Located in front of the courthouse at 531 Dewey Street*
*in Foley*

[Front] When Minnesota's original nine counties were
established in 1849, only three—Benton, Washington,
and Ramsey—officially opened to settlers. They lay in a
triangle of land between the St. Croix and Mississippi
rivers that reached north beyond Lake Mille Lacs—land
ceded by the Dakota and Ojibwe Indians twelve years
earlier.

In choosing names for these new counties, territorial legislators turned for inspiration to the country's
distinguished political leaders. Benton County honors
Thomas Hart Benton, a longtime U.S. Senator from
Missouri, whose work on the country's homestead laws
in the 1820s won him the gratitude of white settlers
throughout the West.

Fur trading and lumbering first drew settlers to
Benton County, largely from eastern states and Canada.
The first census of the county, in 1850, counted 418
white and mixed-blood residents. The population grew
slowly until the 1870s, when large numbers of people
from Norway, Sweden, Germany, and Poland arrived to
farm. By 1880, much of the land in Benton County
had been claimed.

During the territorial years, Minnesota legislators kept busy redrawing old county boundaries and creating new counties. Benton County changed shape several times before the present boundaries were set in 1859.

The county seat, however, kept moving. Originally located in Sauk Rapids, it moved twice as the population shifted. Finally, in 1901, the Foley brothers, powerful Benton County lumbermen, brought it to a vote. Seeking a more central location—and, no doubt, wishing to promote their own interests—they pulled off a win for their namesake town.

Today, faming is still central to the Benton County way of life. But now large, consolidated farms dominate the countryside. What was once the backbone of the county's economy—the small family farm—is gradually disappearing.

**Minnesota Territory 1849–1858**
[Back] On March 3, 1849, during his last hours in office, President James Polk signed a bill adding a new name to the American political landscape, Minnesota Territory. A vast land, it stretched from the St. Croix River and Lake Superior on the east to the Missouri River on the west, and north to the Canadian border. Totaling more than 166,000 square miles, Minnesota Territory was divided into nine counties: *Wabashaw, Dakotah, Washington, Ramsey, Benton, Itasca, Wahnahta, Mahkahta,* and *Pembina.*

In those feverish years of American expansion, pressure built to organize the lands along the upper Mississippi River. Iowa and Wisconsin had already entered the Union and were rapidly filling with settlers. The story of frontier settlement was soon to be repeated in Minnesota, as a thin stream of farmers, lumbermen, and land speculators turned into a tidal wave.

The same places being claimed and named by these settlers and Washington politicians had been the homelands, hunting grounds and burial places of Indian people for thousands of years. And since the later 1600s, small numbers of Europeans and Americans had lived here together with Native people, trading furs and goods, making families, and creating new traditions.

In 1849 that world of relatively peaceful coexistence was about to collapse, sometimes with brutal force. During the territorial years, Dakota and Ojibwe peoples signed treaties that ceded nearly all of their lands in Minnesota to the U.S. government in exchange for money, promises, and reservations.

Meanwhile, settlements such as St. Paul, Stillwater, and St. Anthony mushroomed into cities. Farms and towns spread across the prairies. The booming populations, which had grown from less than 5,000 settlers in 1849 to more than 100,000, clamored for statehood. It was granted in 1858, just nine short years after the creation of the territory. 2001

Boundaries of the original counties in Minnesota Territory

# CASS COUNTY

### 274.   SUGAR POINT BATTLE

*Located on state highway 200 on Leech Lake 2 miles
east of Whipholt*

When a federal marshal with about 100 troops of the
3rd Infantry tried to arrest the Chippewa chief Bugo-
naygeshig at Sugar Point opposite here on the northeast shore of the lake, a sharp fight occurred October 5,
1898. The whites lost 7 killed and 16 wounded and the
arrest was never accomplished.

# CLAY COUNTY

### 275.   LAKE AGASSIZ   △

*Located on U.S. highway 10 in a wayside park at Hawley*

Toward the close of the last or Wisconsin stage of glaciation about 10,000 years ago, the ice front receded from
central Iowa toward the north and, in the latitude of
Browns Valley, crossed the continental divide between
the Mississippi River and the drainage to Hudson Bay.
After the glacier had retreated north of this divide the
meltwaters, unable to follow the natural drainage
northward, were confined between the ice and the
divide to the south.

Thus Glacial Lake Agassiz was created. At its maximum it was 600 feet deep and larger than the combined
area of the five Great Lakes today.

The outlet of the lake was at Browns Valley. There
the Glacial River Warren had its source and carried the
overflow from the lake through the valley of the present Minnesota River. When the northern ice eventually
melted away the impounded water escaped to Hudson
Bay and left behind on the floor of Lake Agassiz the
lake sediments which are now the rich soils in the Red
River Valley region.

Erected by the Geological Society of Minnesota and the Department of Highways, State of Minnesota aided by a grant from the Louis W. and Maud Hill Family Foundation. 1955

## 276. ST. JOHN'S EPISCOPAL CHURCH
*Located on U.S. highway 75 at 120 Eighth Street South in Moorhead*

St. John's Episcopal Church was designed on an Elizabethan model by the noted architect, Cass Gilbert, among whose other significant buildings is the present Minnesota State Capitol. Construction of St. John's began on August 1, 1898. On February 12, 1899, the church was consecrated and the first confirmation held.

Episcopal church services in Moorhead date from 1872 when the Reverend James A. Gilfillan conducted a service in a Northern Pacific Railroad passenger coach. With the arrival of Benjamin F. Mackall, a licensed lay reader, regular services began on May 13, 1873. When the parish was organized in 1875, Mackall was elected Senior Warden, an office he held for 62 years. The movement to construct the present church was led by Mackall and W. H. Davy, who donated the land on which St. John's stands.

St. John's Episcopal Church was designated a State Historic Site in 1967.

## 277. THE SOLOMON GILMAN COMSTOCK HOUSE Ⓜ
*Minnesota Historical Society Historic Site*
*Located on U.S. highway 75 at 506 Eighth Street South in Moorhead*

Born in Maine in 1842, Solomon G. Comstock worked on the family farm until he came of age and then followed the pioneers west. After reading law in Bangor, he studied at the University of Michigan, then went to Omaha and Minneapolis. Finally, in the fall of 1871, "poor, but full of vigor, hope and talents," Comstock established a successful legal practice in Moorhead. His sound judgment and solid statesmanship won him appointment as Clay County attorney and then election to the state legislature as representative and senator and to the United States House of Representatives.

In the late 1870s Comstock donated six acres of valuable city property for the establishment of a state normal school, later to become Moorhead State College. His belief in higher education was also reflected in the career of his daughter Ada Louise, who became a noted educator and third president of Radcliffe College.

Comstock built this imposing eleven-room frame house in 1883 for his wife Sarah and their children. One of the few remaining urban homes to boast the spacious grounds typical of the late 1800s, the house was donated to the Minnesota Historical Society for restoration and preservation in 1965 by Mr. and Mrs. George Comstock. 1971

### 278. BONANZA FARMS IN THE RED RIVER VALLEY
*Located on I-94 at the tourist information center near Moorhead*

The fertile areas along both banks of the Red River of the North were once the bed of a huge lake known to geologists as Glacial Lake Agassiz. When the last glacier retreated and the lake slowly drained some 9,000 years ago, the plain left behind contained some of the richest farmlands in North America.

The flat valley lands were well suited to the new farm machinery of the 1870s and 1880s. Settlers followed the railroads west and sent their huge wheat crops back to the growing flour mills in the Twin Cities. Many of the "bonanza" farms of the valley were more than 2,000 acres in size, and the largest was more than 30,000 acres.

Farm protest movements followed the wheat belt,

because the single-cash-crop farmers with heavy machinery investment were especially vulnerable to price fixing by the railroads, grain buyers, and milling monopolies. The Farmers' Alliance, the cooperative marketing movement, the Nonpartisan League, and the Farmer-Labor Party in turn found strength in the Red River Valley.

Although wheat is still grown, sugar beets, sunflowers, and potatoes are today the staples of valley agriculture, which is still characterized by large-scale operations, high capital investment, and the employment of seasonal workers. 1985

### 279. BLUE STAR MEMORIAL HIGHWAY
*Located on I-94 at the tourist information center near Moorhead*

A tribute to the Armed Forces that have defended the United States of America
    Sponsored by Federated Garden Clubs of Minnesota, Inc. In cooperation with State of Minnesota Department of Highways. 1950

### 280. HUDSON'S BAY FUR TRADING POST, GEORGETOWN, MINNESOTA
*Located off U.S. highway 75 on the west side of Georgetown*

Hudson's Bay Company was chartered by King Charles II of England on May 2, 1670, on its agreement to pay "two Elkes and two Black Beaver" in rent for rights of trade, commerce, and governmental powers over the territories lying within the entrance of Hudson Strait. The region encompassed the drainage basin of the Red River of the North, an area equal to 1/3 North America. Rents were to be paid whenever the reigning sovereign of England set foot on "Rupert's Land." First immigrants to Minnesota were Scotchmen from Red River Settlement established near present-day Winnipeg in 1812.
    Fur trading and barter were the way of life of the

territories. Fur trading posts were built on Red River, the one on this site being erected in 1859. Reconstructed around this marker is the warehouse in which furs were stored for transportation by dog team, oxcart, and pirogue to York Factory in Hudson Bay and shipped by sailing vessels to London.

Georgetown was named after Sir George Simpson, Governor-in-Chief of Rupert's Land. It marks the confluence of the Red and Buffalo rivers and a crossing of the first overland highways in Minnesota—the Red River Oxcart Trails.

Erected by the Clay County Historical Society. 1968

# CLEARWATER COUNTY

### 281.  ITASCA NATURAL AREA
*Located off U.S. highway 71 in Itasca State Park*

Itasca Natural Area has been designated a registered natural landmark under the provisions of the Historic Sites Act of August 21, 1935. This site possesses exceptional value in illustrating the natural history of the United States.

U.S. Department of the Interior, National Park Service. 1965

### 282.  ITASCA BISON SITE
*Located on Wilderness Drive in Itasca State Park*

About 9000 years ago nomadic hunters killed the now extinct "prehistoric bison" (*Bison occidentalis*), camped and prepared stone tools along this stream.

Discovered in 1937, this site was extensively excavated from 1963–65. The project was supported through the University of Minnesota by the Hill family and National Science Foundation.

## 283.  THEODORE AND JOHANNA WEGMANN
*Located off county road 117 in Itasca State Park*

Theodore and Johanna Wegmann built their pioneer home at this place in 1893, one building being used as a store and postoffice.

An act of the Minnesota Legislature in 1945 authorized acquisition of the homestead as an addition to Itasca State Park.

Dedicated in grateful memory of the services of Theodore Wegmann, 1861–1941, and Johanna his wife, 1865–1944.

## 284.  SEARCH FOR THE MISSISSIPPI'S SOURCE
*Located off state highway 200 on county road 38 in Itasca State Park*

The romantic 19th-century quest for the source of the Mississippi River brought many explorers—among them Zebulon Pike, Lewis Cass, and Giacomo Beltrami—to northern Minnesota. The search ended when Ojibwe chief Ozawindib guided Henry Rowe Schoolcraft to Lake Itasca in 1832.

Sent by the United States government to help negotiate a treaty between the Dakota and Ojibwe, Schoolcraft used the opportunity to explore the Mississippi's headwaters area. The expedition, numbering 30, left Sault Ste. Marie in early June and traveled by way of the

Theodore and Johanna Wegmann, about 1895

St. Louis River and Savanna Portage to Sandy Lake, then up the Mississippi to Cass Lake. From there Ozawindib guided them to Lake Bemidji and up the Schoolcraft River, and over a portage to the river's source.

Sorely tried by "voracious, long-billed, and dyspeptic musketoes" and portages knee-deep in mud, the little band caught their first glimpse of the lake on July 13. It was known to the Indians and traders as "Omushkos" or "Lac la Biche," both meaning Elk Lake, but Schoolcraft renamed it "Itasca" from a combination of the Latin words for "truth" and "head," *veritas caput.*

Although public interest focused more on the long-sought source, the Schoolcraft expedition also collected valuable scientific information, inspected fur posts, vaccinated 2,000 Ojibwe against smallpox, and achieved an intertribal peace treaty. 1990

### 285. JACOB V. BROWER
*Located at Brower Inn in Itasca State Park*

Jacob V. Brower Explored the Itasca basin in the fall of 1888 and was commissioned by the Minnesota Historical Society in February, 1889, to conduct an official survey of the area. Largely as a result of this detailed exploration of the sources of the Mississippi, especially in 1889 and 1891, Itasca State Park was established by act of the Minnesota legislature in 1891. Brower was named first commissioner of the park. [1939]

### 286. OLD NORTHWEST TERRITORY
*Located on state highway 200 at the headwaters of the Mississippi River in Itasca State Park*

The First Colony of the United States. Herein, under the Ordinance of 1787, began the westward expansion of this nation. The American Bill of Rights first nationally recognized. Human slavery prohibited. Primogeniture abolished. And the great new principle of colonies becoming equal in rights with parent states was established.

Itasca Lake, source of the Mississippi River, discovered by Henry R. Schoolcraft in 1832.

The Treaty of Paris, 1783, provided that the United States' northwest boundary should extend from the Northwest Angle of Lake of the Woods to the Mississippi River. Itasca was on this boundary. This tablet is erected 1938 by the Northwest Territory Celebration Commission.

Franklin D. Roosevelt, President of the United States; George White, Chairman; Mrs. Leland S. Duxbury, Mrs. George Baxter Averill, Mrs. John S. Heaume, Mrs. Samuel James Campbell, Miss Bonnie Farwell, Mrs. George O. Schermerhorn, Vice-chairmen; Congressman Robert T. Secrest, Treasurer; Rev. Joseph E. Hanz, Secretary; United States Senators Arthur H. Vandenbergh, Frederick Van Nuys; Congressman Thomas A. Jenkins; Paul V. McNutt, E. M. Hawes, Exec. Director.

### 287.   REV. JOSEPH A. GILFILLAN
*Located in Itasca State Park near the Mississippi*
*River headwaters*

Rev. Joseph A. Gilfillan preached the first sermon at the source of the Mississippi River in May 1881, on the knoll approximately 200 feet northwesterly of this tablet.

Text: "Then had Thy peace been as a river."

### 288.   GEOLOGY OF MINNESOTA △
*Located at Peace Pipe Springs in Itasca State Park*

The diversified scenery of Minnesota—of which the Itasca Park area is one phase—is due to the location of the state in the approximate center of the continent. Situated midway between the Atlantic and Pacific oceans, Hudson Bay and the Gulf of Mexico, the state has within its boundaries three principal divides in the watersheds of North America. Minnesota lacks the rugged topography and high elevations found in most continental divides. Its highest elevation, 2,300 feet on the Mesabi Range, is in close proximity to its lowest, the surface of Lake Superior, 602 feet above the sea.

The general surface of the state slopes from the north-central portion near Itasca Park, in four directions toward its distant and opposite corners.

The 10,000 lakes of Minnesota cover 5,600 square miles, an average of 1 square mile of water for every 15 of land. This unprecedented supply of water, which has a surface exceeding the water area of any other state, finds its way to the ocean through Hudson Bay, the Great Lakes and the Gulf of Mexico.

Erected by the Geological Society of Minnesota and the Department of Conservation, State of Minnesota aided by a grant from the Louis W. and Maud Hill Family Foundation. 1954

### 289. ITASCA STATE PARK CENTENNIAL 1891–1991
*Located in Itasca State Park*

The name "Itasca" was coined specifically from the Latin words "Veritas Caput"—literally meaning "true head"—by Henry Rowe Schoolcraft in 1832. Led by Ozawindib, an Ojibwe guide who knew the upper reaches of the Mississippi River and its headwaters lakes, Schoolcraft was able to document the true source of America's greatest river, a feat that had eluded many previous explorers, including Zebulon Pike, Lewis Cass, and Giacomo Beltrami.

More than a half century passed before surveyor Jacob V. Brower, known today as the "father of Itasca," began his efforts to establish the area as a state park. At a time when most of Minnesota was not yet homesteaded and logging was the state's major industry, Brower struggled against tremendous odds and opposition to preserve this special place for future generations. Finally, in 1891, the legislature passed by one vote an act establishing 20,000 acres around Lake Itasca as Minnesota's first state park. Brower was named the first park commissioner, a position from which he staunchly fought poachers, politicians, and lumbermen. While he only partially succeeded in stopping logging before his death in 1905, he predicted that Itasca "will become easily accessible and of great value as a public resort," a remarkably accurate vision.

On the centennial of this park, 32,000 acres are now protected and enjoyed by over a half million visitors each year. Efforts are underway to begin a major pine restoration program to ensure the existence of giant pines and a diverse northwoods ecosystem for the next century and beyond. 1991

A lone camper at Lake Itasca in 1898

# CROW WING COUNTY

### 290. GEOLOGY OF LAKE MILLE LACS ⛰

*Located on U.S. highway 169 in a wayside .2 mile south of Garrison*

This part of Minnesota was covered by glacial ice a kilometer or more thick at least four times during the last million years. As the glaciers moved in from Canada, they brought with them enormous quantities of glacial drift (silt, sand, gravel, and boulders) that was deposited under the ice and at its margin, in sheets or in irregular hills and depressions.

About 15,000 years ago, near the end of the last, or Wisconsin, glaciation, a tongue-shaped lobe of ice, called the Superior lobe, advanced into this area from the Lake Superior region. During the final decline of this ice lobe, it temporarily advanced again; and at its point of furthest progress, it deposited a pile of drift, called an end moraine, along its margin. This end moraine encircles Lake Mille Lacs on the north, west, and south. With the land on the eastern shore already of higher elevation, the moraine blocked the drainage to the south. As a result, the bounded area was flooded, and one of the largest lakes in the state was formed.

Mille Lacs is 29 kilometers long and 22 kilometers wide. Its surface is 381 meters above sea level, and its depth of 8 to 11 meters is rather uniform throughout. Overflow from the lake is discharged to the south through the Rum River, which flows from Vineland about 112 kilometers to Anoka, where it empties into the Mississippi River.

Erected by the Geological Society of Minnesota in partnership with the Minnesota Department of Transportation, the Minnesota Geological Survey, and the Minnesota Department of Natural Resources. 1998

### 291. MILLE LACS LAKE
*Located on U.S. highway 169 in Garrison*

Named from the fur traders' phrase "the thousand lake region," this lake is 1250 feet above sea level and covers about 200 square miles. It formerly included much low ground and several adjacent lakes. When visited by Du Luth in 1679, Sioux villages, now indicated by numerous burial mounds, lined the lake shore.

Concourse designed and constructed by Minnesota Highway Department, National Park Service, Village of Garrison, Civilian Conservation Corps.

## 292.  FORT RIPLEY
*Located on state highway 371 on the east bank of the Mississippi River, about 8 miles north of Camp Ripley Junction*

Fort Ripley typifies the role of the United States Army on the western frontier. It was built on the west bank of the Mississippi River, across from this point in 1848–1850 to protect the Winnebago Indians living on a nearby reservation and to prevent, if possible, the never-ending skirmishes between the Sioux and Chippewa.

Originally known as Fort Marcy and later as Fort Gaines, the name was changed to Fort Ripley on November 4, 1850. The post became a vanguard for the extension of settlement by serving as a post office and furnishing business to farmers and traders in the area.

In July, 1857, the United States War Department concluded that the Chippewa were peaceful and that the fort could be evacuated. As soon as the troops left, the Chippewa pillaged the surrounding area. The soldiers returned, and the post was reactivated. During the Sioux Uprising of 1862 settlers took shelter in the fort's frame buildings.

A fire destroyed most of these buildings in 1877, and Fort Ripley was abandoned in 1880. The ruins of a powder magazine, the only stone structure at the post, are all that remain of this pioneer fort. The site of the old outpost is now within the Camp Ripley Military Reservation used by the Minnesota National Guard. 1967

## 293.  OLD CROW WING
*Located on county road 27 in Crow Wing State Park, about a mile west of its junction with state highway 371*

Few spots in Minnesota are richer in historical lore than Old Crow Wing. Here in 1768, the Sioux suffered a significant defeat in their long struggle to regain central Minnesota from the invading Chippewa. A British fur trader wintered at the mouth of the Crow Wing River as early as 1771, and by 1823, the American Fur Company may have established a post under Allan Morrison. During the next two decades, he and others like Benjamin F. ("Blue Beard") Baker, Clement H. Beaulieu, and William A. Aitkin operated trading stations here. With the decline of the fur trade in the 1840s, Crow Wing became an outfitting center, serving the oxcart trains on the "woods" Red River Trail, which crossed the Mississippi here.

The 1850s saw Catholic and Episcopal missions established, and the village became headquarters for the powerful Chippewa chief, Hole-in-the-Day. Crow Wing reached its peak in the 1860s, with a population of nearly 600 and thirty or so buildings including another mission, this one operated by German Lutherans. Rotgut whiskey flowed freely; brawling and robbery were commonplace. In 1868, the Indians were removed to the White Earth Reservation, and in 1871, the Northern Pacific Railroad bypassed Crow Wing, building to Brainerd instead. Within a half dozen years, the old trading settlement had become one of Minnesota's many ghost towns. 1968

### 294.  BRAINERD REGION  △
*Located on state highway 371 at the end of Long Lake, 8 miles northwest of Brainerd*

Toward the close of the Wisconsin stage of glaciation about 12,000 years ago, the waning lobe of the ice sheet in the Brainerd area retreated westward, leaving in its wake many stagnant ice blocks which had become separated from the main ice field. Water flowing from the surface of the receding ice deposited sand and gravel around and over these severed parts of the glacier and formed an outwash plain studded with huge blocks of partly buried, motionless ice.

On melting, the detached blocks—some of which were miles in extent and scores of feet thick—left permanent, water-filled depressions in the gravel plain. The lakes so formed, including those portrayed on this tablet, do not follow the original shape of the ice blocks but are commonly round or elliptical due to subsequent shore line changes.

Erected by the Geological Society of Minnesota and the Department of Highways, State of Minnesota aided by a grant from the Louis W. and Maud Hill Family Foundation. 1954

### 295.  PORTSMOUTH MINE  △

*Located on state highway 6 in a wayside .4 mile north of Crosby*

The Portsmouth was one of many iron and manganese mines that operated along the Cuyuna Range during the period 1911–1978. As much as 60 meters of glacial sediment cover the iron-bearing bedrock in this area; there are few natural rock exposures. Most ore deposits were discovered by magnetic surveys using a dip needle, which resembles a compass set on its side. During the 1890s, Cuyler Adams used this method to map much of the iron-formation. The name "Cuyuna" is derived from his first name, "Cuyler," and the name of his canine assistant, "Una."

At the Portsmouth Mine, about 13 million tons of iron and manganese ore were extracted from the slate, sandstone, and chert bedrock. These rocks were once clay, sand, and chemical precipitates that were deposited in an ocean about two billion years ago. They were subsequently buried deep in the earth where they were metamorphosed by heat and folded in a complex manner. The folding and associated fracturing provided pathways for fluids that precipitated the metal minerals and leached away silica. These processes concentrated the metals and created the high-grade ores, which have as much as 65 percent iron and 20 percent manganese.

The open-pit mining method used at the Portsmouth and other Cuyuna Range mines required the continual removal of water from the working pits, which could be more than 100 meters deep at some locations. When mining ceased, water slowly filled the pits, creating deep lakes with shorelines composed of glacial sediment. As a result, mine workings in the bedrock are no longer visible, and information about the rock is derived from the reports of mining geologists.

The Cuyuna Range remains an important potential source of manganese, and mining may one day resume. The fact that one can barely see that a mine was here is a tribute to the effectiveness of mine-land reclamation practices and the natural growth of vegetation.

Erected by the Geological Society of Minnesota in partnership with the Minnesota Department of Transportation and the Minnesota Geological Survey. 1998

### 296. THE CUYUNA RANGE
*Located in Crosby*

Named for entrepreneur Cuyler Adams and his faithful dog Una, the Cuyuna Range lies at the westernmost edge of a ring of iron ore that circles Lake Superior. The smallest of Minnesota's three northern iron ranges, the Cuyuna was also the last to be opened. By the time ore was shipped from the first Cuyuna mine to Duluth in 1911, Minnesota had already become the leading iron ore producer in the country.

The Cuyuna-Duluth Mine at Ironton in 1911

In many ways, this range differs from Minnesota's other two great ranges. Here the ore quality varies—some is soft like that scooped from the Mesabi's open-pit mines, some is hard like the ore drilled in the Vermilion's underground mines. The Cuyuna Range is also rich in manganese, an ore at first avoided by miners and later valued for steel production. When World War I cut off U.S. imports of manganese, demand for Cuyuna ore soared. In 1918, one of the Cuyuna's peak years, 27 mines produced nearly 2.5 million tons of ore.

Another difference in the Cuyuna's story can be found in its settlement. Many towns, like Brainerd and Aitkin, were well established before the ore was discovered nearby. Other towns like Crosby and Ironton sprang up when mining began. This meant that vast tracts of land were difficult for developers to obtain. So the Cuyuna Range remained in the hands of smaller, independent mining companies, not the large, consolidated mining operations that dominated the other ranges.

Because much of the Cuyuna's ore lay under lakes and bogs, early attempts to mine it had met with failures as shafts filled with water. Indeed the 1924 Milford mine disaster was the worst in Minnesota mining history. But far-sighted businessmen like Adams and George Crosby persisted, turning the Cuyuna Range into an important supplier of iron ore for the steel industry that fueled the nation's growth. Mining on the Cuyuna Range ceased in the 1970s. 1999

# DOUGLAS COUNTY

### 297. KNUTE NELSON HOUSE
*Located at 1219 South Nokomis Street in Alexandria*

Knute Nelson, who was known for his courage and common sense, served the people of Minnesota as a public officeholder for over 50 years. Born in Norway in 1843, he was elected to the Minnesota legislature and to two terms in the United States Congress before becoming the state's first foreign-born governor in 1893. He then served with distinction for 28 years in the United States Senate, where he championed such causes as conservation, a federal income tax, and pure food and drug legislation.

A Civil War veteran, Nelson homesteaded here in Douglas County in 1871 and a year later built a simple L-shaped house. In 1915 a second story and west wing were added to the structure. It remained the Nelson family home until his death in 1923, when it was willed to the American Lutheran Church to be used for services to the aged. 1978

### 298. STAGE STATION
*Located on state highway 27 in Osakis*

Osakis was one of the stops on the Burbank Minnesota Stage Company line to the Red River, established in the spring of 1859 upon the opening of the Fort Abercrombie military road. During the Sioux Outbreak of 1862 the maintenance of this line of communication was vitally important, and the route was constantly patrolled by troops.

### 299. MINNESOTA WATERSHEDS
*Located on I-94 (east bound) in Lake Latoka rest area*

Lying at the center of the North American continent, Minnesota embraces three great watersheds—areas of land from which all surface water eventually flows into a single stream. From Minnesota's watersheds, water runs off in three directions to three different seas:

In the largest of the watersheds, water flows south through the Mississippi River and its tributaries to the Gulf of Mexico.

From northeastern Minnesota and its St. Louis River system, water drains eastward into Lake Superior and moves through the Great Lakes to the Atlantic Ocean.

In northwestern Minnesota, water flows north by way of the Red River of the North and the Rainy River into Canada's Lake Winnipeg and on to Hudson Bay.

These three areas have very different physical features. The St. Louis River watershed is rough, hilly and heavily wooded. Many of its streams have swift currents, abound with waterfalls, and rarely overflow their steep, rocky banks.

The watershed of the Red River of the North lies largely on flat prairie land. Riverbanks are low and currents sluggish. Minnesota's north-flowing streams are particularly prone to spring flooding, when runoff from melting snows and warm rains in the southern part of the watershed reaches northern areas still frozen over or clogged with ice flows.

The Mississippi watershed combines features of the other two. Generally the upper portion is heavily forested, with rolling terrain and swift streams. Farther down, currents slow as streams meander through open prairies, where they may overflow their banks in times of high water.

Since 1909 state and federal agencies have been charged with regulating Minnesota's waters. In addition watershed districts today oversee such activities as water supply, drainage, flood control, and pollution control. Such regulation helps conserve Minnesota's abundant water resources for use and enjoyment today and by future generations. 1997

# LAKE OF THE WOODS COUNTY

### 300.  GREAT FIRE OF 1910
*Located off state highway 72 in a roadside park at the end of the Baudette International Bridge*

Northern Minnesota forests were tinder dry during the fall of 1910. Marshes and streams shriveled. Small fires smoldered here and there in the peat bogs and underbrush.

On October 4 a forest fire consumed the communities of Williams, Cedar Spur, and Graceton. The flames, fed by loggers' slashings, crackled onward and three days later completely destroyed all the buildings in the little town of Pitt except the depot.

The fire approached Baudette and Spooner on the evening of October 7. As the towns rapidly became furnaces of flames, the citizens gathered at the depot for safety. Victims of a typhoid epidemic were evacuated by train before a whirlwind of flame swept away the two towns and the bridge over the Baudette River that connected them.

Before morning almost everything at Baudette was leveled, leaving what one survivor called "a desolate plain" covered by charred ruins. Only the sawmill at Spooner remained standing.

Forty-two persons lost their lives in the great fire of 1910. About 300,000 acres were burned in ten townships, including much valuable timber and many homesteads and livestock. 1966

Rescue workers in Baudette after the fire

## 301. MASSACRE ISLAND
*Located off state highway 72 in a roadside park at the end at the Baudette International Bridge*

Tradition is woven of fact and fiction. Two islands in the Lake of the Woods are named "Massacre," one on the Canadian, one on the American side of the boundary. The Canadian island, the larger of the two, is heavily wooded. The American island is small, rocky and barren. These islands were so named because of the following events.

In 1732, Pierre Galtier de Varennes de la Vérendrye, French-Canadian explorer and trader, built Fort St. Charles at Northwest Angle Inlet on Lake of the Woods. From this base he traded with the Cree and Assiniboine for furs to finance explorations for a passage to the Western Sea.

Early in June, 1736, La Vérendrye sent his son, Jean-Baptiste, with the priest, Father Pierre Aulneau, and nineteen voyageurs eastward for supplies. At their first campsite, a small rocky island "seven leagues" from the Fort, they were attacked and killed by a Sioux war party. The bodies were decapitated and placed in a row. The heads of the voyageurs were wrapped in beaver pelts and left near the bodies. Those of Jean-Baptiste and Father Aulneau may have been carried off as trophies.

Several weeks after the massacre, a party of Chippewa passed a small island and discovered the victims of the massacre. Out of reverence for the priest, and because they could not dig a grave on the rocky island, they raised a stone cairn over his body.

When he learned of the tragedy, the elder La Vérendrye had the remains of the men taken to Fort St. Charles and buried near the chapel. They were found there in 1908 by an archaeological party from St. Boniface College, Manitoba, Canada.

The island where the massacre occurred has never been satisfactorily identified. 1966

### 302. PIERRE GAULTIER DE VARENNES, SIEUR DE LA VÉRENDRYE

*Located in the Northwest Angle on the site of Fort St. Charles on Magnuson's Island, Lake of the Woods, and accessible by boat from Angle Inlet*

Fort St. Charles was established in the summer of 1732 by the Sieur de la Vérendrye, an enterprising Canadian explorer and fur trader, lured into the wilderness by Indian tales of a great "Western Sea." Traveling by way of the Grand Portage and Rainy River to Lake of the Woods, La Vérendrye made his headquarters at this spot and from it built a chain of five or six other posts in the vicinity of Lake Winnipeg. In 1738–39 he made an expedition to the Missouri River in western North Dakota, and in 1742–43 two of his sons traveled over the plains to the south and west, probably as far as the Big Horn Mountains in Wyoming. On another expedition, the youngest son, Louis-Joseph, also penetrated to the northwest as far as the forks of the Saskatchewan River.

La Vérendrye was plagued by misfortune, menaced by the hostile Sioux tribe, and frowned upon by French authorities for his failure to reach the Western Sea. Nevertheless, his seventeen-year effort pushed French influence far onto the northern plains and established the fur trade northwest of Lake Superior.

Erected by the Minnesota Historical Society and the Minnesota Fourth Degree Knights of Columbus. 1968

# MILLE LACS COUNTY

### 303. IZATYS

*Located on U.S. highway 169 at Vineland on the south shore of Mille Lacs Lake in Mille Lacs-Kathio State Park*

In this vicinity stood the great Sioux village of "Izatys" where Duluth planted the French arms on July 2, 1679. The settlement was visited by Father Hennepin in 1680.

About 1750 the Chippewa, moving westward from
Lake Superior, captured the village, and by this decisive
battle drove the Sioux permanently into southern
Minnesota. 1940

### 304.   BATTLE OF KATHIO  Ⓜ
*Minnesota Historical Society Historic Site*
*Located on U.S. highway 169 in front of Mille Lacs Lake*
*Indian Museum on southwest shore of Mille Lacs Lake,*
*12 miles north of Onamia*

This museum is located on the site where the first day's
fighting occurred in a decisive three-day battle between
Chippewa and Sioux Indians about 1750. A large war
party of Chippewa, armed with guns, marched from
Lake Superior and made an early morning raid on the
Sioux village near the base of Cormorant Point. Fighting with bows and arrows that were no match for the
invaders' firearms, the surprised Sioux made a brave defense but were overwhelmed. A few escaped southward
to the main Kathio village along the outlet (Rum River)
of Mille Lacs. There, on the second day, the Chippewa
again wiped out most of the Sioux, who tried to take
refuge in their semi-permanent lodges. Gunpowder,
dropped by the Chippewa through smoke holes at the
top, exploded in lodge fires and killed most of the Sioux
occupants. A remnant of the Sioux escaped after dark
to a third village on Aquipaquetin Island at the north
end of Lake Onamia. They made a last stand there on
the third day, then fled by canoe down the Rum River.
The Battle of Kathio drove the Sioux forever from their
ancient Mille Lacs villages southwestward to the prairies
and ensured the Chippewa a permanent home in northern Minnesota's forest and lake country. 1962

### 305.   KATHIO SITE
*Located on U.S. highway 169 in front of Mille Lacs Indian*
*Museum on southwest shore of Mille Lacs Lake*

Kathio Site has been designated a Registered National Historic Landmark under the provisions of the Historic Sites Act of August 21, 1935. This site possesses exceptional value in commemorating and illustrating the history of the United States.

U.S. Department of the Interior, National Park Service. 1964

### 306. GEOLOGY OF THE LAKE MILLE LACS REGION △

*Located on state highway 47 at a scenic overlook 2 miles north of Isle on the eastern shore of Lake Mille Lacs*

Almost all the lakes in Minnesota were formed by glacial action. Many small lakes formed after the glaciers receded and blocks of ice buried in the sediment melted, leaving holes, called kettles, that filled with water. Other lakes occupy basins that were scraped out of solid rock by glacial ice. Lake Superior is a prominent example of a lake bottom scoured by glacial ice. Lake Mille Lacs, by contrast, is not really in a basin. It is surrounded on the north, west, and south sides by a moraine—a ridge of sediment (silt, sand, gravel, and boulders) left along the edge of a glacier. With the land on the eastern shore also being of higher elevation, the moraine effectively dams the drainage to the south to form one of the largest lakes in the state.

The Mille Lacs moraine was formed about 15,000 years ago near the end of the last, or Wisconsin, glaciation, by a tongue-shaped lobe of ice called the Superior lobe, which flowed into the area from the northeast. This ice carried sediment derived from rock along the Superior basin and the North Shore, which was later deposited beneath the ice and at its margin. At its maximum, the Superior lobe extended beyond Minneapolis to the south and St. Cloud to the west. Its decline was punctuated by several minor readvances, such as the one that deposited the Mille Lacs moraine.

About 12,000 years ago, another lobe of ice advanced from the northwest and overrode the northern part of the Mille Lacs moraine, sending its meltwater into Lake Mille Lacs. Once this influx of meltwater ended, precipitation and small streams maintained the water level in Lake Mille Lacs, much as they do today.

Erected by the Geological Society of Minnesota in partnership with the Minnesota Department of Transportation and the Minnesota Geological Survey. 1998

### 307.  GLACIAL CROSSROADS BECOMES A LAKE  △
*Located on state highway 27 in Father Hennepin State Park, 2 miles west of Isle*

About 20,000 years ago, during the peak of the last glacial period, a glacier called the Rainy lobe advanced from the Ontario region through what is now the Boundary Waters Canoe Area and covered most of the Lake Mille Lacs region. As it moved, the Rainy lobe picked up, crushed, and deposited fragments of the underlying bedrock. As the glacier receded, streams of meltwater carried sand and gravel from the ice and dropped it in front of the glacier, a deposit called an outwash.

About 15,000 years ago, another glacier, called the Superior lobe, advanced from the Ontario region through the Lake Superior basin and into the area of central Minnesota. It crossed over the outwash that the Rainy lobe had deposited, and pushed up the sand and gravel into a formation of big elongated hills, called a moraine. When the Superior lobe finally receded, it left a layer of reddish sediment over this moraine and buried some stranded blocks of stagnant ice. The reddish color comes from iron oxide in the sediment that the glacier eroded from bedrock in the Lake Superior basin.

The enlarged moraine acted as a natural dam, blocking rivers and streams from draining glacial meltwater to the southwest as before. As a result, the meltwater from the receding ice collected behind the moraine and formed the early Lake Mille Lacs. Water from this growing glacial lake spilled over the moraine into the Rum

River through an outlet about five meters higher than the present outlet. The original outlet ceased to flow when ice blocks, buried in the moraine, melted enough to open a lower outlet, and the lake level dropped. The lower outlet, which also found drainage via the Rum River, is the one flowing today.

Erected by the Geological Society of Minnesota in partnership with the Minnesota Department of Transportation, the Minnesota Geological Survey, and the Minnesota Department of Natural Resources. 2003

# MORRISON COUNTY

### 308.  THE RIPLEY ESKER ⛰

*Located 7 miles north of Little Falls on state highway 371, then .7 mile east on county road 48, then 1 mile north on county road 282*

An esker is a landform built of sand and gravel deposited by a meltwater stream that flowed beneath a glacier. The Ripley esker is a classic esker; it stands 3 to 18 meters above the surrounding plain, and is about 68 to 76 meters wide. Although the Ripley esker is broken into several segments, it has an overall length of about 11 kilometers.

The narrow, sinuous, steep-sided ridge of sand and gravel that forms the esker is flanked on both sides by a row of small lakes and depressions. A vigorous subglacial stream eroded a channel bed initially wide enough to contain those flanking depressions. The ice that surrounded the stream was under pressure from the glacier's weight. When the stream's flow diminished, the ice squeezed inward to form a narrower tunnel. The smaller, slower stream in the smaller ice tunnel could not carry as much sediment, and it began to deposit it on the streambed. As the sediments accumulated, they raised the level of the streambed and along with it the stream, which continually melted the ice above it and kept an

open passage. This narrow, raised streambed grew to a
height that became the ridge one sees today above the
surrounding plain. The esker slopes down from the
ridge along its length because the sediment slumped
after the glacier melted away.

The Ripley esker was formed beneath a tongue-
shaped lobe of ice called the Superior lobe, which flowed
into this area from the northeast about 20,000 to 15,000
years ago. The esker was deposited as the Superior lobe
receded. The sands and gravels of the esker were derived
from the Lake Superior basin and include reddish volcanic and sedimentary rocks as well as Lake Superior
agate. The pile of glacial sediment (silt, sand, gravel,
and boulders) left at the edge of the Superior lobe at the
point of its furthest advance is the St. Croix moraine. It
is the broad swath of high hills that lies to the west of
the esker.

From this point the best views of the esker are in
the spring and fall, when the trees have no leaves and
the prairie grasses are the dominant feature on the top
of the esker.

Erected by the Geological Society of Minnesota in
partnership with the Minnesota Department of Transportation, the Minnesota Geological Survey, and the
Minnesota Department of Natural Resources. 1998

### 309.  LINDBERGH HOUSE 🄼

*Minnesota Historical Society Historic Site*
*Located at 1620 Lindbergh Drive in Lindbergh State Park,*
*about two miles south of Little Falls*

"I never deserted the farm as the ultimate goal of
my return—and there is my home when I am home,
for the farm unquestionably is the best of all places to
live, and it affords the most independence." Thus wrote
Congressman Charles A. Lindbergh, Sr., about his home
here on the bank of the Mississippi River.

C. A. Lindbergh was born in Sweden in 1859. One
year later, his father, August Lindbergh, a former mem-

ber of the Swedish Parliament, brought his wife and infant son to a farm near Melrose, Minnesota, where C. A. grew up. He came to Little Falls as a young lawyer, became a prominent member of the community, and served five terms as a United States Congressman from 1907 until 1917.

Charles A. Lindbergh, Jr., who became world famous in 1927 when he flew nonstop and alone from New York to Paris in the *Spirit of St. Louis,* spent his boyhood summers here in this house built by his father in 1907. In the years following his landmark achievement in aviation he had an active career in exploration, scientific research, writing, and conservation.

In 1931, the Lindbergh family gave this house and 110 acres of land to the state of Minnesota as a memorial to Charles A. Lindbergh, Sr. 1985

Charles Lindbergh and the *Spirit of St. Louis* in 1927

## 310. GREENE PRAIRIE
*Located on the grounds of Camp Ripley*

The township of Greene Prairie was so named to perpetuate in glorious remembrance Charles H. Greene, Corporal, I Company, Third Minnesota Volunteer Infantry Regiment who with twenty men, several convalescents and a few cooks and teamsters in the evening of July 13th, 1862 resisted two successive charges by Kentuckians and three companies of Georgia troops. It was not until the Confederate General Forest had appealed to the manhood of his superior forces and personally led a third charge that the handful of courageous Minnesota troops were overcome. In this, the Battle of Murfreesboro, Tennessee, Corporal Greene gave up his life for his country.

# OTTER TAIL COUNTY

### 311.   LEAF CITY
*Located on state highway 108, 5 miles east of Ottertail*

Trading post on the Red River trail in 1857, and U.S. Post Office from 1857 to 1860. The settlement was broken up by the Sioux Outbreak of 1862. Dedicated by Otter Tail County Historical Society, June 26, 1938.

### 312.   CRAIGIE FLOUR MILL
*Located on state highway 78 on the southeast shore of Otter Tail Lake*

Near this spot James Craigie of Aberdeen, Scotland, who came to Ottertail County about 1868, built the first grist mill in the county in 1870. The mill stones and wheel were imported from Scotland. Craigie and his wife were drowned in Ottertail Lake in 1872, and after long litigation the mill was torn down.

### 313.   OTTER TAIL CITY
*Located at the junction of state highways 78 and 108, 3 miles south of Ottertail*

Otter Tail City in the 1850's was an important post on the fur trade route from St. Paul and Crow Wing to the Red River Valley. It was once the county seat, and had the U.S. land office for the district. When the county seat was established at Fergus Falls in 1872 the city was abandoned. 1950

### 314.  OLD CLITHERALL

*Follow state highway 210 for 1 mile west of Clitherall and .5 mile south from this point. It is also known as Old Town.*

Founded in 1865 by the Church of Jesus Christ, a separate society, from Manti, Iowa. The church was also known as "Cutlerites."

The first permanent settlement in the county, it was named after George B. Clitherall, U.S. land officer. The community prospered till the coming of the railroad in 1881, when the present town of Clitherall was built. It is still headquarters of the church. 1940

### 315.  MINNESOTA WOMAN

*Located on U.S. highway 59, 4 miles north of Pelican Rapids*

Minnesota woman—the skeleton of a girl about fifteen years of age—was discovered at this point in 1931 by a highway repair crew. Although the skeleton has not been dated exactly, based on the site geology scientists believe it to be perhaps 10,000 years old. This would make Minnesota Woman America's oldest human skeleton.

Two artifacts—a dagger of elk horn and a conch shell—were discovered with the bones. Archaeologists believe that the girl drowned in Glacial Lake Pelican, which adjoined Glacial Lake Agassiz, a huge body of water that covered much of northwestern Minnesota during the last ice age. 1992

### 316.  STEAMBOATS ON THE RED RIVER

*Located on I-94 (west bound) in Lake Hansel rest area*

[Front] The Red River, which today marks the northwest boundary of Minnesota, flows north to Lake Winnipeg in such a series of tight, shallow curves that it was considered by early travelers unsuitable for navigation by water craft much larger than canoes. However, from 1859 to 1879 it was traversed yearly by as many as seventeen large steamboats and numerous barges carrying passengers and freight from Minnesota to the Hudson's Bay Company settlement at Fort Garry, north of present day Winnipeg.

In 1859, thirty teams of horses and oxen hauled the boiler for the first steamboat overland from St. Paul. It was built by, and named after, Anson Northup with $2,000 contributed by St. Paul businessmen planning to expand trade with Canada. Red River trade grew rapidly after 1870 with political stability in Manitoba and the extension of the Northern Pacific Railroad to Moorhead, Minnesota. Freight rose from 500 tons carried annually by the "Anson Northup" for the Hudson's Bay Company, to over 38,000 tons carried by many steamboats in 1875.

The steamboats facilitated their decline by hauling material to construct railroads for the rapidly expanding

The steamboat *Selkirk* on the Red River, about 1872

farm population of the Red River Valley. In 1877, the "Selkirk" transported the first locomotive to operate in Manitoba. In 1878, the Red River Transportation Company, which dominated river traffic, sold two steamers to operate around Winnipeg, and stock of the company contributed to the takeover of the St. Paul and Pacific Railroad by transportation entrepreneur James J. Hill and his associates. That railroad was completed to St. Vincent, Minnesota in December 1878, where it linked with a branch line of the Canadian Pacific Railroad. The following spring faster, year round railroad service began which brought more settlers to the region and drew passengers and freight away from the steamboats.

**Climax of Steamboat Traffic on the Red River**
[Back] The climax in river traffic came in the early 1870s with political stability in the new province of Manitoba and the extension of the Northern Pacific Railroad from Duluth to Moorhead, Minnesota. The creation of the Red River Transportation Company by joining the interests of the Hudson's Bay Company with those of St. Paul entrepreneurs James J. Hill and Norman Kittson, dominated steamboat traffic on the river. The company dominated steamboat traffic on the river eventually operating six steamboats and many barges to Winnipeg, which was incorporated as a city in 1873. Freight rose from the 500 tons carried annually by the "Anson Northup" for the Hudson's Bay Company, to over 38,000 tons carried between Moorhead to Winnipeg in 1875.

After 1875, the steamboats facilitated their own demise by hauling material for the construction of railroads to serve the rapidly expanding wheat farms in the Red River Valley. In 1877, the steamboat "Selkirk" transported to St. Boniface the "Countess of Dufferin," the first locomotive to operate in Manitoba. The next year, Hill and Kittson, seeing the future of transportation moving from river to rail, sold two Red River Transportation Company steamers to a firm that operated on the lakes and rivers around Winnipeg. Stock in the company was used to take control of the St. Paul and Pacific Railroad. In December 1878, the St. Paul and Pacific was completed along the east side of the river to St. Vincent, Minnesota where it linked with a branch line of the Canadian Pacific Railroad constructed south from Winnipeg to Emerson, Manitoba. The following spring faster, year round railroad service began which brought more settlers to the region and took passengers and freight away from the steamboats. 1996

### 317.  MINNESOTA: THE LAND OF TEN THOUSAND LAKES
*Located on I-94 (east bound) in Lake Iverson rest area*

Tourists have come to Minnesota since the mid 1830s to enjoy the climate, the diverse scenery, fishing and other sporting activities. Prior to the Civil War, easterners and southerners took "the fashionable tour," a steamboat excursion on the Upper Mississippi River to St. Anthony Falls and Fort Snelling. Following the war, newly constructed railroads encouraged people in the East and South to travel to "cool Minnesota," and Lake Minnetonka thrived as "the Queen of Minnesota's resorts" in the 1880s.

In the late 1800s, fishing attracted sportsmen to northern Minnesota. In many instances, homesteaders provided lodging for guests, and the region's resort industry was born.

It was the automobile, however, that triggered Minnesota's rapid development as a vacation playground. The automobile opened the north woods to recreational development and popularized travel among the middle class. Recreational development flourished in the 1920s. During that decade the number of resorts increased five-fold to nearly 1,300. At the same time communities across the state established public tourist camps to meet the needs of auto-campers, and Twin Cities real estate firms led the effort to develop affordable cabin sites in many of the state's most accessible lakes.

Canoeing on Lake Insula in Superior National Forest, about 1920

Numerous state and local organizations were established to promote Minnesota's recreational resources. The most important, The Ten Thousand Lakes of Minnesota Association, created in 1917, undertook a nationwide marketing campaign to lure vacationers to "The Land of Ten Thousand Lakes." Their efforts were so successful that by the 1930s tourism had become a mainstay of the state's economy. 1996

### 318. GEOLOGY OF INSPIRATION PEAK △

*Located off county road 38 in Inspiration Peak*
*State Wayside*

At an elevation of 524 meters, Inspiration Peak stands high above the Leaf Hills portion of the Alexandria glacial moraine, affording a spectacular view of the surrounding area. The Alexandria moraine is an area of high hills that extends in a broad arc from western Becker County southeast to southern Stearns County in central Minnesota. The moraine consists of sediment (clay, silt, sand, gravel, and boulders) that was transported and deposited by glacial ice. About 25,000 years ago, glacial ice, which advanced into this area from the northeast, pushed up ice and existing sediment at its southwestern edge, forming the hills of the Alexandria moraine.

About 14,000 years ago, another lobe of ice, the Des Moines lobe, flowed southward from the Manitoba region. This ice lobe followed the lowlands of the Red River valley and the Minnesota River valley, finally reaching south into central Iowa near Des Moines. Occasionally, this lobe grew wide enough to advance eastward over parts of the Alexandria moraine. Locally, the Des Moines lobe reached as far east as Parkers Prairie, which is 18 kilometers east of here. The advancing Des Moines lobe reshaped the Leaf Hills by eroding the Alexandria moraine and redepositing the sediment. When the glacial ice receded, distinct topographic features, such as Inspiration Peak, were left behind.

Erected by the Geological Society of Minnesota in partnership with the Minnesota Department of Transportation, the Minnesota Geological Survey, and the Minnesota Department of Natural Resources. 2003

### 319.  INSPIRATION PEAK
*Located off county road 38 in Inspiration Peak State Wayside*

For Minnesota's Nobel Prize-winning novelist Sinclair Lewis, Inspiration Peak more than lived up to its name. From its "bald top," he wrote, "there is to be seen a glorious 20-mile circle of some 50 lakes scattered among fields and pastures, like sequins fallen on an old Paisley shawl." Praising "the enchanting peace and seclusion of this place for contemplation," Lewis at the same time chided Minnesotans for not knowing about their own "haunts of beauty," and added that he might write the governor, "asking His Excellency if he has ever stood on Inspiration Peak."

The highest point is the Leaf Hills portion of the Alexandria glacial moraine. Inspiration Peak rises some 400 feet above Spitzer Lake. Although off the beaten track and not mentioned in early exploration literature, it has recently been promoted as a northwestern Minnesota landmark, celebrated primarily for its views of the bright rolling country around it. 1989

# POLK COUNTY

### 320. ORIGINAL SITE OF FISHER'S LANDING
*Located on U.S. highway 2 near Fisher*

In the American centennial year of 1876, a settlement called Fisher's Landing on the east bank of the Red Lake River just north of this point was a flourishing community. Trains of the St. Paul & Pacific Railway exchanged passengers and freight at the Fisher's Landing railhead with steamboats plying the Red Lake and Red rivers to and from Winnipeg. Travelers and settlers alike were served by four hotels, a Hudson's Bay Company store, a general store, four saloons, and several gambling tents.

After the extension of the railroad to Grand Forks, Fisher's Landing was moved to higher ground because of annual flooding. The present townsite was platted in 1879, and the town's name was later changed to Fisher.

Erected by the Polk County Historical Society. 1983

### 321. GLACIAL LAKE AGASSIZ
*Located on U.S. highway 2 at tourist information center near Fisher*

As the Wisconsin Glacier slowly began to melt some 12,000 years ago, it created Glacial Lake Agassiz, the largest known glacial lake in North America. At its maximum the lake covered an area of over 110,000 square miles—more than the area of the combined

Great Lakes—spread over parts of areas known today as Minnesota, North and South Dakota, Manitoba, Saskatchewan, and Ontario. Over 400 feet deep in places it extended over 700 miles from its southern tip near Browns Valley to its northern tip near Hudson Bay.

While the glacier moved south during its advance, it built up a moraine on its southern end which ponded the melt waters when the ice began its retreat. Eventually the water overflowed, cutting an outlet which created the present Minnesota River valley. Over approximately 3,000 years, as the glacier continued to melt, numerous beaches were created along the lake's shores. Still visible today, these beaches are named after towns such as Herman, Tintah, Norcross, and Campbell.

About 7,500 years ago, when the glacier had receded far enough north that the melt waters began to drain into Hudson Bay, Glacial Lake Agassiz disappeared. A few undrained depressions—Upper and Lower Red Lake, Lake of the Woods, and Lake Winnipeg—remain today to remind us of the site of the glacial lake. The area it covered in northwestern Minnesota is almost flat and lakeless, and the rich land produces bountiful yields of wheat, sugar beets, potatoes, sunflowers, and other crops. Thanks to Glacial Lake Agassiz, the region is sometimes called "the breadbasket of the world." 1989

# POPE COUNTY

### 322. GLENWOOD REGION ⚠

*Located on state highway 28 overlooking Lake Minnewaska near Glenwood*

The view from this point reveals the effects of major glaciation in its most vigorous form. Some 10,000 years ago, the last glacier, as it receded slowly to the north and west, paused here long enough to deposit, in characteristic fashion, the rock material in the recessional moraine that forms the hills around Lake Minnewaska.

The basin of the lake is chiefly within the moraine itself, but on this, the northeastern side, it is bounded by an extensive outwash plain.

The part of the glacier that filled the lake basin became detached from the main body of ice and remained stagnant for many years. During this time it was partially or completely buried by outwash sand and gravel carried toward the northeast by meltwater from the main ice field. As a consequence, this portion of the basin had a steep ice-contact slope, formed while the ice block supported the loose material.

Lake Minnewaska, lying 230 feet below this elevation, is a typical example of a lake in an ice-block basin.

Erected by the Geological Society of Minnesota and the Department of Highways, State of Minnesota aided by a grant from the Louis W. and Maud Hill Family Foundation. 1955

### 323. FORT LAKE JOHANNA AND IVERSON CABIN
*Located on state highway 104 in a wayside 3 miles east of Terrace*

Pope County settlement history began in the spring of 1862 when four Norwegian emigrant families took homesteads near Lake Johanna. During the August–September 1862 Dakota incident those settlers evacuated to the Paynesville–St. Cloud area. This park was founded on a small portion of the homestead of one of those four settlers.

Resettlement of the area and a renewed threat of hostilities in 1865 resulted in Company C of the 2nd Reg. Minnesota Cavalry being ordered to build Fort Lake Johanna in this vicinity. Fort Lake Johanna was one of a series of defensive posts which formed a line from Fort Abercrombie, on the Dakota border, to the Iowa border near Fairmont. Intended as a defense against the threat of Indian attacks, these crude log fortifications were never to see action. After several months, the fear of hostilities ended, and the fort was abandoned. Area settlers reused the fort's logs to build homes and other farm buildings. A marker has been erected at the Fort Lake Johanna site on the highest ridge of hills northeast of this park.

Less than half a mile northwest of this park, and just south of the West Lake Johanna Church, stands the Iverson Cabin. Urjans Iverson built his home with oak logs taken from the fort in 1866. Over the years, that building served as a school, church, and farm blacksmith shop. Having deteriorated, the cabin was restored in 1991 by local residents, assisted by the Minnesota Historical Society. The restoration included the replacement of some of the logs with logs salvaged from another home that had been built with logs from the fort. Restored as a church, the cabin is open for public viewing and is used on special occasions during the summer.

Erected by Fort Lake Johanna Historic Park Association. Plaque donated by Terrace Sportsmens Club. 1999

# RED LAKE COUNTY

### 324. OLD CROSSING MEMORIAL PARK
*Located off county road 11 in Old Crossing Treaty State Wayside, 8 miles west of Red Lake Falls*

Within the area comprising this park, in the fall of 1863, negotiations were conducted with the Pembina and Red Lake bands of Chippewa Indians by which they ceded to the United States about three million acres of land in northwestern Minnesota and northeastern Dakota. This cession made possible the settlement of the Red River Valley. Here stood the great cottonwood tree which served the early settlers as a post office and here also the ox-cart trains which carried furs and supplies between St. Paul and Pembina, by way of St. Cloud or Crow Wing, forded the Red Lake River.

The monument, representing a Chippewa Indian with the pipe of peace, by the sculptor Carl C. Mose, was erected by the United States under the terms of a bill introduced by Congressman Conrad G. Selvig of Crookston.

The land in this park was donated to the state of Minnesota in 1931 by action of the board of county commissioners of Red Lake County, Sam E. Hunt, Frank P. Grenier, Nels L. Roseen, E. E. Hill and Ole O. Lee.

The site was improved under direction of a committee consisting of H. M. Higinbotham, John Sangstad and Thomas M. McCall.

# ROSEAU COUNTY

### 325. WARROAD FUR POST
*Located on state highway 11 at the west end of the bridge in Warroad*

One mile east of this point, just north of the mouth of Warroad River, stood a post of the American Fur Company, built about 1820.

The French explorer, La Verendrye, and his party probably visited this region in 1732 en route to build Fort St. Charles in the present Northwest Angle. 1932

### 326. FORT ST. CHARLES
*Located at the end of Lake Street in Warroad*

Pierre Gaultier de Varennes, Sieur de la Vérendrye, established Fort St. Charles on Lake of the Woods in 1732. A daring soldier, fur trader, and explorer, La Vérendrye had the ambitious dream of the fabled "Western Sea" and sought to establish French outposts along the way. On Magnusons Island (then connected with the mainland) he built a palisaded fort which he named in honor of Charles de Beauharnois, governor of New France.

Fort St. Charles became the western capital of the French empire in the Northwest. From it expeditions were launched and supplies dispatched to newer posts around Lake Winnipeg. Indians brought furs to trade for white men's goods, and these pelts were sent by canoe to Montreal. The scarcity of food and Indian warfare made life precarious. In 1736 La Vérendrye's oldest son, Jean-Baptiste, nineteen voyageurs, and Father Jean-Pierre Aulneau, a Jesuit priest, were sent on an expedition to the east for supplies. They were massacred by a Sioux war party on a nearby island.

Abandoned after 1760, the fort was rediscovered and marked by a group of Jesuit fathers in 1908. The site was acquired and the buildings reconstructed by the Minnesota 4th Degree Knights of Columbus some forty years later.

Erected by the Minnesota Historical Society and the Warroad Chamber of Commerce. 1968

Restored Fort St. Charles on Magnuson's Island, about 1959

## 327. WARROAD

*Located at Lake Street and First Avenue in Warroad*

The name Warroad bespeaks the Indian heritage of this town, once one of the largest Chippewa villages on Lake of the Woods. The Chippewa fought a long and fierce war against the Sioux for the lake's rice fields. Occupying the prairies of the Red River Valley, the Sioux would frequently invade the territory by way of the Red and

Roseau rivers—a route which ended at the mouth of the Warroad River. This was the old "war road" from which the river and village derive their name.

Erected by the Minnesota Historical Society and the Warroad Chamber of Commerce. 1968

# SHERBURNE COUNTY

### 328.  GEOLOGY OF THE ELK RIVER REGION  △
*Located off U.S. highway 10 just north of its junction with U.S. highway 169 in a wayside park on the Mississippi River*

Minnesota was largely covered by glaciers many times during the last million years. The ice flowed across the state from both the northeast and the northwest. As it advanced along separate paths, it scraped up, crushed, and carried with it thousands of cubic kilometers of rock debris, called glacial drift. This was deposited in a thick layer over much of the state.

About 25,000 years ago, a tongue-shaped lobe of ice called the Superior lobe advanced across Minnesota from the northeast. This ice eroded the mostly igneous bedrock in Ontario and the Lake Superior region and deposited a reddish, sandy, and rocky drift. Soils that developed from this drift are not the most fertile.

More recently, about 16,000 years ago, another lobe of ice advanced across Minnesota from the northwest. This was named the Des Moines lobe because its point of furthest advance was Des Moines, Iowa. Drift deposited by this ice contains crushed pieces of sedimentary marine shales and limestones eroded from the Winnipeg Lowland in southern Manitoba. Soils developed from this drift are typically gray to brown, full of clay, and rich in lime, magnesia, and potash. These soils are quite fertile and good for agriculture.

In the Elk River region, deposits from both the northeast and the northwest occur in close proximity.

Most of the quite fertile material at the surface was deposited by an eastern offshoot of the Des Moines lobe called the Grantsburg sublobe. The older Superior lobe deposits are close to the surface, however, and may be mixed with those above. Thus, the fertility of the soils in the Elk River region will vary depending on the proportionate mix of the two parent drifts.

River terrace deposits of sand and gravel are also common near Elk River. The Mississippi River established its present course during the final decline of the glaciers. Water from the melting ice followed a number of different routes until finally cutting the valley in which the river now flows. Sandy terraces mark former river courses.

Erected by the Geological Society of Minnesota in partnership with the Minnesota Department of Transportation and the Minnesota Geological Survey. 1998

### 329. GRANGE SHRINE—OLIVER HUDSON KELLEY HOME
*Located on U.S. highway 10, 2.5 miles east of Elk River*

The National Grange of the Order of Patrons of Husbandry was founded in Washington, D.C., on December 4, 1867. This date marks the birth of organized agriculture on American soil. Oliver Hudson Kelley first advanced the idea of a farm fraternity. As first secretary and one of the founders of the National Grange, he maintained official headquarters here until 1870. This farm has been purchased by contributions throughout the nation and is preserved in honor of our founders. [National Grange, 1938]

### 330. KELLEY FARM
*Located on U.S. highway 10, 2.5 miles east of Elk River*

This gateway erected in memory of Frank and Hildur Archer, devoted Grange members, who gave unstintingly of time and talent to the Kelley homestead. 1980

### 331.  OLIVER H. KELLEY HOMESTEAD  Ⓜ

*Minnesota Historical Society Historic Site*
*Located off U.S. highway 10, 2.5 miles east of Elk River*
*at the Kelley Farm Interpretive Center*

Oliver H. Kelley Homestead has been designated a Registered National Historic Landmark under the provisions of the Historic Sites Act of August 21, 1935. This site possesses exceptional value in commemorating and illustrating the history of the United States.

U.S. Department of the Interior, National Park Service. 1964

### 332.  LUCY EARLE KELLEY

*Located off U.S. highway 10, 2.5 miles east of Elk River at the Kelley Farm Interpretive Center*

In memory of Lucy Earle Kelley, 1st wife of Oliver Hudson Kelley, buried on the homestead, L.E.K. 1833–1851, L.W.K. 1851–6 mo., placed by Mountain County Pomona Grange No. 4 Connecticut. 1959

### 333.  BABCOCK MEMORIAL

*Located off U.S. highway 10 at the Sherburne County Courthouse in Elk River*

Erected on the homesite of Charles M. Babcock by the people of Minnesota in grateful appreciation of his lofty concept of duty and distinguished service for the common good. Member State Highway Commission 1910–1917, Commissioner of Highways 1917–1932. His vision, ability, and untiring efforts made the Minnesota Trunk Highway system a reality. 1947

### 334.  FIRST GRANITE QUARRY

*Located on U.S. highway 10, about 2 miles southeast of St. Cloud across from the entrance to the Minnesota Correctional Facility (St. Cloud Reformatory)*

In the spring of 1868 the firm of Breen & Young opened the first commercial granite quarry in Minnesota on the site of what is now the St. Cloud Reformatory. Their first order was for stone for the corners, steps, and trimmings of the U.S. Custom House and Post Office in St. Paul.

Nearly as old as the earth itself, granite is one of the strongest, most durable stones on the planet. In Minnesota substantial outcroppings of granite lie along the Minnesota River valley near Ortonville and Redwood Falls. It is also found in the St. Cloud area of eastern Stearns County and adjacent parts of Benton and Sherburne counties.

In the mid-1800s most of the commercial granite in the U.S. came from New Hampshire and other rocky areas of the East. The market for granite was relatively small in the sparsely settled Midwest, and transportation costs made it difficult for Minnesota companies to compete for work in faraway eastern cities. Many quarries failed, but others survived as new uses for granite were developed. Prosperity came to the St. Cloud-area quarries in the 1890s when monument work began to replace paving, bridge, and foundation blocks as their principal product.

The "busy, gritty, granite city," as St. Cloud came to call itself, continues to be a major supplier of granite. Prized now more for its beauty than its strength, granite quarried near here graces such state landmarks as the Capitol and the History Center in St. Paul. 1994

# STEARNS COUNTY

### 335. ST. JOSEPH BLOCKHOUSE
*Located 1 block south of county road 75 at Second Avenue N.W. and Birch Street N.W. in St. Joseph*

At this point the citizens erected one of three pentagonal blockhouses of green timber, with sides 50 feet long, in August 1862, during the Sioux Outbreak.

A second blockhouse stood near the present grounds of St. Benedict's College. These forts effectively protected this important town on the Red River trail against Indian threats. 1940

### 336.  ST. JOHN'S ABBEY AND UNIVERSITY
*Located off I-94 at St. John's University in Collegeville*

St. John's Abbey was founded in 1856 on the west bank of the Mississippi River near St. Cloud and permanently located in the Indianbush, now Collegeville, on the shore of Lake Sagatagan in 1866. St. John's was the first Benedictine abbey in the Upper Midwest, and from the beginning its monks were educators, ministers of the word, and artisans. Their first ministry was among the settlers and Indians throughout Minnesota and North Dakota during the frontier era. Subsequently abbeys and priories were founded in Washington, Saskatchewan, Kentucky, the Bahamas, Mexico, Puerto Rico, and Japan.

St. John's University was chartered by the territorial legislature of Minnesota on March 6, 1857. The campus is also the site of St. John's Preparatory School, the Institute for Ecumenical and Cultural Research, the Liturgical Press, and the Monastic Manuscript Microfilm Library. Several campus buildings, including the renowned Abbey Church, were designed by architect Marcel Breuer. 1974

St. John's Abbey, Collegeville, about 1900

## 337.  THE BENEDICTINES IN MINNESOTA

*Located on I-94 (east bound) in Big Spunk Lake rest area*

Between 1854 and 1857 many Catholics came to the United States from Germany and settled in central Minnesota at Saint Cloud and in the Sauk Valley; their religious and educational needs were met by the Benedictines. The Benedictine Order and Rule were established at Monte Cassino, Italy, in 529, and spread far beyond. In the 1840s Boniface Wimmer, a monk at the Abbey of Metten in Bavaria, promoted mission work in the United States, established a monastery in Pennsylvania where he became the first American Benedictine abbot, and subsequently became an important figure in the creation of Saint John's Abbey and University. In the 1850s Benedicta Riepp, a nun from Saint Walburg Abbey in Eichstatt, Bavaria, spearheaded the movement of Benedictine sisters from Saint Marys, Pennsylvania, to central Minnesota where they founded Saint Benedict's Monastery and eventually, the College of St. Benedict. Both the Benedictine monks and the nuns of the Order of Saint Benedict, originally from Bavaria, arrived in the Saint Cloud area from Pennsylvania in the 1850s. By the mid-1860s they had moved to their present locations, the nuns to Saint Joseph and the monks to Collegeville. These institutions have preserved excellent late 19th and early 20th century buildings which possess historic integrity and importance. Saint John's also preserves several buildings designed by internationally known architect Marcel Breuer, including the famous church.

The Benedictines of Minnesota have established high reputations through their many services to humanity for nearly a century and a half. They created important academies, schools of higher education, hospitals, orphanages, homes for the aged, and missions which extend beyond Minnesota to distant parts of the country and world. In addition, they are pioneers in establishing public radio, the liturgical and ecumenical movements, pastoral work, educational publishing, arts and crafts, and the development of a world-renowned library. 1998

**338. CHARLES LINDBERGH'S MINNESOTA ROOTS**
*Located on I-94 (west bound) in Middle Spunk Lake rest area*

When Charles Lindbergh landed his airplane on May 21, 1927, after becoming the first person to fly solo and non-stop from New York to Paris, he instantly became a national hero. His background and boyhood in Minnesota prepared him for this role. His paternal grandfather, Ola Mansson, had been a member of the Swedish National Parliament and a close friend of King Charles XV prior to his emigration to the U.S. in 1859, when he changed his name to August Lindbergh. He began farming near Melrose, located in central Minnesota, but continued to be very active in civic affairs. His son, Charles August (C.A.), followed his father's model. He also bought a farm, served in Congress, and was a candidate for governor of Minnesota and the U.S. Senate. In 1902, a son, Charles, was born to C.A. and Elizabeth Lodge Land Lindbergh. While C.A. represented Minnesota in Congress from 1907 to 1917, the family spent winters in Washington and summers on the farm near Little Falls.

Following his flight across the Atlantic Ocean, Charles flew his plane, "The Spirit of St. Louis," to all 48 states. During a goodwill flight to Mexico he met Anne Morrow. They married in 1929; together they made flights to South America, Europe, Africa, and the Orient, exploring possible commercial air routes. Anne and Charles each became famous authors.

Like his father, C.A., Charles opposed U.S. entry into the European wars, but when World War II was declared, he supported the war effort in many ways, including flying several combat missions, as a civilian, in the South Pacific. Later, Charles continued to contribute to the development of commercial aviation through his work with Pan American Airways. Before his death in 1974, he devoted much of his time to the protection of the environment.

The farm at Little Falls was given by the family to the State of Minnesota as a memorial to C.A. and is now a state park; the farmhouse in which Charles lived during his formative boyhood years has been restored and is interpreted to the public by the Minnesota Historical Society. 1998

### 339. EXPLORING THE MISSISSIPPI HEADWATERS
*Located on I-94 (west bound) in Fuller Lake rest area*

After the American Revolution, the 1783 Treaty of Paris, signed by those representing the American Colonies and Great Britain, sought to establish the boundary of the new country. In the middle of the continent the boundary was to run east to west along a line from Lake of the Woods to the Mississippi River and then along a line located in the middle of the river to the southern boundary. No one knew the exact location of the river in the north nor did the map used to draw the treaty show its location. To establish the boundary, it became important to find the river's source.

The first American explorer of the Upper Mississippi River was Zebulon Pike, an army officer, who led a detachment of soldiers up the river in 1805. Mistakenly, he declared Leech Lake to be the river's source. Later explorers erroneously named Lake Julia and Cass Lake as its source.

In 1832 Henry Schoolcraft aided by Ozawindib, an Ojibway Indian, led an expedition which correctly identified the lake now regarded as the source of the Mississippi River. By this time the boundary was no longer in dispute, but Schoolcraft continued to search for the source of the mighty river. He gave the lake a new name, Itasca, from portions of two Latin words meaning true head, "Veritas caput."

After Schoolcraft's expedition, geographer Joseph Nicollet, in 1836, explored this region in order to make a detailed map of what is now Minnesota and the eastern parts of North and South Dakota. He visited five creeks flowing into Lake Itasca; regarding the largest he said, "This creek is truly the infant Mississippi."

In 1891 the State of Minnesota set aside a large area around the Mississippi headwaters and in 1893 developed it as the first state park open to the public. Today, people can explore for themselves the source of the great Mississippi River. 1997

### 340. SINCLAIR LEWIS

*Located at 812 Sinclair Lewis Avenue in Sauk Centre*

When Harry Sinclair Lewis was born on a bitter cold February 7, 1885, Sauk Centre was a raw prairie town with an unpaved main street and five or six blocks of false fronts. A gawky, sensitive child who achieved little success in school and was the brunt of every crude piece of horseplay, "Red" Lewis spent most of his youth tagging after his adored older brother and doctor-father, and reading every book he could find. He began to write at age fifteen. Despite the years of lost jobs and false hopes that followed his graduation from Yale University in 1908, he persisted in his determination to be a writer.

With the publication of *Main Street* and *Babbitt* Lewis became a successful novelist and critic of American culture, winning the Nobel Prize for Literature in 1930. He returned frequently to Minnesota; never able to deny his underlying attachment to the Northern Middle West, he described it as ". . . the newest empire of the world . . . a land of dairy herds and exquisite lakes, of new automobiles and tar-paper shanties and silos like red towers, of clumsy speech and a hope that is boundless." Lewis's talent declined and he died alone in Italy on January 10, 1951. As he had requested, his ashes were brought home to Sauk Centre. 1968

Sinclair Lewis and his son, Wells, about 1925

## 341. MAIN STREET
*Located on I-94 (west bound) in Sauk Centre rest area*

Nearly every small town has a Main Street—a town center where residents gather to conduct their business, greet their neighbors, and exchange news of the day.

Today the concept of main street is suffused in a nostalgic glow, as we remember the virtues and simplicity of small-town life. But it wasn't always so. The publication of Sinclair Lewis's novel *Main Street* in 1920 jolted Americans out of their sentimental view of their hometown.

Lewis, a native of Sauk Centre, set his novel in the fictional town of Gopher Prairie, whose residents he depicted in an unflattering light. Soon the term "Main Street" took on a negative meaning, becoming synonymous with narrow-minded, small-town provincialism.

Although Lewis intended Gopher Prairie to represent the American village in general, it quickly came to be associated with his own hometown of Sauk Centre. The local newspaper expressed its displeasure by waiting six months before acknowledging any connection to the nation's most talked-about novel. As the book gained popularity, however, Sauk Centre came to appreciate its celebrity status.

Gradually the phrase "Main Street" lost its negative meaning as American film makers and writers in the 1930s and 1940s returned to the glorification of small-town virtues. Sauk Centre's association with Lewis's novel, which had at first brought ridicule, eventually conferred on the town a special dignity.

Now Sauk Centre's Main Street stands as the living symbol of the American small town. In 1994, to recognize its importance in our cultural history, this Main Street was placed on the National Register of Historic Places, the nation's official list of properties worthy of preservation. 1997

# STEVENS COUNTY

### 342. WADSWORTH TRAIL
*Located at Seventh and California Streets in East Side Park in Morris*

Established in 1864 from St. Cloud to Fort Wadsworth, later called Fort Sisseton.

This trail was used by soldiers and traders who came up the Mississippi River by boat. It passed through Sauk Centre, Gager's Station (which was located four and one-half miles north and east of this spot), Toqua, Browns

Valley, and the government agency on the Sisseton
Reservation.

Erected by Wadsworth Trail Chapter, Daughters of
the American Revolution. 1929

### 343. THE DORMITORY AT THE MORRIS INDUSTRIAL SCHOOL FOR INDIANS

*Located on Cougar Circle in front of the Minority Resource
Center at the University of Minnesota-Morris*

This building is all that remains of the former Morris
Industrial School for Indians. Built in 1899, it along
with a classroom building, a superintendent's residence,
a laundry, a bath house, and a barn were added to the
Indian mission school originally established by Mother
Mary Joseph Lynch and the Sisters of Mercy in 1887.

The Sisters of Mercy mission school at Morris housed
Chippewa Indians from Turtle Mountain Reservation in
North Dakota and Dakota Indians from Sisseton Reservation in South Dakota. The mission school was operated
under a contract with the federal government, whose
policy prior to 1887 had been to isolate Indians on reservations. After 1887, the Dawes Severalty Act emphasized
assimilation of Indians into mainstream culture. Mission
boarding schools were established to fill the need for an
education system. In Minnesota, many of these boarding
schools, including the Morris school, were administered
by the Bureau of Catholic Indian Missions.

In 1896 federal policy changed again, and administration of the Morris Indian mission school was transferred to the federal government. The Indian Industrial
School in nearby Clontarf was closed and its students
were transferred to Morris, where they were offered
both industrial and academic classes. The combined
school at Morris continued to operate until 1909.

Facing growing opposition to Indian boarding
schools, the federal government again changed its policies and abandoned the concept. The Morris Industrial

School for Indians was one of the first five federal Indian schools to be transferred to state governments for use in their general education systems. In 1909, the school was renamed the West Central School of Agriculture, and in 1960, changed to the University of Minnesota, Morris. 1999

# SWIFT COUNTY

### 344. MONSON LAKE MEMORIAL
*Located on county road 95 off state highway 9 in Monson Lake State Park*

Near this spot in Monson Lake Memorial Park thirteen settlers—members of the Anders P. and Daniel P. Broberg and Andreas L. Lundborg families—were killed during the Sioux Uprising on August 20, 1862.

This marker was presented by the Swift County Historical Society to the Monson Lake Memorial Association at a Centennial observance on Sunday, August 19, 1962.

# WILKIN COUNTY

### 345. FORT ABERCROMBIE
*Located on U.S. highway 75 at its junction with the road to McCauleyville, 1 mile northwest of Kent*

On the west bank of the Red River, at the head of navigation, about one mile west of here, stood Fort Abercrombie, begun by U.S. troops in August 1857 to protect the northwest frontier against the Indians.

The post withstood several Sioux attacks during the outbreak of 1862, and was garrisoned until its abandonment in 1877.

## 346. BRECKENRIDGE

*Located on U.S. highway 75 at the north edge of Breckenridge*

Named for John C. Breckenridge, vice-president of the United States from 1857 to 1861, the town was laid out in 1857. On August 23, 1862, its citizens were warned that the Sioux Indians were planning a raid on the town, and most of them fled to Fort Abercrombie. Scoffing at the warning, three men—Edward Russell, Charles Battle, and Martin Fehrenbach—stayed behind and were killed by the Indians. After the Sioux Uprising, Breckenridge remained a virtual ghost town until 1871 when the St. Paul and Pacific Railroad reached here and ushered in a period of booming growth.

# WRIGHT COUNTY

## 347. THE DUSTIN MASSACRE

*Located on U.S. highway 12, about 1.5 miles west of Howard Lake*

A state of terror prevailed on the Minnesota western frontier for many months after the Sioux Uprising of 1862. Roving bands of Sioux continued to elude pursuers and attack settlers. The Dustin massacre occurred on June 29, 1863, one third mile northwest of this spot.

Amos Dustin was moving his family to a new claim in the southwestern part of Wright County. There were six in the party: Amos Dustin, his wife Kate, their three children, Alma 6, Robert 4, and Albert 2, and Dustin's widowed mother, Mrs. Jeanette Dustin. Their wagon was drawn by an ox team. A party of Indians fell upon them from ambush, shot three to death with arrows, and mortally wounded a fourth. Alma and Albert were left unharmed. The victims are buried in a cemetery at Waverly.

It has always been believed, although never proved, that the massacre was perpetrated by members of Little

Crow's party who were in the vicinity at the time. Four days later Little Crow was shot and killed near Hutchinson while picking berries with a son.

Erected by Wright County Historical Society June 29, 1963.

### 348.  MINNESOTA'S HIGHWAYS
*Located on I-94 (east bound) in Enfield Woods rest area*

Minnesota's system of highways evolved gradually. The earliest routes were Native American trails linking major waterways—trails later used by fur traders. Next came military and stage roads, the main routes of overland travel until railroads crisscrossed the state at the end of the 19th century.

Where other roads were needed, each township built its own. But unskilled labor and lack of planning resulted in miles of unconnected, poor-quality roads.

As the state's population grew, so did the need for roads that travelers could count on. Farmers wanted dependable roads to get their crops to market. Merchants hoped better roads would increase their trade. In the 1890s, together with proponents of a new national fad—bicycling—they formed the Good Roads Movement, joining a nationwide crusade for all-weather, all-season thoroughfares.

The advent of the automobile at the turn of the century and the use of heavy trucks in WWI increased the demand for good roads. Motorists yearned to travel to faraway vacation spots but poorly marked roads made it difficult to get there. To encourage tourism, community boosters throughout the country mapped out interstate tourist routes known as blazed trails, each given colorful names and marked with distinctive signs. The goal was to persuade state and federal governments to take over the tourist routes. It worked.

Minnesota's state highway system took its present shape in 1921 when a state constitution amendment authorized the Minnesota Highway Department to oversee the design, construction, and maintenance of all state highways. This new era of state management meant better planning, and safer, more dependable roads.

The 1940s and 1950s saw passage of national laws to create a new system of high-speed interstate highways connecting the country's major cities. Three of them—I-35, I-90 and I-94 cross through Minnesota border to border.

Today's road system combines many classes of road—township, municipal, county, state, and federal—that together form a well-integrated transportation network. 1997

Traffic stopped on highway near Anoka in 1939 after a tornado

# INDEX

## PICTURE CREDITS

The picture on page 161 is from the Carleton College Archives. All others are from the Minnesota Historical Society. Photographers and source information are known for many of the photographs; that information is as follows: Page 6 (Whitney's Gallery), 21 (Benjamin Franklin Upton), 26 (*Minneapolis Journal*), 31 (W. H. Jacoby & Son), 35 (Norton & Peel), 44 (A. F. Raymond), 65 (*St. Paul Pioneer Press*), 92 (John Runk), 95 (Joel E. Whitney), 115 (Thomas J. Lutz), 118 (Joel E. Whitney), 125 (anonymous), 135 (Hiram J. Jacoby), 143 (Diana Mitchell), 150 (Joel E. Whitney), 165 (Schaefer Studio), 183 (Steve Plattner), 189 (Charles A. Zimmerman), 192 (Matthew B. Brady), 202 (Laurence Oliphant, *Minnesota and the Far West* [Edinburgh, 1855], 190), 212 (William F. Roleff), 240 (*Minneapolis Tribune*), 252 (William W. Folwell, *A History of Minnesota* [St. Paul: Minnesota Historical Society, 1957], 1:247), 267 (Charles J. Hibbard), 285 (United States Forest Service), 308 (*Minneapolis Tribune*).

## ACKNOWLEDGMENTS

The compiler wishes to thank Ellen Green, Dave Nystuen, Tim Glines, Tom Ellig, Douglas Zbikowski, Laura L. Anderson, Merlin Johnson, Rebecca Rubinstein, and staff members at Anoka, Blue Earth, Cook, Goodhue, Nicollet, Scott, Stevens, and Washington County Historical Societies, Afton Historical Society, Iron World USA, Fort Snelling State Park, Carleton College Archives, and Hull-Rust-Mahoning Mine for their assistance.

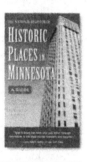

## JOIN THE MINNESOTA HISTORICAL SOCIETY TODAY! IT'S THE BEST DEAL IN HISTORY!

The Minnesota Historical Society is the nation's premier state historical society. Founded in 1849, the Society collects, preserves, and tells the story of Minnesota's past through innovative museum exhibits, extensive collections and libraries, educational programs, historic sites, and book and magazine publishing. Membership support is vital to the Society's ability to serve its ever-broadening and increasingly diverse public with programs and services that are educational, engaging, and entertaining.

What are the benefits of membership?

Members enjoy:

• A subscription to the quarterly magazine *Minnesota History;*

• *Member News* newsletter and events calendar;

• Unlimited free admission to the Society's 25 historic sites;

• Discounts on purchases from the Minnesota Historical Society Press and on other purchases and services in our museum stores, library, Café Minnesota, and much more;

• Reciprocal benefits at more than 70 historical organizations and museums in over 40 states through Time Travelers; and

• Satisfaction of knowing your membership helps support the Society's programs.

Membership fees/categories:

• $55 Household (2 adults and children under 18 in same household)

• $50 Senior Household (age 65+ for 2 adults)

• $45 Individual (1 adult)

• $40 Senior Individual (age 65+ for 1 adult)

• $100 Associate

• $250 Contributing

• $500 Sustaining

• $1,000 North Star Circle

Join by phone or e-mail. To order by phone, call 651-296-0332 (TTY 651-282-6073) or e-mail membership@mnhs.org. Benefits extend one year from date of joining.

Printed in the USA
CPSIA information can be obtained
at www.ICGtesting.com
JSHW021432130524
63055JS00001B/45

9 780873 514569